Born in Christchurch, New Zealand, in 1991, Ben Stokes moved to Cumbria with his family at the age of 11. He made his debut for Durham CCC in 2009, and just two years later pulled on an England shirt for the first time.

He has scored the fastest Test century at Lord's and England's fastest Test double-century. His bowling spell of 6-36 at Trent Bridge in August 2015 helped England to regain the Ashes.

In July 2019 Stokes received the Player of the Match accolade in the ICC Cricket World Cup final as England won the tournament for the first time. In the summer's Ashes series, he scored 441 runs at an average of more than 55, including two centuries and two fifties. His 135 not out in the second innings at Headingley will be remembered as one of the greatest innings in Test history.

Stokes has played for the Melbourne Renegades in Australia's Big Bash League, and Rising Pune Supergiant and the Rajasthan Royals in the Indian Premier League.

He is married with two young children.

Praise for Ben Stokes:

'He is the Special One, and I intend to call him that for the rest of his career' Sir Ian Botham, *Daily Telegraph*

'There are not enough superlatives to describe Ben Stokes' Nasser Hussain, *Daily Mail*

'The undisputed hero of English cricket' *The Times*

'Stokes is unstoppable now, a colossal superman' Michael Vaughan, *Daily Telegraph*

'He was a giant, spinning the planet with his foot, his bat producing mighty claps of thunder' Martin Samuel, *Daily Mail*

Also by Ben Stokes and available from Headline

Firestarter

BEN STOKES

ON FIRE

My Story of England's
Summer to Remember

with Richard Gibson

HEADLINE

First published in 2019 by
HEADLINE PUBLISHING GROUP

First published in paperback in 2020 by
HEADLINE PUBLISHING GROUP

1

Cataloguing in Publication Data is available from the British Library

ISBN 9781472271280

Offset in 10.56/14.94 pt Warnock Pro by Jouve (UK), Milton Keynes

Printed and bound in Great Britain by Clays Ltd, Elcograf S.p.A.

HEADLINE PUBLISHING GROUP
An Hachette UK Company
Carmelite House
50 Victoria Embankment
London
EC4Y 0DZ

www.headline.co.uk
www.hachette.co.uk

To Clare, Layton, Libby, Mam, Dad, Jane and all those
involved with the England cricket team.
For all your love and support.

CONTENTS

THE ASHES 2019

PROLOGUE

Years like this do not come around very often. For the few England players like me who are members of both the Test and one-day international set-ups, a fixture list that included a World Cup and an Ashes series on home soil offered a once-in-a-lifetime experience.

Quite simply, these events represent the two biggest prizes in cricket, and just to be involved in matches of this magnitude is an unbelievable thrill. Justifiably, however, we were not just looking at participating but winning. We knew we were as prepared as we could be for double success.

To be crowned a world champion is a highlight in any professional athlete's career. People associate such triumphs with great planning in the build-up, but I view things slightly differently. It is not as though you get to the start of a tournament and begin formulating a strategy that is going to make you successful, embark on the kind of physical work required to get you through a schedule of up to 11 matches in seven weeks, or talk about the challenges that conditions will throw up.

The seeds of success for this England team had not been planted overnight but in 2015, when the ECB's director of cricket Andrew Strauss made a couple of key appointments:

Eoin Morgan as captain and Trevor Bayliss as coach. The pair of them created a no-limits environment in which players were able to work out for themselves what they needed to do to thrive at the top level: how to react in certain match situations, the fitness levels necessary, and the development of mental resilience. These facets are all acquired through experience and that experience comes through consistency of selection. The planning for the on-field success was only possible once the foundation stones were put in place.

We were able to achieve our long-term goal of winning the World Cup because the team was allowed to develop over time. The best learning is done on the job and the lessons, good and bad, were delivered over a four-year cycle.

Naturally, there was disappointment that we were unable to win the Ashes, but I think if we had been offered the summer we have had back at the turn of 2019, we would have taken it. It has provided some unforgettable drama.

Nowadays, thanks to social media, it's very hard not to be aware of how the country is affected by big sports events, and so it was nice to see the videos of fans at football grounds, people at local cricket clubs, in pubs and in their front rooms, and the crowds gathered in Trafalgar Square watching the big moments of the summer – the nail-biting Super Over victory against New Zealand at Lord's on 14 July and the one-wicket thriller at Headingley on 25 August – and indeed their reactions.

We heard countless stories of people who did not previously like cricket being glued to their television sets. To discover that over eight million people were engrossed in the latter stages of the World Cup final was absolutely mint. To know that we are reaching that far out, and are not just limited to the established cricket community, is one of the most pleasing aspects of our success. This summer has made cricket in this country feel so much bigger.

And it's the reach to the next generation that is so import-ant. We want to inspire them to take up the game themselves. We want to be their heroes and role models.

One recent episode highlighted for me how our on-field feats have made us more recognisable figures. I was at the Metro Centre in Newcastle when my six-year-old son Layton clocked that three lads had stopped and were chatting among themselves nearby. Layton has recently developed an aware-ness of the attention that playing for England can draw. He just went up to them and said: 'Do you want a picture of my daddy?' I was a bit embarrassed but, yes, they wanted a photo. So many more people have wanted similar things this year. We are accustomed to the regular groups of autograph hunters outside our hotels, but even that has gone to a different level with young children now joining the queues with their mums and dads. It actually gave me goosebumps to see how many kids had turned out when we paraded the World Cup silverware at the Oval on the morning of 15 July.

Let's face it, we all play cricket for the love of the game. It's why we all fell for it when we were eight-, nine- and ten-year-olds ourselves. For the moments of sheer joy it can deliver. The indescribable feeling of achievement. The times when you liter-ally celebrate like schoolkids. That's what it felt like when we ran about the Lord's outfield after Jos Buttler had removed the bails to run out New Zealand's Martin Guptill.

The double-tie that saw England claim a maiden 50-overs trophy, 44 years after first trying, followed by the narrowest of victories over Australia at Headingley, 42 days later – those were amazing games to be part of. And amazing games in which to be able to contribute meaningfully to the end result.

The unbeaten innings of 84 and 135, I realise, will be talked about for years to come. I am proud that is the case. I enjoyed being the person out there trying to get England over the finishing line. I want to win games for this team. For my country. For my teammates. We are not only teammates, we are mates.

Stuart Broad said he had been travelling on the Underground while in London and there was someone across from him in the carriage holding a newspaper with a picture of me on the front page and another picture of me on the back page. He said he wanted to shout out: 'I know him, I know him!'

But as I said to him: 'I bet you weren't saying that two years ago when I was on the front page, were you?'

In all seriousness, one of my biggest disappointments was to miss the Ashes series of 2017–18 through events that happened away from a cricket field. To be caught up in something that I should not have been. I want to be known as a cricketer that wins matches for England, not misses them.

The tight nature of these two wins made for the greatest drama possible. Hopefully, as great as it was to be part of, I will never be involved in the like again. To be honest, it all got a bit too close for comfort at times.

People have asked me how I coped with the expectation. How I managed to keep calm and collected when the odds were stacked against us in both scenarios.

My answer is: that it is what I have trained to do. Batting at number five for a long period of time in a career presents repeatable scenarios. It's usually one thing or the other when you arrive at the crease. It's either dig in, work hard and build an innings because the team needs to rebuild, or give yourself a quick look for a quarter of an hour before launching into an attack. Being exposed to those two contrasting situations so many times over the last four years has helped me to avoid putting pressure on myself when I'm batting for England.

Not that preparation makes you infallible. Pressure situations in games can really alter what human beings do. Take Jason Roy fumbling the ball late on during New Zealand's Super Over. He is a superb fielder and it shows you even the best can err when the game is on the line. Then there was Nathan Lyon's fluffed run out late on at Headingley. These were moments that contributed to the theatre.

When Jack Leach charged down the pitch for a single in Leeds, clearly doing his best impression of Monty Panesar from Cardiff in 2009, I could have had a conversation with him, he was that close. In just a couple of seconds, the Ashes were gone and then alive again. It must have been gripping viewing.

When Mark Wood joined me in the middle for the final delivery of our 242-run chase at Lord's, I wanted to ensure that we got a minimum of one run. 'Get your running boots on and if you have to bring your imaginary horse out and jump on it then do it,' I told him. He knew what he had to do, but unfortunately I couldn't quite get the ball where I wanted it.

At Headingley, I got my pitching-wedge distance just right at the right times in hitting some of those eight sixes. Some will tell you it's because of the amount of golf I played between matches.

Not everything was perfect in terms of my stroke play, but the main thing was that I delivered on my pledge to be there at the end by calculating my way through situations. Earlier in my career, there was a time when I didn't think, I just did. I played the ball as I saw it. These days, there is a lot more thought that goes into what I am here to do – to perform, to contribute to England winning.

And I have an overwhelming respect and gratitude for those who have performed alongside me with the three lions on their chest. When Jack Leach walked out at number 11 on that stupendous Sunday, we required 73 runs to win. Whatever he goes on to achieve, those are likely to be the most important balls he will ever face in his Test career. His single off his 17th and last one, the most important run. Remember, it takes two to tango.

Yes, I am so glad that my individual displays appear to have caught the mood of the nation but this is a team sport. We win together, we lose together.

You can take a lot of personal pride when you receive man of the match awards as I have done, but arguably the most is taken from putting in the effort for those sat alongside you in the dressing room. Such accolades can't be compared to collective success.

I only found myself in the positions I did because of what other guys in the England squad have achieved as well. What we have done as a team in 2019 is phenomenal: to win the World Cup and draw the Ashes has been a fantastic summer and something I am proud of personally and as a team. This is my story of how it came together.

1

FIRESTORM

For a short period during my time with the Rajasthan Royals at the Indian Premier League in the spring of 2019, I feared that my World Cup might be over before it had begun.

All that work over four years suddenly felt like it might be for nothing after injury had struck in my left hamstring, the damage done in the home match versus Chennai at Jaipur while I was fielding on the boundary. *What was that?* It had made me jump a bit when I stopped the ball and turned to throw, but as I was full of adrenaline I ignored it at the time.

It felt like chronic cramp, but on the day of the incident I could hardly lift my leg up to get on the team bus, and later, at the hotel, I realised how stiff I was. So when I woke up still feeling sore the next day, I knew that I'd have to go for a scan. I was worried to death that I had torn the damned thing, as that would have kept me sidelined for eight weeks.

When the scan failed to show up anything, it made me feel a lot better on one hand but a bit of a fraud on the other as my teammates were asking what was up and I was having to tell them that the simplest answer was 'nothing'. Happiness that it was nothing serious was offset by the fact certain people would think I was soft.

The problem turned out to be an inflamed tendon that caused me to miss a couple of matches. Thankfully, it was only a week before I was passed fit to play as a batter, and although I wasn't quite 100 per cent fit, it was a much better outcome than I had first feared. As an all-rounder there have been several times during my career when I have been unable to bowl due to injury and it is frustrating not to be able to contribute to my full capacity. But you have to get used to taking it easy and fielding in unusual positions, like the inner ring rather than on the boundary, to minimise the running and chances of aggravating any issues. One of the psychological challenges for someone like me, who likes to do everything at 100 mph, is to remember my limitations when carrying such a niggle.

Bearing in mind that I was an England player in India expected to play every game – especially given the huge amount of money they had spent on me in the auction – I could not have received better treatment from Rajasthan. The medical team never forced me to do anything I wasn't comfortable with during recovery, taking the view that my interests were the only interests they were bothered about.

As a player, it felt like such a boost to receive this kind of message, that my welfare was the only thing as a franchise that they were concerned with. It was the same message coming from the physio John Gloster as from the two big chiefs Manoj Badale and Ranjit Barthakur, the owner and chairman of Rajasthan respectively. There was never any pressure to get back on the field to play in the away fixtures against Mumbai and Kings XI Punjab over the following days, and knowing that made things a lot easier for me.

As things turned out, I didn't bowl in my remaining three

appearances for Rajasthan ahead of a pre-World Cup camp in Cardiff, or for a week or so after that for that matter. It meant I faced a race against time to get my workload up in training so that I was ready to fulfil the role of sixth bowler when the England matches came around. What playing out in India did do, however, is hone my big-match mentality. Every game out there is a huge event played in front of sold-out stadiums and that is ideal preparation ahead of a major global event.

There was less than a fortnight between my final IPL match on 25 April and the first of five England matches against Pakistan, a series that acted as a World Cup warm-up. The medical advice in the build-up was that it was important not to overdo things in matches, so that meant limiting my overs to between three and four at a time while making sure I bowled plenty of spells in the nets. Across the five games, I contributed 17 overs, wicketless ones, but the important thing was to get through them without my hamstring reacting at all.

My fitness programme was designed to make sure that I hit the ground running and was ready to bowl a full 10 overs – if required by Eoin Morgan – at the most important time of the summer; that, of course, being when the fifth World Cup on English soil was scheduled to begin at the end of May.

•

For me personally the Pakistan series was a chance to switch modes, having spent five weeks playing Twenty20 cricket, and from a team perspective it was an important time for some players to press their claims for a place in the final 15-man squad for the World Cup. At that stage it was clear that 17, or even as many as 18, had a genuine claim to a final spot.

One player who did miss out on selection was Alex Hales, despite having being picked originally in the 17-man preliminary squad. The rest of the England players, myself included, were truly taken aback when we found out that he was missing some cricket within the first month of the English season, citing personal reasons. It was subsequently reported in the press that his absence was due to a 21-day suspension for failing two recreational drugs tests. The group of senior players within the squad had no idea that he had been suspended because the ECB's rules require it to keep such suspensions confidential.

We were at the England team's fitness testing at the Vale of Glamorgan Hotel prior to the summer's first one-day international against Ireland in Dublin when the news came to light. It was soon clear that I was not the only one questioning how we had not known anything about it. It was not that any of us wanted to pry into the troubles of one of our teammates; rather that Alex as an individual had not felt able to share his struggles with a group that he'd spent so much time with, in a team environment over the past few years, that bothered us. I can't help but think that if he'd handled things better it might have all worked out so differently.

No-one knew what had been going on and it felt like a player in his situation should have been able to sit down with the rest of the lads and let us know what was going on. We had been a tight-knit team throughout Eoin Morgan's captaincy period and so reading the finer details in a newspaper was not a great way for us all to find out. The collective feeling was that he should have felt comfortable enough in the environment that we had created to let on what was happening.

Over the weekend of 28 and 29 April, Eoin Morgan made it

his business to seek out the senior players within the squad to canvas their views as to what should be done about Alex's situation. When asked directly what I would do, I came straight out with it: 'No. I can't have him in the squad.' I was speaking as someone with first-hand knowledge of what it's like when an off-field issue is hanging over a team. I went into all the details about my experience of what happened on the 2017–18 tour of Australia and posed the question as to whether Hales was the level of player that we could make an exception for.

Was he so indispensable that he was worth keeping in the squad no matter the sideshow that might ensue? No. This was the resounding response from myself and other senior players when asked by Eoin to provide our input on whether or not we should stand him down.

From Eoin's perspective a series of one-on-one chats, with people who Alex had played a lot of international cricket with, was probably the best way to come to a consensus on the issue. Sometimes, if you try to make such decisions in a group situation, individuals can be led by what others say. This was a way of obtaining independent, impartial opinion. I obviously don't know exactly what everyone else said, but I'm pretty sure it would have been along the same lines as what I offered.

When Eoin addressed the gathered media in Malahide for the one-off international against Ireland, he said: 'Unfortunately, Alex's actions have shown complete disregard for our values. This has created a lack of trust between Alex and the team.' Several players had spoken to Alex between his break from cricket being announced and the England team camp, of which he was due to be a part, and he had assured everyone he was okay.

As I say, the question became whether we benefited more from having Alex's undoubted quality as a player in the team, or whether the other stuff that would come with him – and the spotlight and scrutiny placed on him – would be floating around causing an unnecessary distraction. We were within sight of the prize we'd worked so hard for and we wanted our heads to be on winning the World Cup, not thinking about other issues. What was bigger? What was more important? In the end, it came down to us protecting the culture and environment we had built.

A World Cup only comes around every four years and retaining Alex as a squad player would have proved too much of a distraction. You don't need an issue that draws extra attention hanging around a team for weeks. I know this from personal experience, and I didn't like it when I was the one that was the focus of such attention in the aftermath of the Bristol incident that contributed to me missing the last away Ashes.

The thing I hated most throughout that period of time was that other players were constantly being asked questions about me. Press conferences were taken in a completely different direction and had nothing to do with what had happened on the field that day. That really upset me. As Trevor Bayliss, the England coach, said of my absence from that tour of Australia: 'It's something you'd much rather not have to deal with, but that's life. It's happened, and we will have to get on with it. The Australian media will hammer away and try to put the pressure on in other areas as well. We have to try to deal with that and keep it separate from what we are doing on the practice field and in matches.' Sometimes that is easier said than done, though.

There were guys out in Australia wearing England shirts, trying to win the Ashes, and they shouldn't have had to deal with that kind of situation. Things are tough enough on the field in a Test series against the Australians without having the diversion of off-field situations to think about that really aren't your concern. There are only so many times you can see your teammates having to answer questions that they really shouldn't have to, and don't know much about, before it really gets to you. I was left wondering when it was all going to stop.

Unfortunately, it would have been a similar case if Alex had been in our World Cup squad. We needed to focus on the task at hand. Off-field distractions only serve to limit what you are trying to achieve on it. If we brought in someone of similar quality, but without the baggage, then we would not be having to deal with the backlash and unwanted attention of everything else.

As it was, the omission of Hales gave James Vince a chance to stake his claim against the Pakistanis, having not originally been named in the squad. Vince is a player who has been in and out of England squads since I first began establishing myself with England in 2013, and someone I always want to do well. When you play for England you always want everybody to do well, of course, but you come across a handful of guys in your international career who you tend to look out for. Guys who you are desperate to do well for themselves, cementing their places for months and years to come. Vince has always been one of those to me.

I have known him since we played alongside each other for England Under-19s. We've always spent a lot of time together when we've been in national teams and squads, and I also know from experience of playing against him over the years what a good player he is. At times, when you are on the opposition he just looks a million dollars and you can be left in awe.

To be fair, on nearly every occasion he has played for England he has looked like that too. He just hasn't quite managed to turn in that one performance that defines a career. Against Pakistan, there were a couple of times he looked like providing it, only to get out when well set, but the selectors obviously recognised his potential by picking him as Hales' official replacement when the 15-man squad was finalised ahead of the 23 May deadline.

When he got his chance to deputise for the injured Jason Roy through the middle of the tournament, he put himself under too much pressure to do what Roy does. I know for a fact that if he had his time again, he would go out not worrying about trying to replicate someone else but play like himself. He's a much better batsman when playing his natural game.

Undoubtedly, he tried to play in a hyper-aggressive way because he thought his task was to fulfil the Roy role in this England team. What Jason has done with his positive intent and clean ball-striking has been a major part of why we have had such a successful team over a long period of time. But James really should have had the confidence in his own ability to extend the team's success through his own highly-thought-of credentials.

•

Over the space of five matches in 11 days, everyone got enough game time to influence the final World Cup squad selection. There was an unusual mood about the place at this time, I guess, because so many individuals seemed to be vying for one fast-bowling spot. Without doubt, the guys knew who they were and who they were up against in trying to avoid missing out on a World Cup on home soil. It showed exactly where we had come from as a squad over a journey of four years that there were five guys all up for selection and that each and every one of them deserved to be there with the performances they had put in.

The truth is that across a quintet of Mark Wood, Tom Curran, David Willey, Liam Plunkett and Jofra Archer there was not an individual among them who would let the England team down. The fact that they were in a five-way fight really seemed to inspire their performances against Pakistan. It is true that whenever you play a one-day international you are always so keen to do well, but this extra edge really got the competitive juices flowing within the group.

None of it in a selfish way, mind. People were unquestionably raising their games but never solely for their own ends. That's what has always been good about this team. The main focus has always been on how any one individual can contribute to a win. It said a lot about the team spirit that the five who were up against each other trained together, helped each other, spent time away from the field together. There was none of the selfishness that you might expect would develop from such a scenario.

The way they conducted themselves was exemplary. Never once was their attention deflected from trying to make the team as successful as possible and their performances did not speak of players being under pressure. Only later did players like Liam Plunkett reveal that they had felt that pressure as the days ticked closer to the squad announcement and the main event itself. The reason it couldn't be detected was that performances were being turned in that said 'pick me'.

Arguably, the best thing about competition for places is that it creates a perfect competitive environment. Within a bigger picture it suggested that if they were able to perform under that kind of scrutiny then they could also do it when the stakes were raised even further. It showed what a healthy mental state the group was in. Nobody deserved to miss out in that 15 and it felt like we could have picked 17.

This was one of those problems that selectors say they like to have. Whoever missed out was going to be unlucky but from a team perspective we knew that whoever was chosen would go out and have a go, deliver their skills and show what they were about on the biggest stage.

During the two weeks leading up to the series, there were a lot of words spoken and a lot of words twisted in relation to the equation being reduced from five guys to four. The four guys established for some time were all asked how they felt about Jofra, only qualified since mid-March and without a cap to his name, winning one of the places.

Headlines made it look like they were suggesting his selection should not happen. I know as a group they were disappointed with how some of their interviews were portrayed by the media. They were simply saying how tough it would be for someone who had been a fixture in the squads for the best part of four years to miss out at the final hurdle. It's hard to see a long-term teammate lose out like that. The last thing they wanted to do was upset a guy coming into the squad like Jofra and it led to several text exchanges to explain what they had actually said.

What Jofra has to offer made his selection non-negotiable in my eyes. You cannot ignore a guy like that. I got to know him playing with Rajasthan at the IPL. He is the kind of player that makes any team better. With the ball in hand, he offered something that England had not seen in a long time. He bowls in excess of 90 mph, is one of the best death bowlers in the world and has great control of all his skills. You just can't look past someone with those qualities.

I would be lying if I said I wasn't confident he was going to be a part of our World Cup plans as soon as it became public that he would be available in the spring of 2019. When it comes to cricket, he is a very confident individual, someone who literally thinks there is nothing he cannot do. It means that he never backs away from any situation. Having seen how he performed at the IPL, I knew international cricket would not faze him because he lives to perform on the biggest stage possible. He really wanted to be a part of the World Cup and was desperate to become a Test cricketer this summer. He just wanted as many people as possible to see him do his thing.

One thing that has developed is a bit of lighthearted fun from the team towards Jofra because of how easy he finds things on the cricket field. We refer to these as 'Jof-isms'. Things come so easily and naturally to him, he doesn't understand that this isn't the case for everybody. So anything he can do he just considers to be the norm. During group chats among the bowlers, someone will discuss bowling a certain delivery and he explains how to do it so matter of factly, as if it is the easiest thing in the world. Of course, for a normal person it isn't. His general attitude is 'yeah, I just run up and do it.' That's a Jof-ism.

Against Bangladesh, it was obvious that we were going to win. We needed three wickets and, in a team huddle, Jofra was saying: 'Come on, get me back on, let's finish this off.' Nobody else would say that. It just shows great confidence for such a young player.

If you didn't know him you would think he was bordering on arrogance, but he's not. He's just that naturally gifted. He started work on a knuckle ball during the World Cup, something that it might take months for a top-level performer to perfect. Yet, there he was rocking one out in the Super Over of the World Cup final. It got belted for six by Jimmy Neesham, but it shows the confidence in his ability to even contemplate going with it in a situation like that.

Only top players can do that and he has a real desire to show everybody that he can do everything – bowl this ball, that ball, play this shot, that shot. It's like he's addicted to being the best cricketer he can be. It is a reflection of how talented he is that he can bowl 90 mph with his right arm and decent spin with his left arm. He's the kind of guy that sees someone else do something, tries to copy them, and does so perfectly, perhaps even better than the original.

A lot of this determination to succeed must have stemmed from the disappointment that he felt when he was younger and was not selected for West Indies for the Under-19 World Cup; a disappointment made worse when, amid a number of injury problems, he was unsure of which way his career was heading. Thankfully for English cricket, he decided to resurrect his career in the land of his father Frank's birth.

I have no doubt that this particular period in his life, when he moved from Barbados to play club cricket in Sussex – something that takes a lot of guts for a 19-year-old – has developed the desire to be the person that he has become. He is someone who has made the most of being given another crack at the highest level, having feared it might have gone for ever when so young, and he wants to make the very most of every opportunity he is given.

•

There was quite a difference in attitude between England and Pakistan during the bilateral series. It felt like the Pakistan batsmen were using it as a bit of a net for the main event that was to follow, being a bit careful, and playing for themselves. They perhaps saw it as an opportunity to get some time out in the middle in English conditions.

In contrast, our intention was to go out and win the series comprehensively. There were no thoughts of individual gain. One thing we have found over a long period of time is that your team only gets better if you are always on it, wanting to be dominant in every match you play. Winning matches is what improves teams and individual performances.

The difference in approaches during our 4–0 series win was highlighted in the game at Bristol when Pakistan scored 358 and we cantered home, winning with more than five overs to spare. We simply chased down one of their biggest ever one-day international totals with ease. Of course, it happens when you have experience of scoring big. Several times we have scored 350-plus batting second, winning matches against New Zealand and West Indies when doing so, and when you know you can make 400, as we had managed four times since the first match of the 2019 World Cup cycle began, it provides a belief that a game is never out of reach.

So we never walk off the field feeling as though a game is gone at the halfway stage, and there was certainly no suggestion that anybody was daunted with what we were facing when we were set 359 in Bristol. There is a calmness around the dressing room in such situations that you might not have been able to believe could exist under previous regimes. But once you have done something, it becomes easier to do it again and again. Our mood doesn't really change with differing sizes of target. Even when opponents score in excess of 300, you will find the same attitude recurring, with batsmen saying 'well done' to the bowlers.

What's more, when Jason Roy and Jonny Bairstow are going at the kind of scoring rate they managed that day, they are almost unstoppable. It's almost become a competition as to which one of them can maintain the highest strike rate and who can hit the biggest six. That's the way they play and we have been successful because no-one has tried to rein them in. They set the template for how we want the entire team to bat. By the time they were separated on this occasion, the whole dynamic of the contest had changed. A partnership of 159, leaving just 200 to get in 32.3 overs with nine wickets intact, meant it was a totally different game from there.

When you have two guys at the top of the order who average well in excess of 40, scoring at quicker than a run-a-ball on all surfaces, dominating opposition, why would you ever want to change it? They always go out with that positive intent and so if the ball is there to hit – allowing them to score 76 off 55 balls and 128 off 93 respectively on this occasion – they do so. However, just like the rest of us they have come to realise that not all pitches allow you to score 400 and sometimes you have to respect a surface on which 270–280 is a good total. They have developed a way to play on 400-type wickets and another to play on 280-type surfaces.

Assessing conditions is certainly an improved area of my batting. The more cricket I've played, the greater understanding I have developed of my role in the team, and the start of the 2019 summer was arguably a time when I began to show this consistently. One thing that I have definitely learned from experience is that the game is never won until it's won. The number of times that I got out in my England career for 30 or 40 – often drawing praise for my contribution, despite there still being 70 runs left to get for victory – was far too high for the player I want to be. I was sick of going out and playing eye-catching innings that ultimately meant nothing.

So I made a conscious decision to cut out these types of innings from my game. My target was to take games as deep as I could because I know that if I am still there at the end we have a much better chance of winning, especially given how long our batting order is in 50-overs cricket. We bat all the way down to number 10 and I have learned that it is important not to think about completing the win too early. It leaves you vulnerable if you lose a couple of wickets and two batsmen have to start again.

I've never been someone who is happy with a few showy shots if the team is losing the game. The most important thing when I pull on an England shirt is winning, and I want to be the guy who plays a part in that more often than not. So, it was pleasing for me to play a major part in the fourth match of the season, the one which saw us take an unassailable 3–0 lead.

We had made a good start in pursuit of 341 and, when

Jason Roy was out for yet another hundred, we were beyond 200 with only two wickets down. Within a couple of overs, however, we were 216–5 and the nature of the innings changed. I am not even sure exactly when the penny dropped for me, I just know from experience of lots of different situations that I have the knowledge of what it takes to get teams over the line from this position. It's been a natural progression for me over the last two or three years, discovering that even in a game limited to a certain number of balls there is always enough time if you can keep a clear head.

I just don't panic now if I've got 10 runs off 25 deliveries because I know I can catch up. Certainly, during the last World Cup cycle if I hadn't hit a boundary during the first 25 balls of my innings, and my strike rate was 30, I would start to get stressed about how I was playing and feeling under pressure to kick things on, but I now trust my game. And I trust my judge-ment of how to play the game. So I still felt in control when, with 37 from 45 balls to my name, we entered the final 10 overs needing 83.

It's only 8.3 runs an over, I told myself. *Be here at the end and we have a better chance of winning the game.*

What has contributed to me keeping my composure better is developing an understanding of how all my teammates are going to play and what abilities they have. For example, during this successful run chase in Nottingham, I knew exactly how Tom Curran would approach his batting when he joined me in the middle with 60 deliveries remaining. We didn't need to say anything to each other. I knew he would be aggressive and look to put the pressure back on the bowlers, so I had to concentrate on ticking along as I was and let him chance his arm. That's just about knowing your teammate's strengths. I would still look to score and punish any bad balls, but I also considered that he would play the role of aggressor and if he didn't come off it would be me who then had to take on that attacking role. In that kind of situation, it's important not to let your ego get in the way, instead taking a more pragmatic view. Tom was the one who was really making them think about how they were going to stop us from scoring, while I was quite relaxed about how I was playing, knowing where my boundary options were and continuing to strike the ball as hard as I could whenever I could. I absorbed a few dot balls and then went big when I had the chance. Even with 19 runs needed off the final two overs, I didn't panic and that was pleasing.

The bowlers are under more pressure than I am. One boundary. Just one boundary and the game is ours. We won with three balls to spare.

It's always important to learn from experience, and the Champions Trophy semi-final defeat to Pakistan in 2017 was a big example to us of how you can go wrong in 50-overs cricket. We'd played on absolutely belting pitches throughout the tournament and were then asked to play on something completely different for the semi-final match. At that stage of the team's development, we were out of our comfort zone when challenged with a slow and sluggish surface like the one presented to us at Sophia Gardens. We lacked clarity in our thinking about what a good score was and made a total mess of our innings, limping to 211 all out. Pakistan beat us easily that day.

People have highlighted that match as one of great importance, and rightly so, although there is another example of how a defeat shaped our thinking. It came the following year in Dunedin when we went from 267–1, in the 38th over of an ODI, to 335–9 and New Zealand's Ross Taylor levelled the series, batting on one leg. On this occasion, Jonny Bairstow and Joe Root had scored hundreds.

However, our middle order failed to capitalise in terms of contributing runs, with Jos Buttler, myself, Eoin Morgan and Moeen Ali offering a combined nine runs. That's not something that usually happens. It was a one-off and so when, during our dressing room chats after the game, coach Trevor Bayliss asked us whether we had done the right thing during that particular phase of the game, we stuck to our guns.

Everyone was adamant that when we found ourselves in positions like that in a limited-overs match, we would play our shots and try to impose our aggressive characteristics on the opposition. When the top three sets the platform like that, we put our foot on their throats and aim as high as we can. We don't play within ourselves to finish on 350 with six wickets down. We hadn't played the wrong way; we just hadn't played well enough. There was nothing wrong with our mindset, so if faced with a similar situation again, we'd do exactly the same. Just do it better.

'We didn't execute things properly but that's the way I want this team to play,' said Morgan.

Bayliss tended to speak less often in one-day cricket than in Tests but his over-riding message for both forms was 'positivity'. In one of his early one-day series as England coach, against Pakistan in the United Arab Emirates in 2015, he spelled out exactly what he meant by the word. I was missing because of a shoulder injury but it's one of the lads' favourite stories about Trevor.

'Be positive in all you do. That includes communication out in the middle,' he said in a team meeting.

'If you're calling for a single, it's not yes, it's Y-E-S-S-S-S!'

Several people got the fright of their lives, causing them to jump from their seats – he was that loud.

His message in Test cricket was similar but got misconstrued by those outside of the England environment.

'Being positive is not about hitting fours and sixes,' he would say. 'It's about positive in your feet movement, positive in the way you defend the ball, positive in the way that you leave it.'

To get better in our ODI cricket, we needed to retain our positive way of thinking but be smarter on not such good surfaces. I wouldn't call these two matches in question turning points: rather they were two signposts on our journey. Moments that showed us the pitfalls. Trevor might have been asking the questions in that changing room in Dunedin but he wasn't challenging our methods. He believed in that way of playing too and I am sure that he was looking for the group to reiterate our commitment to this attacking ethos. He is a man of few words and he knows exactly what he's doing every time he speaks. He knew what reaction he was getting and he simply wanted it said out loud.

Those experiences told us we had to be more adaptable if we wanted to achieve the levels that could see us become world champions. When our journey started four years earlier, we put 400 on the board against New Zealand at Edgbaston. Because it was so new to us, we were like a group of kids, saying 'wow, check this out'. A couple of years later we were thrown onto slow slag-heaps in the Caribbean where 240 was a good score. What we've come to realise is that you can suffer if you're always trying to score 350. Some disappointing results helped shape the batting unit we became at the tournament.

The scores generally throughout its seven-week duration certainly weren't what we expected when we entered 2019. After all, the year had started with a series in the Caribbean which saw ourselves and West Indies share 46 sixes in an ODI of 807 runs.

Thankfully, though, as we headed into a tournament for which we knew we were favourites, we had a more diverse way of playing. Being able to play effectively in multiple ways allowed us to embrace that favouritism rather than being fearful of it. We had been world number ones for some time and felt we deserved that status. But we also knew that as well as we had played to get to the top, it didn't give us a God-given right to lift the trophy in mid-July. The rankings would count for nothing once things got going, and at a tournament in which everybody plays everybody else you can win even if you're ranked number seven. Play well enough over a certain space of time and that's good enough.

Equally, Eoin Morgan spent the time from our squad camp in Cardiff onwards reminding us of the importance of concentrating on ourselves and how we wanted to play over anything else. Yes, we should take note of the opposition, but our focus should be on what we did well because we had proved over a sustained period that it was good enough to beat every other team in the world. If we could play our best game, it would beat everybody else's best game. With that message in our ears, we began our quest.

ICC
CRICKET
WORLD CUP
2019

2

FOCUS

One thing was for sure as we embarked on the first World Cup to be held on our own soil for 20 years – we were the fittest England limited-overs team in that period.

For me, pre-season is always a time when training goes through the roof in terms of gym work and aerobic fitness. Then throughout an international summer – a World Cup followed by an Ashes series in this instance – it is about maintaining a certain level. Once you are into a routine of a couple of practice days followed by a match, your general fitness tends to be okay, so it's just about being at the right level in terms of your strength and stamina.

Things were slightly different for me in 2019, heading into a home season immediately after the Indian Premier League and having to keep on top of my hamstring injury, making sure I did the right work to keep it protected and my body strong.

Thankfully, the bulk of my regime designed to get into peak condition had been done months earlier on the tours of Sri

Lanka and the Caribbean. As an England player abroad, at a start of a tour, you often have a period of about 10 days to a fortnight before the first international fixture. So, in terms of preparation this is the final push for being in the optimum physical shape.

I got my head around the extra work I would require ahead of what was shaping to be the biggest season of my life as we headed out to Colombo in October 2018. After net sessions, I would go off and do extra fitness, such as running or heading to the gym. It was something I did on both our overseas trips and by the end of the Caribbean leg, I felt I was at a level of fitness that I'd never reached before.

The key to it all was lots of 2 km runs and interval sprints, challenges that improve endurance and increase the anaerobic threshold. The 2 km runs are an excellent way of judging whether or not your overall fitness is improving, simply by monitoring your own times, and I was determined to get mine down throughout the winter. They also condition your hamstrings for competitive action. The thing I like about the interval sprints – run as hard as you can for 30 seconds, rest for 30 – is that this is exactly the kind of activity replicated on a cricket field during a match.

To be a cricketer you need to practise lots of sprints, as the work we do from a physical perspective tends to be short and sharp: like running in to bowl or chasing the ball in the field for 40 metres. Sometimes, you might have to run as fast as you possibly can to the boundary to haul in a ball, and then be faced with the same prospect from the next delivery. You generally tend to get 30 seconds rest in between throwing the ball back and being in position for the bowler to run in again, and if you get two chases to the boundary in a row it can absolutely ruin you.

In early 2019, I made a video for the World Cup with Red Bull, who I have worked with for three years. The video was shot at a disused Sunderland dockyard that highlighted how high impact cricket can be. I was smashing balls delivered from bowling machines into orbit, bowling at full pelt, hurtling headlong into one-handed catches and then springing back up to throw down a target from 30 metres, with constant running in between around this specially designed course. It took eight hours to film and proved a really tough physical challenge, but the end product was awesome in that it accurately painted the physical picture of what is required at the highest level.

People from the outside might dismiss the fitness levels required, but what we do is very demanding when you get to a certain level. Players will focus differently on their training depending on their role in the team. Batsmen need to have decent stamina if they are going to be batting for long periods of time, for example, while a bowler tends to need more explosive-type fitness.

As an all-rounder, I do a bit of everything and so I need to have all the different dynamics covered for when I get onto the field. In a one-day international, I might find myself batting for the best part of 50 overs, then be bowling a spell of six overs in the second innings, followed by a period in which I am fielding out on the boundary during the demanding, business end of the game, between overs 35 and 50, having to hurtle around the ground and throw myself full-length on occasions to stem the opposition's runs. That can be fairly demanding and requires power-based training.

For example, the day before an international fixture, I will do lots of heavy lifting – Romanian deadlifts and more traditional deadlifts – to help me produce power and reach high velocity. At the start of 2019, I was lifting a bar with an overall weight of 100 kg. Usually it will just be low repetitions, something like three of each exercise, and I am always looking to push myself, so by the end of the summer I was up to 140 kg.

I do however struggle to push on at times because my right-hand grip is not so good due to surgery earlier in my career. It means I use grip chalk whenever it is lying around in the gym; or the liquid variety that goes chalky when squeezed onto your hands. Imagine my surprise one day in the Lord's gym then when I was preparing to lift 140 kg and the liquid had not changed its properties. Puzzled, I double-checked the bottle. I was not going to get anywhere with massage oil, was I?

The rest of the strength work features bent-over rows (the combination of a push and pull exercise stops your upper body becoming like Arnold Schwarzenegger's) and bench presses using dumbbells of 42 kg in each hand. As Phil Scott, our strength and conditioning coach, says: 'Your chest is your engine, but there is no point in having a Ferrari without any brakes.' The pulling elements develop those brakes and allow you to go faster in on-field competition.

In a summer like the one we've just experienced, the last thing you want is to be unable to fulfil your technical skills due to physical issues, and so it has been a mid-career focus of mine to improve all aspects of my fitness. In years gone by, I suffered horrendously badly with cramps. I still do to an extent but they tend to come less often now and that is down to the work I have done with the England and Wales Cricket Board's medical team.

Undoubtedly, it has helped that I am in tip-top condition, but there has also been some invaluable advice from the doctors that work with the England team. My main problem has always been that I am a very bad eater on game days. Not that I am tucking into a burger and fries or anything like that. Quite the opposite, actually. During matches, I tend to lose my appetite, and no matter the interval break, whether it be lunch or tea, I have no desire to eat.

It means I almost have to force-feed myself with the encouragement of the medics, literally scoffing as much food down as is physically possible. Our strength and conditioning coach Phil Scott always tries to look out for me during game days, offering me protein shakes and popping extra vitamins in my drinks because he knows of my reluctance to eat.

Emma Gardner, our nutritionist, is always hot on what we are putting into our bodies. Throughout a week, I have to log what I've eaten, and when she first analysed my intake she told me I was putting in less than half of what my body needed. If you are not preparing your body properly, and that goes for the fuel you are providing it with as well as your physical preparation, it won't work as efficiently as you want it to. So now I tend to load up on carbohydrates the day before a game, such as potatoes and pasta.

The team's improved overall fitness is undoubtedly due to the influence of Jos Buttler, and it was Jos' fitness regime that caught my eye going back to the summer of 2017. He was the first one to go off and do extra stuff on his own at the end of a day. I noticed that he would be asking for 20 minutes' work with Phil Scott and when a teammate is willing to go the extra yards I've always been the kind of person to follow suit. I don't want to think that others are working harder than me.

Jos and I are numbers one and two in the 2 km runs, going on our group results, but gradually everyone started following our example and by the start of 2019, it had become a regular practice for guys to finish England training sessions and then begin their own aerobic activities. For instance, it became very noticeable on the Test tour of the Caribbean that Moeen Ali and Adil Rashid had taken it upon themselves to do extra running on the outfield every time the bats, balls and stumps were packed away.

Mo is one of the funniest guys I know. And he's not averse to taking the mickey out of himself. During this increased period of fitness, he would take his top off in the dressing room and parade himself around in body-builder pose as if to say: 'I'm ripped, bro!' He's not got the best rig but he was prepared to poke fun at his efforts to get fitter.

Mo and Adil were doing their interval sprints daily and it clearly caught the attention of Jonathan Agnew, the BBC's cricket correspondent, as he waited to do his pre-match interviews at the Kensington Oval, Barbados. Aggers ended up asking Mo on air about it and was told that he and his spin twin Adil did not want to let the team down when it came to the fitness side of things.

That was exactly the kind of attitude that the current England environment promotes. When you are committed to a team you don't want to be lagging behind everybody else, letting the group down because you are tired. You wouldn't ever want to think that one of the factors in a loss was that you simply weren't fit enough.

Equally, when you see guys like Mo and Rash doing that, you know that the message of the team, and the culture that it stands for, is strong. It's not that Jos and I were particularly trying to influence our teammates, it was just that it became a normal habit for us. But once you get into a habit of using downtime to top up your exercise, it is something that you naturally maintain. I remember one day in Sri Lanka when it chucked it down and we couldn't practise – but I still wanted to get out there and do some running.

Other players have gradually introduced it into their regimes as well. That particular tour was the first for Ollie Pope and I got the impression that he thought this kind of behaviour was just the norm. I don't think that's a bad thing. None of it is compulsory but it certainly promotes a good team culture when others buy in. People have expectations to get through whatever challenge they have set themselves physically, and the fact that everyone wanted to improve shows the dedication that has gone into a team trying to become the best it can be.

A tournament like the World Cup lasts for a month and a half and features a lot of cricket, with matches all very close to each other, so the fitter you are the better you are going to be at handling that kind of schedule. To go through a tournament like that without injuries, other than to Jason Roy's hamstring and Mark Wood's side in the very last over he bowled, said something for the shape we'd got ourselves into. It gave us the option of nearly playing our best XI in every single game and that's important when you are faced with different conditions.

The excellent fitness levels made sure we always had all bases covered.

•

From the start of the World Cup, we knew we were going to have amazing support; that wherever we travelled around the country we would be treated to an incredible atmosphere and that we could make the most of home advantage that partisan crowds provided. We knew that apart from the two games in which we were due to play India and Pakistan, we would have a raucous following, and there was constant chat among the squad about how good it was to be playing in a home World Cup.

It felt like we had captured the imagination of the British public before a ball was even bowled, and with the Ashes to follow we were so fortunate to be in a position where we had these two massive events at home with no other major global sport event, such as an Olympics, to compete with. Certainly, from the perspective of an English cricketer this felt like the biggest summer of our lives.

I am not a supporter of a football team, although I have come to enjoy watching the big matches, and like the rest of the nation I was gripped by the football World Cup in 2018. I've never been so involved in football before, to be honest. I was so excited to watch it, and you could see Gareth Southgate's squad really did inspire the nation.

During our Cardiff weekend of fitness testing, Gareth dropped in for an hour-long chat in which he charted how his England team had changed during his three years in the job. He talked us through what he did from the moment he took charge and how he wanted to go forward.

The stuff he told us was 90 per cent of what we had done ourselves during a slightly longer period, and it was awesome to know other teams from a completely different sport were thinking like that. He spoke about how he and his players had embraced higher expectations and changed some of the thinking of England teams in the past.

The message Southgate said he'd tried to get across to his England squad before the football World Cup 12 months previously was that although the media would focus on past failures, these were not related to the present.

'You aren't that team. You are the team of 2018. We are four years, eight years, twelve years further on,' he told us he had said to them during their tournament preparations.

'You have the opportunity to write your own destiny.'

We weren't the team of 2015 either. We were not a team focused on the past but on the present.

Southgate's England set a benchmark for how to engage with aspiring players and fans, and this for us was an opportunity to do the same for cricket: to make the next generation want to take up our sport. The responsibility to perform on the pitch, and promote the game as best we could, was something we took seriously. My target was to influence games to help us win. Not necessarily target hundreds or five-for's but to perform at the critical moments in matches. I have always been someone who has placed winning over any personal milestones.

The rise in expectations that the England footballers had to cope with was also something we had become accustomed to. Our own supporters had us down as World Cup favourites and that is not a very English attitude, being so confident heading into a global trophy.

But there was no getting away from it. As we travelled the country, the World Cup was everywhere. Arriving in a new city for a game, you would see yourself and teammates on advertising billboards, and when we got into London, the Mall was flying the flags of every participating nation. That looked awesome.

In normal summers, people stop you in the street from time to time but the World Cup undoubtedly blew everything up for us, and the number of people who so desperately wanted us to do well was inescapable.

One aspect we had no control over, despite being the home team, was the pitches. In bilateral series we get quite a big say on this issue, but that's not the case when it comes to ICC events. So while having the fans behind us was a massive thing, we weren't necessarily playing on the pitches that suited us best. Had we been given the choice we would have liked every pitch to be quick and true, whereas we knew some would be slower and might take some spin. In this regard, we realized that we would have to be adaptable as we switched from venue to venue.

One of the other advantages of playing in England, so I was told, was that it meant we could all escape home between matches. Well, not if you live in the northeast. Sure, others might have got to spend some extra nights with their families, but until the final group match against New Zealand at Chester-le-Street, I'd only spent three nights sleeping in my own house during the previous six weeks.

Geography, and fear of developing a bad back, did for me. If we had a game scheduled in the Midlands, most of the team were no more than one and a half hour's drive away, but for me to head to Durham could take up to four hours. Then I'd be faced with a similar car journey a day or two later. So, while others did get back to see their loved ones, I tended to hang around the cities where matches had just taken place. Not seeing as much of my wife Clare and my children Layton and Libby as I would have liked was undoubtedly a sacrifice for me. On the other hand, it certainly meant my golf improved.

•

When we did get our campaign under way, we made the most terrible of starts as Jonny Bairstow got a first baller against South Africa. Up in the Oval dressing room, everyone was asking each other what the hell was going on? For the previous 18 months this kind of thing just hadn't happened. We were used to our opening batsmen walking out into the middle and whacking it. First-ball dismissals were pretty rare for us, but it did take us back to the start of our four-year World Cup cycle when Jason Roy hit one straight to point against New Zealand at Edgbaston during the ODI series which followed the 2015 tournament.

As I looked around at my England teammates, I told them: 'This is definitely down to Ottis Gibson. This is Gibbo's work!' South Africa had opened the bowling with the leg-spinner Imran Tahir, a tactic not designed for Bairstow as it happened but for his opening partner Jason Roy. Gibson, our former bowling coach, had seen opposition teams throwing the new ball to their spinners against J-Roy in the past, thinking that they always had a chance against him if they could get the ball turning away from the bat, so it was slightly ironic when Tahir got one to spin just enough to do for Jonny instead.

Perhaps it was the loss of that early wicket that contributed to his thinking but Jason did not burst from the blocks as he so often does, taking his time and amending his tempo to the game situation, as well as the character of the pitch. That showed another side of our cricket, that we had developed an ability to adapt. Jason played sensibly for the conditions he was batting in. At the other end, Joe Root played in his normal way to set the platform alongside him.

When they were separated after fifties apiece within the space of four deliveries, it left myself and Eoin Morgan to rebuild from 111–3. However, although I remained at the crease from the 20th over to the 49th, at no stage did I ever feel *in*.

This is tough going. If I am finding it this hard, it's going to be doubly so for anyone coming in to start their innings from scratch.

I knew the onus on me was to be there at the back end to cash in, if possible.

The lack of fluency was undoubtedly the reason I was able to preserve that chance – because I was never confident enough to play in any different way. My aim was to get through for as long as I could, in the hope that the more time spent in the middle the easier hitting the ball would become.

To be honest, apart from a spell of eight balls just before I reached 50, when I struck four fours, things didn't get any easier. I hit 53 singles in the innings, which told its own story, and the brief period of fluency, when I played some shots with real confidence, came from my own manufacturing.

After running down the wicket a couple of times in an attempt to create my own pace on the ball off the bowling of Dwaine Pretorius, which reaped a couple of boundaries, I anticipated that with wicketkeeper Quinton de Kock coming up to the stumps in reaction, that the next delivery was going to be full. With third man also re-positioned inside the 30-yard circle, there was no chance Pretorius was bowling a short ball and so, in my mind, I knew what I was going to do. If I got any kind of bat on a deflection behind the wicket it was going for four. Thankfully, my reading of the situation proved correct and the connection I made with a reverse scoop was perfect.

During that spell I thought I could break the shackles but the ball kept sticking in the pitch. All the slower balls were gripping to an extent, so despite the brief respite the rest of the innings took on the characteristics of the start, being something of a struggle, which meant I had to leave it as late as possible before considering anything outrageous.

Even then, the outrageous didn't really materialise until I slapped a reverse pull straight to point off Lungi Ngidi, having made 89. I knew that any score over 300 would be a really good one on that surface and it being the opening match at a World Cup. Our chats out in the middle reflected this and we agreed that 280 was the minimum defendable target as the innings advanced to 135–3 at the halfway stage.

'If we aim for 290, that's a good score,' Morgs said. 'If we get there before the end of the innings, we might have a bit left in the tank to go higher.'

As it was, we got there in the 48th over and ended up adding another 20. This wasn't a situation for clearing the ropes towards the death, more of a scrambling for ones and twos.

So when South Africa responded to the loss of two early wickets for 44 runs in the powerplay – a period which saw the retirement of Hashim Amla after Jofra Archer struck him in the helmet with a bouncer – with De Kock and Rassie van der Dussen playing a shot a ball, I was thinking: *Flippin' hell, these guys are serious.* I've never felt like that while fielding, never felt anxious about how another team is playing. But they were climbing into their shots, timing them on a surface that had proved so tricky for us to do so.

Thankfully, as he so often does, Liam Plunkett came on, dismissed De Kock via a mishit cross-bat shot and changed the course of the innings. Two more quick wickets followed. I had a hand in both, catching JP Duminy at long-off after he was deceived by Moeen Ali, and running out Pretorius at the start of the next over, the 27th of the innings, to leave the South Africans 144–5.

Neither incident was of note, unlike my next involvement in the game. Let me be honest here, though, the catch that I took to dismiss Andile Phehlukwayo was a fluke. South Africa required 131 from 16 overs when, with the returning Amla for company and four wickets standing, Phehlukwayo swept the first ball after drinks from Adil Rashid.

What happened next? Well, I completely messed up. Phehlukwayo hit the ball flat and hard, but as I was running in from the square-leg boundary I totally misjudged the trajectory of his stroke, thinking he had clothed it when he had struck it cleanly. Suddenly, I realised the ball was flying over my head and left shoulder. I didn't have time to think about things so I readjusted, twisted my body, and leapt up and stuck my right hand out in a reverse-cup position.

At that point it almost felt like a movie. You know, when a certain incident in a film happens, they use special effects like slow motion to emphasise it. Suddenly, everything goes quiet.

That's exactly what it felt like as the ball sunk into my hand. It was like a scene from *The Matrix*. Then I hit the floor. For a split-second my world had been suspended. Then, the volume returned once more and I was hit by a wall of cheers.

It was such an amazing thing to experience: coming up with the ball in my hand, and then turning around to celebrate with the crowd. Watching everyone and hearing everyone around me was a real *wow* moment.

A lot was made of how spectacular the catch was, but it was not as if I was trying something spontaneously that I'd never done before. We practise those kinds of catches all the time in training – catching reverse-cup, over our heads, behind our backs, all that kind of stuff.

When we do those fielding drills, the situations that the coaches create are designed for us to fail. So you might be surprised at how often they come off. In a match situation, when one comes off you might refer to it as a five-percenter, a catch that might make a difference between whether you win or lose, but we work hard at all aspects of our game.

We do a lot of work on catching next to the boundary rope: jumping and attempting catches over our heads; with our arms behind our backs, running at full pelt and trying to stay inside the rope before throwing it back to ourselves and completing the catch inside the field of play; and catching steeplers right on the rope, sometimes arching our backs or throwing ourselves into the air to relay a throw to a teammate standing five or ten metres away.

We are always trying to make practice as hard as we can for ourselves in order to make it feel that little bit easier when we are in a match scenario. So although one-handed catches look

43

spontaneous and improvised, this is only true to a certain extent because so much preparation has gone into perfecting this kind of catch.

People were flagging it up as the best one I'd ever taken. Others were comparing it to the low chance I took just above the turf during the Ashes of 2015, when I snared Adam Voges off Stuart Broad. They were very different catches, one being on the boundary and the other being at slip, but the fact is that one was a misjudgement and would have been nowhere near as spectacular if I'd managed to get myself into the right position in the first place, whereas the low grab at Trent Bridge was a complete reflex reaction from where I was positioned. That just happened. There was no time at all for any adjustment. I had a split-second to react to a ball that had just gone behind me and I grabbed it. One I had time to think about, the other I didn't.

England v South Africa   The Oval, 30 May 2019, Match 1 of 48

Result: England won by 104 runs

ENGLAND innings

ENGLAND innings	R	B	4s	6s	SR
Jason Roy c Faf du Plessis b Andile Phehlukwayo	54	53	8	2	101.88
Jonny Bairstow c Quinton de Kock b Imran Tahir	0	1	0	0	0.00
Joe Root c JP Duminy b Kagiso Rabada	51	59	5	0	86.44
Eoin Morgan (capt) c Aiden Markram b Imran Tahir	57	60	4	3	95.00
Ben Stokes c Hashim Amla b Lungi Ngidi	89	79	9	0	112.65
Jos Buttler (wk) b Lungi Ngidi	18	16	0	0	112.50
Moeen Ali c Faf du Plessis b Lungi Ngidi	3	9	0	0	33.33
Chris Woakes c Faf du Plessis b Kagiso Rabada	13	14	1	0	92.85
Liam Plunkett not out	9	6	1	0	150.00
Jofra Archer not out	7	3	1	0	233.33
Extras (w 8, lb 2)	10				

Total (8 wickets, 50 overs) 311

Fall of wickets
1-1 (Bairstow, 0.2 ov), 2-107 (J Roy, 18.4 ov), 3-111 (J Root, 19.1 ov), 4-217 (E Morgan, 36.5 ov), 5-247 (J Buttler, 41.2 ov), 6-260 (M Ali, 43.6 ov), 7-285 (C Woakes, 47.3 ov), 8-300 (B Stokes, 48.6 ov)

Bowling	O	M	R	W	Econ
Imran Tahir	10	0	61	2	6.10
Lungi Ngidi	10	0	66	3	6.60
Kagiso Rabada	10	0	66	2	6.60
Dwaine Pretorius	7	0	42	0	6.00
Andile Phehlukwayo	8	0	44	1	5.50
JP Duminy	2	0	14	0	7.00
Aiden Markram	3	0	16	0	5.33

SOUTH AFRICA innings

SOUTH AFRICA innings	R	B	4s	6s	SR
Quinton de Kock (wk) c Joe Root b Liam Plunkett	68	74	6	2	91.89
Hashim Amla c Jos Buttler b Liam Plunkett	13	23	1	0	56.52
Aiden Markram c Joe Root b Jofra Archer	11	12	2	0	91.66
Faf du Plessis (capt) c Moeen Ali b Jofra Archer	5	7	1	0	71.42
Rassie van der Dussen c Moeen Ali b Jofra Archer	50	61	4	1	81.96
JP Duminy c Ben Stokes b Moeen Ali	8	11	1	0	72.72
Dwaine Pretorius run out (Ben Stokes/Eoin Morgan)	1	1	0	0	100.00
Andile Phehlukwayo c Ben Stokes b Adil Rashid	24	25	4	0	96.00
Kagiso Rabada c Liam Plunkett b Ben Stokes	11	19	2	0	57.89
Lungi Ngidi not out	6	5	0	1	120.00
Imran Tahir c Joe Root b Ben Stokes	0	1	0	0	0.00
Extras (w 1, b 4, lb 5)	10				

Total (all out, 39.5 overs) 207

Fall of wickets
1-36 (A Markram, 7.4 ov), 2-44 (F du Plessis, 9.3 ov), 3-129 (Q de Kock, 22.6 ov), 4-142 (JP Duminy, 25.5 ov), 5-144 (D Pretorius, 26.2 ov), 6-167 (R van der Dussen, 31.5 ov), 7-180 (A Phehlukwayo, 34.1 ov), 8-193 (H Amla, 38.1 ov), 9-207 (K Rabada, 39.4 ov), 10-207 (I Tahir, 39.5 ov)

Bowling	O	M	R	W	Econ
Chris Woakes	5	0	24	0	4.80
Jofra Archer	7	1	27	3	3.85
Adil Rashid	8	0	35	1	4.37
Moeen Ali	10	0	63	1	6.30
Liam Plunkett	7	0	37	2	5.28
Ben Stokes	2.5	0	12	2	4.23

England v Pakistan,
Trent Bridge, 3 June 2019, *Match 6 of 48*

While our fielding was of the standard we had come to expect in the opening match, this was not the case in our second match a few days later. During our growth as a team, we are never happy to be outplayed but downright furious when we are outfielded, and to be so by Pakistan, a team not renowned for its athleticism and agility, left us furious.

If an opponent bats better than us or an attack bowls well to restrict us, we can accept that on occasion, but fielding is something in which we set the highest bar. We have genuinely good fielders in our squad but what has made us good is our attitude towards being out there in the field. The desire for our teammates to do well is genuine, and so when someone is bowling the other ten players out there with him are desperate to do everything they can to make his figures the best they can be. If you make mistakes, or are not as efficient as you should be, and when it's hurting someone else's performance, that hurts you too. More so, in fact, than if it was you bowling and someone else fielding.

Eoin Morgan was forthright afterwards in expressing just how disappointed he was that we had been outperformed by Pakistan of all teams. Quite frankly, we'd somehow gone from what was widely accepted to be one of our best fielding performances in four years against the South Africans to quite possibly our worst. All within a matter of four days.

It was hard to quantify how badly things really affected us because we missed the chance to dismiss man-of-the-match Mohammad Hafeez very early when Jason Roy dropped him. It was a straightforward skier to mid-off and Jason somehow fluffed it. If he had ten more chances like that in a row, he wouldn't drop any of them. He is right up there with our very best fielders.

Not that it was one individual's fault. This was one of those days. As a collective we were hopeless: the number of times we dived and failed to cut balls off, allowing them to go for four, was embarrassing. We weren't cutting out the twos, as we have become accustomed to doing, and there were some overthrows pitched in for good measure. It was inexplicable.

This is no defence of what happened but I have often felt how you start a game can be a huge influence on what transpires later. We made our first misfielding errors as early as the first over and it carried on for the entire allocation of 50. This isn't just applicable to us as a team; you see examples of it in cricket all the time. It's like a disease that spreads. It starts somewhere on the field and, before you know it, it's infecting everyone. Equally, if someone pulls off a blinding stop or takes a remarkable catch, it can be just as infectious.

It hurt us all and we accepted afterwards in the post-match debrief that it was the difference in our 14-run defeat. We hadn't lost on our batting or our bowling performance, we had simply allowed a team an extra 20 runs and that proved crucial. Considering we were playing at such a high-scoring ground – we were not bad with the ball at all and two players, Joe Root and Jos Butler, scored hundreds – we could hardly be critical of the way that we had put the two sides of our game together.

As for suggestions that we had lost focus with the ball to try to copy the West Indies' tactic of bouncing out the Pakistan batsmen, that was codswallop. This England team has never tried to replicate what other teams do. We have operated in our own way and it has been hugely successful for us. We have never focused on other teams. It is always us, then them.

Trent Bridge, the home of a really flat pitch, is usually a ground where we blow teams away, either batting first and powering out of range, or by chasing huge targets thanks to our great depth of stroke players all the way down the order. Turn up at Trent Bridge and the batsmen usually have smiles on their faces while the bowlers can be heard chuntering 'here we go again'. It's funny how many bowlers' hamstrings feel sore a week or two before we have a one-day match there.

When faced with totals of around 400 or more, our opponents are naturally intimidated and start questioning what they are going to do. Conversely, we are never daunted by any kind of target when we are playing in Nottingham, as was the case back in 2015 when we knocked off 350 against New Zealand with five overs to spare.

At the halfway stage of this game, despite Pakistan's score of 348, we had the same confidence. The pitch at Trent Bridge is such a true surface that you always feel the runs are there as long as you take the game as deep as possible. The way that Joe and Jos played for the fifth wicket meant they both deserved to be the guys to take us to victory at the end. Quite honestly, until Jos got out, immediately after bringing up his three figures, with 61 runs required off 33 balls we were still very much in the game. But we just didn't manage to get over the line.

Despite the loss, I feel there isn't a venue in the country

that better suits the way we have wanted to develop our white-ball cricket during this period. Our entire bowling line-up is used to bowling on very flat wickets. Our batting unit took all the plaudits building into the World Cup, having broken so many records – including the one-day international high of 481 versus Australia at Nottingham in 2018 – but credit should also go to the bowlers for the job they have done in containing opponents in that time. It takes a decent group of bowlers to defend at venues where the par score is around seven runs per over.

The bigger picture is that totals everywhere have been going up over the last few seasons and in 10 years' time, when this team is no longer together, I suspect you will have bowlers getting to 50 one-day international appearances with economy run rates well in excess of a run a ball. It is the way the game is going. Just think back to a decade ago when a bowler's economy for a career tended to hover somewhere between 4.7 and 5.

Not that it means you have to accept going for more runs an over. In fact, I had a chat with Eoin Morgan before the start of the tournament about my role in the bowling attack, following several conversations with Moeen Ali about his mindset when playing one-day international cricket. My target for this World Cup was to return an economy rate of under six. I thought this was a realistic goal but would mean I needed to change the way I went about things when thrown the ball.

Throughout the 4–0 series win over Pakistan a few weeks earlier, I was asking Mo how he had turned himself into such a successful limited-overs spinner – because from my experience of such a role it can be tough. If the pitch is not gripping, you can be on to a hiding to nothing and so I wanted to know what he looked to do to counter batsmen. He's been so successful and although we are different types of bowler, me being a seamer and him a spinner, I could see similarities between what we were being asked to do.

'Bowling in one-day cricket, I have found you need to change your mindset,' he told me. 'It's not about trying to get the batsmen out. The building of pressure will lead to wickets.'

He put it in my mind that there was a different way to go about things when he told me he remained focused on going at less than sixes and how he didn't care if his wickets came caught at deep midwicket and long-off. Squeezing can effectively be more dangerous than attacking.

To some people, aiming to go at a run a ball might seem high but as a bowler, and particularly a sixth bowler in a one-day team, conceding runs at that rate means that the opposition should not be getting totals much above 300, and in the modern game you'd settle for that kind of threshold every time. In this form of the game, it's more about creating the pressure to buy a wicket.

As Mo suggested, a batsman will eventually succumb to the run squeeze and hit the ball straight up in the air, or pull one straight down someone's throat on the boundary. Of course, you're not thinking about obtaining that kind of dismissal, you're just concentrating on running up and putting as many deliveries in the same kind of area as possible to strangle the scoring. In among the stock balls, throw in the odd bouncer and slower ball to ensure they cannot be second guessing everything that you are bowling to them in that period, and you are filling a role that is invaluable to the team.

I knew I would generally only get four or five overs per match. Previously, if I knew I had that amount to bowl I might be thinking that I needed to take a couple of wickets, which is a much more attacking mindset but isn't necessarily a more effective strategy in one-day cricket. It is a different way of looking at things but I considered that sending down five or six overs for no more than 30 runs, regardless of wickets, would be perfect. If I could do that on a game-by-game basis, Morgs would always have enough options elsewhere to be able to rotate the bowlers to suit the conditions.

I left Nottingham satisfied from a bowling point of view, having contributed seven overs for 43, but sharing the disappointment of my England colleagues that our fielding had been dire. At least after just two matches, there was still plenty of time left in the group stage to put things right, but we knew that as the hosts and favourites, other teams wanted to knock us off our pedestal.

On their day, Pakistan are a seriously good team. They can be at the other end of the spectrum on occasion too, but this was one of their better performances and was certainly a step up from a few weeks earlier when we had beaten them easily four times in a row. On this particular day they outbatted, outbowled, and, most frustratingly of all, outfielded us.

England v Pakistan   Trent Bridge, 3 June 2019, Match 6 of 48

Result: Pakistan won by 14 runs

PAKISTAN	R	B	4s	6s	SR
Imam-ul-Haq c Chris Woakes b Moeen Ali	44	58	3	1	75.86
Fakhar Zaman st Jos Buttler b Moeen Ali	36	40	6	0	90.00
Babar Azam c Chris Woakes b Moeen Ali	63	66	4	1	95.45
Mohammad Hafeez c Chris Woakes b Mark Wood	84	62	8	2	135.48
Sarfaraz Ahmed (wk) c & b Chris Woakes	55	44	5	0	125.00
Asif Ali c Jonny Bairstow b Mark Wood	14	11	0	1	127.27
Shoaib Malik c Eoin Morgan b Chris Woakes	8	8	0	0	100.00
Wahab Riaz c Joe Root b Chris Woakes	4	2	1	0	200.00
Hasan Ali not out	10	5	0	1	200.00
Shadab Khan not out	10	4	2	0	250.00
Extras (w 11, b 1, lb 8)	20				
Total (8 wickets, 50 overs)	348				

Fall of wickets

1-82 (F Zaman, 14.1 ov), 2-111 (Imam ul-Haq, 20.1 ov), 3-199 (B Azam, 32.5 ov), 4-279 (M Hafeez, 42.4 ov), 5-311 (A Ali, 46.1 ov), 6-319 (S Ahmed, 47.2 ov), 7-325 (W Riaz, 47.5 ov), 8-337 (S Malik, 49.1 ov)

Bowling	O	M	R	W	Econ
Chris Woakes	8	1	71	3	8.87
Jofra Archer	10	0	79	0	7.90
Moeen Ali	10	0	50	3	5.00
Mark Wood	10	0	53	2	5.30
Ben Stokes	7	0	43	0	6.14
Adil Rashid	5	0	43	0	8.60

ENGLAND	R	B	4s	6s	SR
Jason Roy lbw Shadab Khan	8	7	2	0	114.28
Jonny Bairstow c Sarfaraz Ahmed b Wahab Riaz	32	31	4	1	103.22
Joe Root c Mohammad Hafeez b Shadab Khan	107	104	10	1	102.88
Eoin Morgan (cap) b Mohammad Hafeez	9	18	1	0	50.00
Ben Stokes c Sarfaraz Ahmed b Shoaib Malik	13	18	1	0	72.22
Jos Buttler (wk) c Wahab Riaz b Mohammad Amir	103	76	9	2	135.52
Moeen Ali c Fakhar Zaman b Wahab Riaz	19	20	1	0	95.00
Chris Woakes c Sarfaraz Ahmed b Wahab Riaz	21	14	1	1	150.00
Jofra Archer c Wahab Riaz b Mohammad Amir	1	2	0	0	50.00
Adil Rashid not out	3	4	0	0	75.00
Mark Wood not out	10	6	2	0	166.66
Extras (w 5, lb 3)	8				
Total (9 wickets, 50 overs)	334				

Fall of wickets

1-12 (J Roy, 2.1 ov), 2-60 (J Bairstow, 8.6 ov), 3-86 (E Morgan, 14.5 ov), 4-118 (B Stokes, 21.2 ov), 5-248 (J Root, 38.5 ov), 6-288 (J Buttler, 44.3 ov), 7-320 (M Ali, 47.5 ov), 8-320 (C Woakes, 47.6 ov), 9-322 (J Archer, 48.4 ov)

Bowling	O	M	R	W	Econ
Shadab Khan	10	0	63	2	6.30
Mohammad Amir	10	0	67	2	6.70
Wahab Riaz	10	0	82	3	8.20
Hasan Ali	10	0	66	0	6.60
Mohammad Hafeez	7	0	43	1	6.14
Shoaib Malik	3	0	10	1	3.33

3

ATTITUDE

England v Bangladesh,
Sophia Gardens, 8 June 2019, *Match 12 of 48*

One area in which we were extremely consistent in midsummer was in the totals we were posting during the World Cup. Against Bangladesh in Cardiff, we made it a record seventh consecutive total of 300 or more.

Our no-limits attitude to batting was key to this impressive sequence: we hit 14 sixes, twice as many as any England team had managed in a World Cup match previously, and soared to 386–6, another tournament high. Unsurprisingly, it was also the biggest score in a one-day international at Sophia Gardens.

All powered by a typical innings from Jason Roy. Whenever he gets runs, they tend to be made in a similar fashion. J-Roy starts positively, gets to a point where he is set and the team is in such a good position that he decides to put his foot down and accelerate. He takes the view that if he comes off, the team is going to benefit.

On this occasion, once he got to 110, he produced some

unbelievable hitting. He really took the Bangladesh bowlers to the cleaners. When I say unbelievable hitting, it was actually unbelievable batting. He just went up into the highest gears, to hit 43 off his final 18 deliveries, something he was able to do because he played himself into a position of strength. When he explodes in this manner, there are few who can match him in the world game.

Jason had made his mind up to go for six sixes in an over from the off-spinner Mehidy Hasan but unfortunately succumbed on the fourth. He was really toying with the Bangladeshi attack by this stage.

Bangladesh were the latest team to open the bowling with a spinner, in the form of Shakib Al Hasan, in a bid to counter the attacking stroke play of Jason and Jonny Bairstow. Teams had undoubtedly calculated how powerful they can be up front against the pace bowlers and opted for a change of pace, as spin has generally been more successful against the England opening pair, especially at the start of an innings.

Normally, if you walk out to bat at the start of a 50-over innings as an opener it's against two seamers, a new ball and a bit of swing. But Jason and Jonny's ability to take the best bowling attacks apart was forcing more and more opponents into a change of tactics, asking our first-wicket duo to take on a different challenge.

Yet here they still combined for another century partnership. Then, Jos Buttler, promoted to number four, showed an equal disdain for the bowling in hitting 64 off 44 balls.

The trouble that Jos found himself in while batting was of his own making. He had been hit on the hip by the Pakistan left-armer Wahab Riaz in the previous game, doing damage to the top of his IT band, the tendon that runs down the outer length of the thigh.

Here, it was causing him more and more issues throughout his innings, and there was a shot, when he rocked back to a slightly short ball and punched it off the back foot over long-on and out of the ground for a six off Mosaddek Hossain, that triggered a huge grimace on his face. The wincing, as he grabbed his hip, was a big concern for us. Whenever a player of his ability suffers an injury mid-match it always causes concern. He'd started the tournament well with a hundred and a 50 and we all know what a matchwinner he can be.

The pain from his hip was affecting his movements. Thankfully, though, with Jonny also in the squad it meant that we could err on the side of caution and keep Jos off the field for our defence of a 387-run target.

Bangladesh are not dissimilar to Pakistan in terms of their unpredictability. They can be an extremely competitive team on their day and showed this by beating South Africa and running New Zealand so close in the opening fortnight of the tournament. They can also be hugely disappointing and you are never sure which one of the two you are going to be up against.

It means you have to disregard what they've done in their most recent outings and focus very much on the present. Putting a huge total on the board was obviously key. There are some teams that you feel you can bowl well at but still get outplayed, because of their ability with the bat. Bangladesh aren't one of them. They don't have the depth of others, so we knew the win was ours unless we bowled really poorly.

Our bowling attack had actually taken on a new dimension. This was the second match of the tournament in which Jofra

Archer and Mark Wood bowled together and it was like one was trying to outdo the other for pace. They were both getting it through in rapid fashion. First Jofra bowled a 95 mph delivery. Then Woody came up with an even faster one.

I'd never seen Woody put together so many high-quality performances in an England shirt as he was managing during this period. This was stretching back to the winter tour of the Caribbean all the way into the home season and deep into this tournament, the biggest of our careers.

Woody's not just a Durham teammate, or a work colleague, but a friend, so it was great to see him come through like this. Throughout his career to that juncture there had been a repeated pattern. He would play four or five games, often impressing, and bowling at the kind of speed that no other England bowlers could muster, and then injury would strike. That would set him back to square one. Hats off to him, he always came back, but to go through three ankle operations must have taken its toll mentally. It would have done the same to anyone.

The absence of any reaction in his left ankle was undoubtedly at the heart of Woody's improved performances. He clearly took confidence from the fact that he backed up games against Pakistan before the World Cup and didn't have the worry of breaking down any more. That was always the big thing for Woody: getting to a place where he could be 100 per cent confident that his body was not going to give way. Once these worries were removed, he could concentrate on what he does best – bowling fast.

He certainly wasn't carrying any questions with him into this World Cup and that's why we saw him do what he did. Against Pakistan it could have been the first time he'd gone into any series for England without some nagging doubts at the back of his mind. It was awesome to see firsthand what a fit Mark Wood can do.

In this World Cup, he bowled as fast as he could in every single game and showed himself to be at his absolute best. Add the fact that we had Jofra Archer, operating at the same kinds of speed at the other end – it was an amazing spectacle to watch as a teammate in the field. Having two guys able to bowl at 90 mph plus for 20 overs of an innings was a great weapon for us.

On a slower pitch like this one in Cardiff, it must have been a nightmare to face the pair of them because although you know at what speed the ball is coming out of the hand, you are never quite sure at what speed it will come off the wicket.

If the ball stuck in the wicket for Jofra, it bounced a bit more, encouraged by his height, while others popped through the top of the surface. At the other end, Wood, because he is shorter, didn't tend to get much bounce at all, the ball skidding on a bit instead. You don't have much time to react to him anyway but it's much more difficult to do so on a slower wicket.

An indication of the pace at which Jofra was operating came when he bowled Soumya Sarkar and the ball deflected off the top of the stumps and travelled over Jonny Bairstow's head to clear the boundary. What we were seeing at this very early stage of his career was that there was unrelenting accuracy from his bowling too. Meanwhile, my commitment to bowling dot balls reaped three wickets: reward for the job I'd set out to do a few weeks earlier.

At this point in the tournament, it was just good to be on the field to get results like this 106-run victory. Over the course of its second week, four games fell foul to the weather. It just rained constantly. There was some grumbling about the lack of reserve days, but in a tournament in which every team plays each other it would have been a logistical nightmare, and the fact that you had nine scheduled games per team also meant that you had a cushion if you had a bad performance. There was always a chance to catch up if you lost a game to the elements.

England v Bangladesh   Sophia Gardens, 8 June 2019, Match 12 of 48

Result: England won by 106 runs

ENGLAND	R	B	4s	6s	SR
Jason Roy c Mashrafe Mortaza b Mehidy Hasan	153	121	14	5	126.44
Jonny Bairstow (wk) c Mehidy Hasan b Mashrafe Mortaza	51	50	6	0	102.00
Joe Root b Mohammad Saifuddin	21	29	1	0	72.41
Jos Buttler c Soumya Sarkar b Mohammad Saifuddin	64	44	2	4	145.45
Eoin Morgan (capt) c Soumya Sarkar b Mehidy Hasan	35	33	1	2	106.06
Ben Stokes c Mashrafe Mortaza b Mustafizur Rahman	6	7	0	0	85.71
Chris Woakes not out	18	8	0	2	225.00
Liam Plunkett not out	27	9	4	1	300.00
Extras (nb 1, w 7, lb 3)	11				
Total (6 wickets, 50 overs)	386				

Fall of wickets
1-128 (J Bairstow, 19.1 ov), 2-205 (J Root, 31.3 ov), 3-235 (J Roy, 34.4 ov), 4-330 (J Buttler, 45.2 ov), 5-340 (E Morgan, 46.5 ov), 6-341 (B Stokes, 47.1 ov)

Bowling	O	M	R	W	Econ
Shakib Al Hasan	10	0	71	0	7.10
Mashrafe Mortaza	10	0	68	1	6.80
Mohammad Saifuddin	9	0	78	2	8.66
Mustafizur Rahman	9	0	75	1	8.33
Mehidy Hasan	10	0	67	2	6.70
Mosaddek Hossain	2	0	24	0	12.00

BANGLADESH	R	B	4s	6s	SR
Tamim Iqbal c Eoin Morgan b Mark Wood	19	29	1	0	65.51
Soumya Sarkar b Jofra Archer	2	8	0	0	25.00
Shakib Al Hasan b Ben Stokes	121	119	12	1	101.68
Mushfiqur Rahim (wk) c Jason Roy b Liam Plunkett	44	50	2	0	88.00
Mohammad Mithun c Jonny Bairstow b Adil Rashid	0	2	0	0	0.00
Mahmudullah c Jonny Bairstow b Mark Wood	28	41	1	1	68.29
Mosaddek Hossain c Jofra Archer b Ben Stokes	26	16	4	0	162.50
Mohammad Saifuddin b Ben Stokes	5	8	0	0	62.50
Mehidy Hasan c Jonny Bairstow b Jofra Archer	12	8	2	0	150.00
Mashrafe Mortaza (capt) not out	4	9	0	0	44.44
Mustafizur Rahman c Jonny Bairstow b Jofra Archer	0	3	0	0	0.00
Extras (w 10, lb 9)	19				
Total (all out, 48.5 overs)	280				

Fall of wickets
1-8 (S Sarkar, 3.2 ov), 2-63 (T Iqbal, 11.6 ov), 3-169 (M Rahim, 28.6 ov), 4-170 (M Mithun, 29.3 ov), 5-219 (S Al Hasan, 39.3 ov), 6-254 (M Hossain, 43.1 ov), 7-261 (Mahmudullah, 44.6 ov), 8-264 (M Saifuddin, 45.4 ov), 9-280 (M Hasan, 48.2 ov), 10-280 (M Rahman, 48.5 ov)

Bowling	O	M	R	W	Econ
Chris Woakes	8	0	67	0	8.37
Jofra Archer	8.5	2	29	3	3.28
Liam Plunkett	8	0	36	1	4.50
Mark Wood	8	0	52	2	6.50
Adil Rashid	10	0	64	1	6.40
Ben Stokes	6	1	23	3	3.83

West Indies v England,
Ageas Bowl, 14 June 2019, *Match 19 of 48*

One of the early features of our World Cup campaign was that contributions were coming from across the entire squad. In contrast, we were up against a team renowned for individual brilliance in our next match at Southampton.

West Indies are dangerous. So dangerous. There's no other way to do them justice when describing their batting. On any given day, players like Chris Gayle and Andre Russell can take any bowling attack apart.

They have an X factor, as was demonstrated during our 2–2 ODI series draw in the Caribbean in early 2019. We'd seen what Gayle could do to England throughout his career but particularly during that series, when he showed his 39 years did not weigh heavily upon him, striking 424 runs, 66 per cent more than his nearest rival Eoin Morgan. Equally, Russell goes around the world playing in the Twenty20 leagues, hitting 120-metre sixes with one hand!

Gayle is the kind of guy who can dominate opponents and influence a match result if you don't get on top of him. No matter how he starts an innings, one thing is key – you've got to get him out. Sometimes, he's very happy to start off in a cautious manner, and this is because he knows he can start unloading once he feels confident he has grasped the nature of the pitch and the conditions. You almost have to disregard the scoreboard when he is on one of his slow starts, because he can catch up comfortably later on.

That's why he's never a batsman that you are looking solely to contain. Dismissing him is so important because he can change tempo at the flick of a switch and take anybody down. He's a typical West Indian in that he is so laid back, but this should not disguise the fact that he's clinical with a bat in his hand.

You get the impression that he lines up his bowlers, picking on one that he's going to score heavily off and then launching into him. He does this every time he bats. He has such an amazing limited-overs record and for me this makes him one of the greats of the game. To do what he's done – scoring 25 ODI hundreds and surpassing all others to become West Indies' top scorer – has been phenomenal. Then, you remember that he has in excess of 150 wickets with his off-spin as well.

So we knew what to expect from Gayle for our World Cup match at the Ageas Bowl. Given what a game-changer he can be, it was a real miss from our perspective when Mark Wood dropped him at third man early on in his innings. A couple of us had even told Woody to get ready for a catch the ball before, but the ball spiralled so high and did all sorts on its way down. It had been a typical Gayle attempt to lash this particular delivery from Chris Woakes out of the ground. Woody got in a full-length dive but couldn't cling on, much to his complete and utter devastation. I told him to shut up and get his head up because he'd just made an unbelievable effort to get us the prize scalp.

In the greater scheme of things, that miss on 15 was not a costly one as Liam Plunkett's bang-in ball enticed Gayle into a skyscraper off a top-edged pull and he was out for 36 off 41 balls. But there were other things to worry about in the field, as Eoin Morgan went in the back and J-Roy pinged his hamstring.

This is not what's meant to be happening, I thought. It was a good job, with neither able to bat and us effectively chasing with nine men, that the bowling unit had managed to restrict the Windies to 212.

Between innings, there were a few discussions going on in our changing room about the batting order. The chat was that Chris Woakes would be promoted to number three and Joe Root would open.

'What's the point in that?' I asked Eoin, arguing that Joe had been our regular number three for so long that it made more sense to promote Woakes from eight all the way up to open rather than him come in first wicket down. It seemed like less disruption to me.

In the end, Root opened and got a hundred and Woakes came in at number three and played like the genuine batter he is. In fact, having someone as versatile as him in the XI meant that losing a couple of our top-order players wasn't the biggest of concerns.

The one surprise, to be honest, was the West Indies' tactics. Defending such a modest score, they knew that they had to dismiss us. The Ageas is such a big ground, with lots of space to knock ones and twos, that runs come quite freely. Early wickets would have helped, but on a pitch that was offering a little bit of sideways movement, I was amazed the Windies were obsessed with trying to blast out our top order with the short ball. It was obviously a ploy they thought would work against us, and they persisted with it throughout the innings.

I would have questioned it had I been a member of their coaching staff. Yes, they had talked about it in the build-up, clearly thinking that this ultra-aggressive tactic might work because it had done so against Pakistan. But we have some very fine players of the short ball, I feel, and in my mind, on pitches that nibble about, you have to have discipline in bowling a good line and length, or show plenty of variations. You're not going to intimidate a team with 10 bumpers hooked to deep square-leg. Sure enough, we won the game with 17 overs to spare and only two wickets down.

Result: England won by 8 wickets

WEST INDIES	R	B	4s	6s	SR
Chris Gayle c Jonny Bairstow b Liam Plunkett	36	41	5	1	87.80
Evin Lewis b Chris Woakes	2	8	0	0	25.00
Shai Hope (wk) lbw Mark Wood	11	30	1	0	36.66
Nicholas Pooran c Jos Buttler b Jofra Archer	63	78	3	1	80.76
Shimron Hetmyer c & b Joe Root	39	48	4	0	81.25
Jason Holder (capt) c & b Joe Root	9	10	0	1	90.00
Andre Russell c Chris Woakes b Mark Wood	21	16	1	2	131.25
Carlos Brathwaite c Jos Buttler b Jofra Archer	14	22	0	1	63.63
Sheldon Cottrell lbw Jofra Archer	0	1	0	0	0.00
Oshane Thomas not out	0	11	0	0	0.00
Shannon Gabriel b Mark Wood	0	3	0	0	0.00
Extras (w 12, lb 5)	17				
Total (all out, 44.4 overs)	212				

Fall of wickets:
1-4 (E Lewis, 2.6 ov), 2-54 (C Gayle, 12.6 ov), 3-55 (S Hope, 13.2 ov), 4-144 (S Hetmyer, 29.5 ov), 5-156 (J Holder, 31.6 ov), 6-188 (A Russell, 36.2 ov), 7-202 (N Pooran, 39.4 ov), 8-202 (S Cottrell, 39.5 ov), 9-211 (C Brathwaite, 43.4 ov), 10-212 (S Gabriel, 44.4 ov)

Bowling	O	M	R	W	Econ
Chris Woakes	5	2	16	1	3.20
Jofra Archer	9	1	30	3	3.33
Liam Plunkett	5	0	30	1	6.00
Mark Wood	6.4	0	18	3	2.70
Ben Stokes	4	0	25	0	6.25
Adil Rashid	10	0	61	0	6.10
Joe Root	5	0	27	2	5.40

ENGLAND	R	B	4s	6s	SR
Jonny Bairstow c Carlos Brathwaite b Shannon Gabriel	45	46	7	0	97.82
Joe Root not out	100	94	11	0	106.38
Chris Woakes c Sub b Shannon Gabriel	40	54	4	0	74.07
Ben Stokes not out	10	6	2	0	166.66
Extras (nb 1, w 15, lb 2)	18				
Total (2 wickets, 33.1 overs)	213				

Fall of wickets:
1-95 (J Bairstow, 14.4 ov), 2-199 (C Woakes, 31.5 ov)

Bowling	O	M	R	W	Econ
Sheldon Cottrell	3	0	17	0	5.66
Oshane Thomas	6	0	43	0	7.16
Shannon Gabriel	7	0	49	2	7.00
Andre Russell	2	0	14	0	7.00
Jason Holder	5.1	0	31	0	6.00
Carlos Brathwaite	5	0	35	0	7.00
Chris Gayle	5	0	22	0	4.40

England v Afghanistan,
Old Trafford, 18 June 2019, *Match 24 of 48*

The versatility of our batting order, which stood up in adversity on the south coast, showed itself to be effective in more conventional fashion four days later in the match against Afghanistan in Manchester.

Although Jason Roy began a spell on the sidelines, it was great news that Eoin Morgan was passed fit for a fixture that was a potential banana skin for us. Before the competition began I envisaged Afghanistan winning games, and not only that, but beating one of the bigger nations. Why? Because they had an abundance of natural ability throughout their squad and in Rashid Khan, Mohammad Nabi and Mujeeb Ur Rahman they possessed three quality bowlers who could strangle opposition batsmen.

Old Trafford is also the ground where you'd least like to face them, as arguably it's the most responsive to spin in the country. Chasing on a pitch that might grip for their main bowlers would not be easy, so when Morgs had a word about what we should do in the event of winning the toss – as he occasionally likes to with other players if he is uncertain – I said to bat as it reduced the chances of Afghanistan coming into the game. If the pitch was going to deteriorate, even an under-par score of 220–230 could prove challenging.

My other advice to Eoin during this match came after we

made another solid start with the bat. Jos Buttler and I are always flexible within our batting order depending on the situation of the game, what the pitch is doing and who is bowling at a certain time. If the pitch is an absolute belter, he definitely goes in before me. His strike rate in the last 10 overs of ODI innings is quite remarkable and so it is easy for me to accept slipping down a place in order for us to make full use of his freakish hitting.

I'm normally at the forefront of calls for him to get his pads on once we get beyond the 20-over mark with plenty of wickets in hand. On occasions such as this one, Eoin Morgan was also deliberating whether to promote him higher, but I persuaded Eoin himself to go in at four, his usual batting position. I was among those encouraging him to leave things as they were simply because he is capable of producing a similarly destructive innings.

My argument was that if he played aggressively and it didn't come off, we still had Jos to come in soon afterwards. If he went out and came off, then great. If he didn't, then few balls would have been wasted and Jos could go in and do his thing all the same.

As captain, the team winning is all Morgs cares about. In this game, however, he showed his ability as a devastating batsman. There are some big lads on the global scene who can muscle it out of the park using their physical attributes. So what's his secret? Well, he might not be the biggest but he is strong. And he's a serious power-hitter because of his lovely bat swing, a little pocket rocket. From a position of 164–2 after 30 overs, the foot went down to the floor and Morgs smacked 148 off just 71 balls. It was an incredible effort.

I am pretty sure that Rashid Khan, a leg-spinner on the shopping list of just about every Twenty20 franchise on the planet, had never been treated like that before. Towards the end, I don't think he wanted to bowl at Morgs. This was a man who had gone at under four runs per over throughout his ODI career, someone who'd only twice previously conceded 60 runs in a match and here he was being taken for 110 in nine overs. It was a phenomenal thing to witness.

Eoin had gone out to bat in a certain manner, so whoever was bowling it was a case of 'look out'. Everyone was going to get the same treatment. When you have set yourself for full-on attack mode, a bowler's reputation goes out of the window. There was a real buzz among us as we watched him shower the stands with those 17 sixes. He's certainly not a one-dimensional player. He will sweep, reverse sweep and run down the wicket. Equally, he's happy to rock back in his crease and swat the ball back over the bowler's head. Such an array of options makes him a nightmare to bowl at.

Afterwards, there was a lot of mickey-taking in the dressing room. 'Bloody hell, Eoin, we all need a bad back next game.'

England v Afghanistan   Old Trafford, 18 June 2019, Match 24 of 48

Result: England won by 150 runs

ENGLAND

ENGLAND	R	B	4s	6s	SR
James Vince c Mujeeb Ur Rahman b Dawlat Zadran	26	31	3	0	83.87
Jonny Bairstow c & b Gulbadin Naib	90	99	8	3	90.90
Joe Root c Rahmat Shah b Gulbadin Naib	88	82	5	1	107.31
Eoin Morgan (capt) c Rahmat Shah b Gulbadin Naib	148	71	4	17	208.45
Jos Buttler (wk) c Mohammad Nabi b Dawlat Zadran	2	2	0	0	100.00
Ben Stokes b Dawlat Zadran	2	6	0	0	33.33
Moeen Ali not out	31	9	1	4	344.44
Chris Woakes not out	1	1	0	0	100.00
Extras (nb 1, w 7, lb 1)	9				
Total (6 wickets, 50 overs)	397				

Fall of wickets

1-44 (J Vince, 9.3 ov), 2-164 (J Bairstow, 29.5 ov), 3-353 (J Root, 46.4 ov), 5-362 (J Buttler, 47.4 ov), 6-378 (B Stokes, 49.1 ov)

Bowling	O	M	R	W	Econ
Mujeeb Ur Rahman	10	0	44	0	4.40
Dawlat Zadran	10	0	85	3	8.50
Mohammad Nabi	9	0	70	0	7.77
Gulbadin Naib	10	0	68	3	6.80
Rahmat Shah	2	0	19	0	9.50
Rashid Khan	9	0	110	0	12.22

AFGHANISTAN

AFGHANISTAN	R	B	4s	6s	SR
Noor Ali Zadran b Jofra Archer	0	7	0	0	0.00
Gulbadin Naib (capt) c Jos Buttler b Mark Wood	37	28	4	1	132.14
Rahmat Shah c Jonny Bairstow b Adil Rashid	46	74	4	1	62.16
Hashmatullah Shahidi b Jofra Archer	76	100	5	2	76.00
Asghar Afghan c Joe Root b Adil Rashid	44	48	3	2	91.66
Mohammad Nabi c Ben Stokes b Adil Rashid	9	7	0	1	128.57
Najibullah Zadran b Mark Wood	15	13	0	1	115.38
Rashid Khan c Jonny Bairstow b Jofra Archer	8	13	1	0	61.53
Ikram Ali Khil (wk) not out	3	10	0	0	30.00
Dawlat Zadran not out	0	0	0	0	0.00
Extras (w 8, lb 1)	9				
Total (8 wickets, 50 overs)	247				

Fall of wickets

1-4 (N Zadran, 1.2 ov), 2-52 (G Naib, 11.5 ov), 3-104 (R Shah, 24.5 ov), 4-198 (A Afghan, 40.5 ov), 5-210 (M Nabi, 42.4 ov), 6-234 (H Shahidi, 45.5 ov), 7-234 (N Zadran, 46.2 ov), 8-247 (R Khan, 49.4 ov)

Bowling	O	M	R	W	Econ
Chris Woakes	9	0	45	0	5.00
Jofra Archer	10	1	52	3	5.20
Moeen Ali	7	0	35	0	5.00
Mark Wood	10	1	40	2	4.00
Ben Stokes	4	0	12	0	3.00
Adil Rashid	10	0	66	3	6.60

Sri Lanka v England,
Headingley, 21 June 2019, *Match 27 of 48*

Up until this point, we had generally played on pitches that allowed us to score heavily in the manner we had made our trademark during Trevor Bayliss' time at the helm. However, this was not true of the pitch that we got served up at Headingley against Sri Lanka.

As I have previously mentioned, a lot of the talk during the development of this team had revolved around being able to adapt to different surfaces, to have plans other than plan A, and this was one of those times when we needed to play differently.

One thing we picked up during Sri Lanka's innings, which was held together by Angelo Mathews' unbeaten 85, was that seamers and cutters were sticking in the pitch. We knew that it was a slow surface and that a relatively small score might prove competitive. Not that we were worried about it when we set off on our pursuit of Sri Lanka's 233.

It was hard to score because there was no pace in the wicket and, although we later faced criticism for going too slowly early in the innings, I would argue this was because we did adapt and play completely differently. This was the one match in the whole tournament that forced us to alter our outlook on batting and we just weren't good enough to get over the line.

We had been relatively well placed to do so at 73–3 and

127–4 but we faltered badly later in the innings. Arguably, the turning point was when Moeen Ali, who had just hit a six, tried a repeat next ball with 63 runs required off 70 and was caught on the boundary. On balance, it was not a shot he needed to play.

As the not-out batsman in the middle, I probably didn't experience the same emotions as those who were sat in the dressing room. From my perspective it was not ideal but you can't worry about the loss of a partner, or the way in which you've been separated, when you have the bigger picture to concentrate on.

Mo came in for a lot of external criticism too, and I can understand why – although let's remember that we have all played bad shots in our careers and that poor shots remain in minds longer than good ones. He had decided that he was going to win the game. A quickfire 25 or 30, and brilliant, we win easily. Unfortunately, he got out.

Mo knows and fully understands what it looks like when he gets out in a situation like that – a situation soon made worse as it began our slip from 170–5 to 186–9 – yet at the same time you have to be careful not to take away the aspects that make him the dangerous cricketer that he is. We all have different ways of how we go about things and so have to remember that Mo is a guy with three ODI hundreds, including one off just 53 balls. You can't always use someone's career record as an excuse, but you must try to strike a balance.

Both Jos Buttler and myself took the chance to speak to Mo after the game. Naturally, he was questioning his methods. My advice was to middle the ball for a while longer before playing the big shots as there's always more time than you think in the kind of situation he'd found himself in. Jos advised him: 'Just have a bit more of a think about it, mate.'

His response was that he'd wanted to smack the part-time off-spinner Dhananjaya de Silva. If Mo decided that he was going to go out there and play a quickfire innings to win us the game then good for him to have the balls to go out there to try to implement it.

My advice to people when we talk about one-day batting is: 'Don't wait until you get out into the middle to decide how you're going to play. Have a game plan in your head while you're watching. Don't make your mind up once you're in the action. Have a visual of how you want to play when you take guard. Tell yourself what you want to do and stick to it.'

This has been key to what I view as my own improvement as a batsman across all formats. Afterwards, I questioned myself on whether I had got my own tactics right in trying to get us to the win and another two group points. Had I played correctly? That's a question I always ask myself when things don't work out.

I had contributed an unbeaten 82 but it's not always the personal numbers that count. The fact is we had lost by 20 runs. Could I have done things differently? Should I have done things differently?

To be honest, even with Adil Rashid and Jofra Archer, numbers nine and ten respectively, for company I was as orthodox as possible. As far as I was concerned, in both cases I was partnered by another batsman, and it was only when Mark Wood came in at number eleven that I tried to face as many balls as possible. There had been no panic previously because I foresaw that if we just batted we would win the game.

But with only one wicket standing, it changed the dynamic.

I knew that with the ball cutting in the pitch that the bowlers were going to be a threat due to the close fielders in the ring being quite tight. It was a danger trying to force shots through them for fear of a mishit providing a catch. It wasn't a pitch on which you could play big drives on the up.

Weighing up the situation, I decided I needed to see off Lasith Malinga even though it would push an asking rate that had begun at just over 4.5 up to 9. I told myself not to throw my wicket away trying to attack him, as I might be able to have success against the other bowlers once he'd got through his full allocation of overs.

I left myself with five overs to get 45. I backed myself to get the runs off the rest. The challenge was to hit boundaries early in the over – consecutive sixes off Isuru Udana were followed by consecutive fours off Nuwan Pradeep. Then, get a single later in the over as I only wanted to give Woody the strike for the last ball, or maximum two, every over.

I need to score these runs. I can't expose Woody to too many deliveries.

The Ben Stokes of five years ago would have played it a lot differently. I've come a long way as a cricketer in that time. I might have been able to play in the same manner from a talent perspective but I would not have been capable of the thought processes that go into managing an innings in this way. I wouldn't have had the capacity to think about playing a different, or more complex, kind of innings back then. I might have had the range of strokes and defensive technique to get through, but I would not have been able to understand or deliver the process.

Arguably, I might have unleashed the big shots at seven or

eight wickets down in the midst of other batsmen being dismissed. The fact I managed to get the game to a later stage is because I'm a much more mature cricketer than I was back then. The Ben Stokes of 2014 would have been playing attacking cricket that would have got us to a certain point. But there would be no guarantees of going past that point.

For example, I'm pretty sure that at some point I would have tried to hit Malinga out of the park. Now I know that it is a way that could possibly deliver victory but one that just as likely can end in defeat. I guess what I'm trying to say is that I'm just better at managing the odds these days. There certainly wouldn't have been calculations about who was most likely to get me out, who was most difficult to face and who were the easiest bowlers to hit. It would have been a case of allowing my ego to take me to wherever the game was going to end.

The only place you learn is on the field, and from experience of lots of different types of matches. The more I've played, the more of those types of situations I've found myself in, and the more I understood that you learn most from your failures. One of my favourite sayings is that you either win or you learn.

I've been in those situations where I've been the one batter left and I've been last man out and we've lost. In days gone by, I would have shrugged it off by saying: 'I didn't have any other option.' I would convince myself that my only choice was to try and slog every ball out of the park.

But you have to read every situation as it presents itself to you. I judged that I could get to our target with a combination of brains and brawn. Unfortunately, Woody got a feather on the final ball of the 47th over and we fell short in the end.

It wasn't a result that did any real damage to our confidence.

We just saw it as a hiccup. It was a performance that was nowhere near what we knew we were able to deliver on a field. You can't dwell too long on matches in the group stage of a World Cup, though. But we also knew we couldn't afford to play like that again if we wanted to go further in the competition. The message was clear: be better.

Sri Lanka v England   Headingley, 21 June 2019, Match 27 of 48

Result: Sri Lanka won by 20 runs

SRI LANKA	R	B	4s	6s	SR
Dimuth Karunaratne (capt) c Jos Buttler b Jofra Archer	1	8	0	0	12.50
Kusal Perera (wk) c Moeen Ali b Chris Woakes	2	6	0	0	33.33
Avishka Fernando c Adil Rashid b Mark Wood	49	39	6	2	125.64
Kusal Mendis c Eoin Morgan b Adil Rashid	46	68	2	0	67.64
Angelo Mathews not out	85	115	5	1	73.91
Jeevan Mendis c & b Adil Rashid	0	1	0	0	0.00
Dhananjaya de Silva c Joe Root b Jofra Archer	29	47	1	0	61.70
Thisara Perera c Adil Rashid b Jofra Archer	2	6	0	0	33.33
Isuru Udana c Joe Root b Mark Wood	6	4	1	0	150.00
Lasith Malinga b Mark Wood	1	5	0	0	20.00
Nuwan Pradeep not out	1	1	0	0	100.00
Extras (w 6, lb 4)	10				
Total (9 wickets, 50 overs)	**232**				

Fall of wickets:
1-3 (D Karunaratne, 1.6 ov), 2-3 (MDKJ Perera, 2.2 ov), 3-62 (WIA Fernando, 12.5 ov), 4-133 (BKG Mendis, 29.4 ov), 5-133 (J Mendis, 29.5 ov), 6-190 (D de Silva, 43.3 ov), 7-200 (NTLC Perera, 45.4 ov), 8-209 (I Udana, 46.4 ov), 9-220 (L Malinga, 48.3 ov)

Bowling	O	M	R	W	Econ
Chris Woakes	5	0	22	1	4.40
Jofra Archer	10	2	52	3	5.20
Mark Wood	8	0	40	3	5.00
Ben Stokes	5	0	16	0	3.20
Moeen Ali	10	0	40	0	4.00
Adil Rashid	10	0	45	2	4.50
Joe Root	2	0	13	0	6.50

ENGLAND	R	B	4s	6s	SR
James Vince c Kusal Mendis b Lasith Malinga	14	18	2	0	77.77
Jonny Bairstow lbw Lasith Malinga	0	1	0	0	0.00
Joe Root c Kusal Perera b Lasith Malinga	57	89	3	0	64.04
Eoin Morgan (capt) c & b Isuru Udana	21	35	2	0	60.00
Ben Stokes not out	82	89	7	4	92.13
Jos Buttler (wk) lbw Lasith Malinga	10	9	1	0	111.11
Moeen Ali c Isuru Udana b Dhananjaya de Silva	16	20	0	1	80.00
Chris Woakes c Kusal Perera b Dhananjaya de Silva	2	4	0	0	50.00
Adil Rashid c Kusal Perera b Dhananjaya de Silva	1	2	0	0	50.00
Jofra Archer c Thisara Perera b Isuru Udana	3	11	0	0	27.27
Mark Wood c Kusal Perera b Nuwan Pradeep	0	4	0	0	0.00
Extras (w 5, lb 1)	6				
Total (all out, 47 overs)	**212**				

Fall of wickets:
1-1 (J Bairstow, 0.2 ov), 2-26 (J Vince, 6.5 ov), 3-73 (E Morgan, 18.4 ov), 4-127 (J Root, 30.3 ov), 5-144 (J Buttler, 32.3 ov), 6-170 (M Ali, 38.3 ov), 7-176 (C Woakes, 40.1 ov), 8-178 (A Rashid, 40.5 ov), 9-186 (J Archer, 43.4 ov), 10-212 (M Wood, 46.6 ov)

Bowling	O	M	R	W	Econ
Lasith Malinga	10	1	43	4	4.30
Nuwan Pradeep	10	1	38	1	3.80
Dhananjaya de Silva	8	0	32	3	4.00
Thisara Perera	8	0	34	0	4.25
Isuru Udana	8	0	41	2	5.12
Jeevan Mendis	3	0	23	0	7.66

Australia v England,
Lord's, 25 June 2019, *Match 32 of 48*

All the talk in the build-up to the group game against Australia at Lord's had focused on the fact that Steve Smith and David Warner were being booed by English crowds since returning from their 12-month bans for their parts in Sandpapergate.

Whenever players within our team were asked about it by the media, while we never condoned it neither did we ask for our own supporters to stop. As far as I am concerned, supporters have the right to boo players as they see fit. The two guys themselves knew they were in for it and had to get ready for some serious stick once they were back in the Australian team again, especially when playing in England.

When a crowd is noisy it doesn't necessarily unsettle you but, even if you are good at blocking out peripheral sound, there is no getting away from the fact that you always know it's there. Not that this was the concern of the England team. Our job was to concentrate on getting them out.

To be honest, I thought it was a little bit rich when Australia coach Justin Langer asked for our supporters to refrain. Of course, coaches are always going to stick up for their players, but it seemed convenient for him to forget comments made by Darren Lehmann, his predecessor, inciting Australian crowds to get stuck into Stuart Broad back in 2013–14. Not to mention the words of Nathan Lyon ahead of that year's Ashes series in which he said he wanted to see Mitchell Johnson end some England careers.

It has been well documented that Langer wants to change the culture of this Australia team and the way Australian cricket in general is looked upon from further afield following a year of scandal in 2018, but people have long memories.

Our memories of playing Australia in one-day cricket were good, although they looked a different team from the previous summer when we achieved a 5–0 whitewash over them, mainly because of the returns of Smith and Warner, plus the return of another world-class performer in Mitchell Starc with the ball. I didn't play in that series either due to injury, but it was not an isolated run of success against them. At the turn of 2018, we had also won 4–1 away. The results matched our outlook: if any other country in the world plays their best game against us, it won't be good enough if we play ours.

Unfortunately, we didn't reach our top levels on this occasion against rejuvenated opponents who had moved to within a victory over us of becoming the first team into the semifinals. Once again, we had not played our best at Lord's, where we have the worst record of any home ground in one-day internationals. Not that I think you could read too much into that for this result. There are some grounds that you do really well at and others not so well, and it's hard to find rhyme or reason as to why.

I thought we were extremely unlucky in the first 15 overs with the ball after winning the toss. Everything seemed to go Australia's way. They say you make your own luck, of course, and the way Aaron Finch and David Warner came out and tried to attack probably worked in their favour. They came quite hard at the ball, so edges were flying over or wide of the slips during what represented a pretty decent start on a tricky surface.

On another day we could easily have had three wickets early on, but the luck was with Australia and on occasions there was only a matter of inches between us missing chances and taking them. James Vince was so close to taking a spectacular catch at point when Finch was on 15, diving away, horizontal to the ground like a goalkeeper. Jofra Archer, who created the opportunity, and Chris Woakes were getting plenty out of the pitch, with the ball carrying through very nicely, bouncing from back of a length and zipping past the outside edge countless times.

Finch went on to make a good hundred, but we brought things back pretty nicely in the second half of the innings and I didn't feel like Australia took advantage of where they were when their luck was in. They'd got to 123 when Moeen got one to bounce a little bit more and Warner cut him straight to point, and so for them to close on 285 was a tremendous effort from our perspective – but for a nice cameo from Alex Carey it would have been even fewer.

The pitch had started off rather sticky and we thought it would improve with some heat on it throughout the afternoon. Unfortunately, unlike the Australians, we lost early wickets. Australia had recalled Nathan Lyon for this match and also called up Jason Behrendorff, who proved almost the perfect bowler for the atmospheric conditions. His lack of speed through the air meant he couldn't afford to bowl short, so he just pitched it up and used the left-arm angle to good effect, getting everything out of that wicket that he possibly could.

Sometimes, bowlers who bowl at 80 mph in conditions like that are almost harder to face than those who can bowl rockets. As a batsman, when you see the ball come out of the hand you line it up but it has longer to do things through the air or on contact with the pitch on its journey towards you.

While Behrendorff bowled at 80 mph and got plenty of swing and nip, at the other end Mitchell Starc was getting it down 10 mph quicker, offering quite a different challenge. The ball with which he trapped Joe Root lbw was an absolute beauty, curving perfectly at pace, and facing him in those conditions proved very tough.

It was also Starc who did for me when he returned later in the innings. Did for me good and proper, in fact, because just as he was about to load up for his delivery stride, he twiddled the ball around in his hands to make me think he was going to bowl a slower ball. He suckered me because it was no such thing. It was actually a 90 mph yorker. I have to say, it was a very good bit of bowling. He double bluffed me, and, as I rose to my feet after having had my stumps rearranged, I kicked my bat in frustration.

Just as in the match against the Sri Lankans a few days earlier, I attempted to stay at the crease for as long as I could, without forgetting to take the odd risk because the run rate was climbing. I had tried to pick my moments and once again, the longer I was at the crease, the greater the chance I believe we had of winning. Losing four wickets for 53 had hurt us but with 89 to my name I had not given up hope when Starc slipped one through my jab down to leave us 177–6 with 13 overs remaining. From there, we were all out for 221, which meant Australia won by 64 runs.

Starc had certainly bowled at high pace for this match but suggestions that Eoin Morgan was scared were just rubbish. The short-ball tactic is one that teams have used against him certainly, especially if they have possessed genuinely quick bowlers. But the word scared was inaccurate. You can't be scared and have a record like his.

It's not something you level at an international batsman who averages 40 in more than 200 ODIs. I suspect he couldn't give a toss what Kevin Pietersen had to say on Twitter, to be honest. And his dismissive response to questions about that in the post-match press conference not only told you this; it also spoke of a more serious issue. We needed to turn our campaign around fast.

Australia v England   Lord's, 25 June 2019, Match 32 of 48

Result: Australia won by 64 runs

AUSTRALIA	R	B	4s	6s	SR
Aaron Finch (capt) c Chris Woakes b Jofra Archer	100	116	11	2	86.20
David Warner c Joe Root b Moeen Ali	53	61	6	0	86.88
Usman Khawaja b Ben Stokes	23	29	1	0	79.31
Steve Smith c Jofra Archer b Chris Woakes	38	34	5	0	111.76
Glenn Maxwell c Jos Buttler b Mark Wood	12	8	1	1	150.00
Marcus Stoinis run out (Jonny Bairstow/Adil Rashid)	8	15	1	0	53.33
Alex Carey (wk) not out	38	27	5	0	140.74
Pat Cummins c Jos Buttler b Chris Woakes	1	4	0	0	25.00
Mitchell Starc not out	4	6	0	0	66.66
Extras (w 4, lb 4)	8				
Total (7 wickets, 50 overs)	285				

Fall of wickets

1-123 (D Warner, 22.4 ov), 2-173 (U Khawaja, 32.2 ov), 3-185 (A Finch, 35.3 ov), 4-213 (G Maxwell, 38.2 ov), 5-228 (M Stoinis, 41.5 ov), 6-250 (S Smith, 45.4 ov), 7-259 (P Cummins, 47.1 ov)

Bowling	O	M	R	W	Econ
Chris Woakes	10	0	46	2	4.60
Jofra Archer	9	0	56	1	6.22
Mark Wood	9	0	59	1	6.55
Ben Stokes	6	0	29	1	4.83
Moeen Ali	6	0	42	1	7.00
Adil Rashid	10	0	49	0	4.90

ENGLAND	R	B	4s	6s	SR
James Vince b Jason Behrendorff	0	2	0	0	0.00
Jonny Bairstow c Pat Cummins b Jason Behrendorff	27	39	5	0	69.23
Joe Root lbw Mitchell Starc	8	9	2	0	88.88
Eoin Morgan (capt) c Pat Cummins b Mitchell Starc	4	7	1	0	57.14
Ben Stokes b Mitchell Starc	89	115	8	2	77.39
Jos Buttler (wkt) c Usman Khawaja b Marcus Stoinis	25	27	2	0	92.59
Chris Woakes c Aaron Finch b Jason Behrendorff	26	34	2	0	76.47
Moeen Ali c Alex Carey b Jason Behrendorff	6	9	1	0	66.66
Adil Rashid c Marcus Stoinis b Mitchell Starc	25	20	3	1	125.00
Jofra Archer c David Warner b Jason Behrendorff	1	4	0	0	25.00
Mark Wood not out	1	2	0	0	50.00
Extras (w 3, b 1, lb 5)	9				
Total (all out, 44.4 overs)	221				

Fall of wickets

1-0 (J Vince, 0.2 ov), 2-15 (J Root, 3.3 ov), 3-26 (E Morgan, 5.5 ov), 4-53 (J Bairstow, 13.5 ov), 5-124 (J Buttler, 27.2 ov), 6-177 (B Stokes, 36.6 ov), 7-189 (M Ali, 39.3 ov), 8-202 (C Woakes, 41.3 ov), 9-211 (J Archer, 43.3 ov), 10-221 (A Rashid, 44.4 ov)

Bowling	O	M	R	W	Econ
Jason Behrendorff	10	0	44	5	4.40
Mitchell Starc	8.4	1	43	4	4.96
Pat Cummins	8	1	41	0	5.12
Nathan Lyon	9	0	43	0	4.77
Marcus Stoinis	7	0	29	1	4.14
Glenn Maxwell	2	0	15	0	7.50

4

SMARTS

England v India,
Edgbaston, 30 June 2019, *Match 38 of 48*

There was no room for manoeuvre now. Defeat to Australia had simplified the equation. To win the World Cup from here, we had to beat both India at Edgbaston and New Zealand at my Durham base of Chester-le-Street.

With eight points from seven matches, we occupied the fourth and final qualifying place, a point ahead of Bangladesh. Sri Lanka and Pakistan, two and three points behind us respectively, each had a game in hand.

India, a point ahead with two games in hand, plus the early pacesetters New Zealand and table-toppers Australia looked home and hosed for the semi-finals. Victories in both remaining group matches would guarantee progress for us too, but there was no getting away from the fact that we were under pressure.

I was certainly feeling the strain and I told David Young, our team psychologist, as much after he invited me for a coffee at Starbucks in Birmingham's Mailbox shopping centre. He asked me how I was feeling about the situation in which the England team found itself ahead of fixtures against two very strong opponents.

'How are things, Ben?' he asked me. 'What are your thoughts on what lies ahead?'

'I'm nervous,' I told him, opening up on exactly what was going through my head.

He then encouraged me to repeat everything I had told him to the rest of the group at a team meeting convened on the large viewing balcony outside the dressing rooms at Edgbaston on our first day of practice ahead of the India fixture.

'Nerves and worrying about the worst that can happen, worrying about your own performance, is something that happens to everybody,' I began.

I wanted to make it clear that it was very common to feel this way. Sometimes I think players sense that they are the only person who feels a certain way, when the truth is that nearly everyone in the dressing room is in the same boat but is afraid to admit it.

When you are feeling anxious and nervous about what's coming up, especially when you know what is on the line, the chances are that all your teammates are going through the same experience.

If you're nervous about the game, about how you are going to do, nervous in the knowledge that without winning you're not going to go through to the business end of the competition, to be able to achieve your dreams, you can feel isolated. You are unlikely to want to speak about it because, as a professional sportsman, you do not like to admit to fragility or weakness. We are conditioned to be tough, unforgiving competitors.

'I am nervous, I am anxious, I am worrying about what happens if we don't win. Believe me, I am worried.'

To be frank, I wasn't only worried about doing my own job but the prospect of other guys not performing and it preventing us progressing beyond the group stage.

'Everybody in our changing room has the exact same thoughts going through their minds, right now, I guess. No-one is alone. It's fine to feel nervous, it's fine to feel anxious, it's fine to worry about what is required to get through to the next round and it is fine to worry about the worst possible thing that can happen. That's all absolutely normal.'

During that group chat, we tried, rather than running away from the situation, to embrace this nervous energy. We knew what was on our shoulders and what we had to do. Rather than dwell in lonely places as individuals, allowing these feelings to eat away at us, we came together and opened up.

Hearing a senior guy like me, someone approaching 100 one-day international caps, saying that I had a few mental gremlins was a huge thing in settling everybody else down. Youngy thought that coming from me it would resonate with the rest of the lads more than anything he could say on the matter. There is nothing more powerful than a player speaking, he told me, over our coffee. It was then that I started thinking more clinically about exactly how I was feeling and made my mind up that I needed to share it.

•

There was another psychological boost for the team at this most crucial time – the return to the team of Jason Roy from a hamstring injury.

It was also a significant factor for India, as they had to bowl at him. J-Roy stands at just over 6 ft tall, has shoulders like granite and looks such a huge man when he's stood at the crease. Having him back – given his form at the World Cup and throughout the previous 20 months, a period in which he passed 50 on a dozen occasions in 32 innings and converted half of them into hundreds – was a massive thing for our team.

He brought such energy to our group at this stage of the competition, and it was refreshing to see him going about his batting in such a confident way after Eoin Morgan won the toss. He has such swagger about him that he retains confidence no matter who is bowling at him. When he's in form, he doesn't care who the bowlers are: he will not let them settle regardless of their names and reputations. I love watching the way he plays cricket.

Getting Jason and Jonny Bairstow back together as an opening partnership was critical. The thing I loved about this particular game was the way that the pair of them played the Indian spinners. They knew that Chahal and Kuldeep Yadav represented the main threat – the two bowlers that India use in the middle overs to block opposition teams off and control the run rate – but they simply hit them out of the park.

Virat Kohli turned to Chahal as early as the sixth over, but from the off Roy and Bairstow struck the ball all around the ground, the latter launching his third ball straight over the bowler's head for a one-bounce four. They used every shot in their repertoires to manipulate the field and when they decided to go big, they went big, regardless of the fact that fielders were back on the boundary. When they opted for the aerial route, they just kept hitting it over their heads, without a second thought.

South Africa, The Oval (London), 30 May – won by 104 runs

Switch-hitting during my innings of 89.

'That catch': a one-handed grab and I'm about to hit the deck.

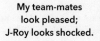

My team-mates look pleased; J-Roy looks shocked.

Joe Root and Jos Buttler both scored wonderful centuries in our total of 334-9.

Jason Roy thrashes another boundary on his way to a fantastic innings of 153.

I'm celebrating the wicket of Shakib Al Hasan - one of my three wickets on the day.

Mark Wood
bowled
beautifully,
taking 3-18.

Skipper Eoin Morgan smashes one of 17 sixes in his remarkable innings of
148 runs from just 71 balls.

Left. A big swing to the leg-side in my knock of 82 not out.

Right. I was pleased with my half-century, but losing the game was really disappointing.

I squeeze the ball past Glenn Maxwell on my way to scoring 89, but we lost to the Aussies.

I feel another switch-hit coming on.
I scored 79 in this must-win game.

Jonny Bairstow's century was pivotal in
our defeat of the Black Caps.

I celebrate another wicket with Adil Rashid. He and Chris Woakes took three wickets
each and restricted the Aussies to a modest total which we chased down with ease.

Lining up for the national anthems.

Trent Boult catches me on the boundary edge but he can't help stepping on the rope and so we get a crucial six runs as a result.

I apologise to the New Zealand team for inadvertently deflecting the ball for a boundary as I slid my bat in to avoid a possible run out.

Left. Running hard with Jos Buttler during the hurly-burly of our Super Over.

Right. Jofra Archer's composure under intense pressure during New Zealand's Super Over was extraordinary.

Jos Buttler runs out Martin Guptill off the final ball of the Super Over.

Flat on my back at the very end of the game.

Above. I can't quite believe I'm holding the World Cup trophy. A truly amazing feeling. Joe has my back.

Above, right. Receiving my Player of the Match award from one of the sport's greatest players – Sachin Tendulkar.

Right. The celebrations continue in the dressing room.

Above. We were excited to be invited to take the trophy to Number 10 Downing Street.

Left. Meeting the then Prime Minister Theresa May, a genuine cricket fan.

It was like they were saying: 'Virat, we know these spinners are your main bowlers through the middle, and you want to get a grip on the game, but we 're not going to let them settle. We're going to whack them.' It was some statement, and I don't think Virat had a clue what to do.

He was obviously not used to seeing his two prized wrist-spinners being treated like that. It was just such a shock to them all but they didn't know how to respond. Tactically, they didn't really have anywhere else to go. Chahal had never conceded as many as 88 runs in an ODI before, while Kuldeep went for 72, the third most expensive return of his 50-over career with India.

Thanks to Bairstow's first World Cup hundred and an equally brilliant 66 off 57 balls from Roy – out to a wonder catch by the substitute Ravindra Jadeja, after India reprieved him by not reviewing a short ball from Hardik Pandya that feathered his glove – India's fightback was only a temporary disruption to our progress. So when I came into bat at 207–3 in the 34th over, I knew there were more than enough deliveries remaining for me to be able to assess what the pitch was doing, and allow myself the best opportunity to get in, with a view to getting to a stage where it was time to apply some pressure of my own.

I went along at just a fraction below a run a ball before deciding it was time to let loose once into my twenties. Part of my calculations on how to play the situation was that I knew Jasprit Bumrah still had some overs left, so while he was not bowling I wanted to capitalise on as many deliveries from the other bowlers as I could. *The risks will have to be taken against the others,* I told myself.

Bumrah is very hard to get away and is rated as the best death bowler in the world for a reason. He always pulls out a performance and is rarely anything other than deadly accurate. But, thanks to all the front-end work that Jonny and Jason did in this innings, I didn't feel under pressure to go too hard against him even when he came back on for the final three overs of his allocation towards the end of the innings.

When your openers set such a great platform it allows the rest of the top six breathing space and the freedom to target the bowlers we feel we can score heavily off while playing those who demand respect with greater caution. So it was a matter of taking what I could off Bumrah in making a third consecutive 50 and trying to milk the runs at the other end with more daring shots against Chahal and Mohammed Shami in particular.

Improvising against Bumrah in the final over of the innings coincided with my eventual departure for 79, off 54 balls, with an attempted scoop flying straight to fine-leg.

A score of 337–7 represented a strong response to the must-win nature of the match, and we followed this with what was our best powerplay period with the ball in the tournament, conceding only 28 runs despite only taking one wicket – that of KL Rahul.

The way that Rohit Sharma and Virat Kohli played was mystifying. I know that we bowled brilliantly well during this period, but the way they went about their batting just seemed bizarre. They allowed their team to get so far behind the game. They showed no desire to put any pressure back onto our team, content instead to just drift along, a tactic that was clearly playing into our hands.

In normal circumstances, when as a batting side you are

chasing a big score like that, the opening 10 overs is where you really try to get on top of things, to cash in on the fact there are only two fielders allowed outside of the circle.

The intention should be to exploit these gaps, to get ahead of the game, do the work early and not force yourself to be burdened throughout the middle overs when run rates tend to drop. Particularly given their quality, I felt the Indian top order should have tried to be more proactive. Instead they just left the rest of the team with too much to do.

Compared to other leading nations, India were still using quite an outdated method of playing to build their totals, keeping wickets in hand in a bid to cash in at the back end of the innings. Yet that can be a dangerous game because the bigger the score, the less margin there is for any error, and the quicker the required run rate climbs once you hit the second half of an innings.

India needed nine an over when Liam Plunkett continued his running theme of the tournament in the 29th over, adding Kohli to his illustrious list of victims. He not only has a habit of picking up wickets but regularly pouches the big ones. He doesn't typically knock them over, rather wearing them down instead, but always seemed to be the one getting the crucial breakthroughs. Pudsey became our World Cup partnership breaker, with his wickets coming after the highest average stand of 63. So it was no longer a shock when he got out the vital players.

On this occasion, when Virat was dismissed, from a miscued drive to point, there were a few shrugs of the shoulders and players muttering with smiles on faces: 'Of course he's got Virat. It's Pudsey.'

Arguably, the way that MS Dhoni played when he came in

with 112 runs needed from 11 overs was even stranger. He appeared more intent on singles than sixes. Even with a dozen balls remaining, India could still have won. Yes, it was a daunting task but it was still possible. Yet there was little or no intent from him or his partner Kedar Jadhav. To me, while victory is still possible you always go for broke.

There is a theory in our camp that Dhoni's way of playing has always been the same. Even if India can't win the game, he takes it right to the end to try to make sure that India's run rate stays relatively healthy. His big thing has always been to give himself a chance of winning by being at the crease for the final over, but he generally likes to stick around to get as close to a target as possible even in a losing cause.

I have witnessed at first hand how successful his tactics can be. During my first season at the Indian Premier League in 2017, I was batting with Dhoni in a match against Sunrisers Hyderabad that was running away from Pune, the team we were representing. When I was dismissed, the equation stood at 56 runs required for victory from 23 deliveries. We won from the last ball of the match; Dhoni was particularly savage on Bhuvneshwar Kumar.

On this occasion it wasn't until the last over that India, through Dhoni, finally cleared the ropes. In the modern game, when one team has struck 13 sixes in their batting effort, that's just odd. Not that we were overly bothered because all we cared about was getting the result.

Yet it was weird to hear India captain Kohli whingeing about the size of the boundaries at the post-match presentation ceremony. He said the toss was vital, adding 'especially looking at the boundary that was quite short. It was 59 metres, which coincidentally is the minimum amount required in an international match. Quite bizarre on a flat pitch. If batsmen are able to reverse sweep you for six on a 59-metre boundary there is not much you can do. And one side was 82 metres.'

I have never heard such a bizarre complaint after a match. It's actually the worst complaint you could ever make. Both teams have to bat out there, and get the same number of balls, so how can the playing area's dimensions be an advantage to one team or the other?

England v India   Edgbaston, 30 June 2019, Match 38 of 48

Result: England won by 31 runs

ENGLAND	R	B	4s	6s	SR
Jason Roy c sub (Ravindra Jadeja) b Kuldeep Yadav	66	57	7	2	115.78
Jonny Bairstow c Rishabh Pant b Mohammed Shami	111	109	10	6	101.83
Joe Root c Hardik Pandya b Mohammed Shami	44	54	2	0	81.48
Eoin Morgan (capt) c Kedar Jadhav b Mohammed Shami	1	9	0	0	11.11
Ben Stokes c sub (Ravindra Jadeja) b Jasprit Bumrah	79	54	6	3	146.29
Jos Buttler (wk) c & b Mohammed Shami	20	8	1	2	250.00
Chris Woakes c Rohit Sharma b Mohammed Shami	7	5	1	0	140.00
Liam Plunkett not out	1	4	0	0	25.00
Jofra Archer not out	0	0	0	0	0.00
Extras (w 4, b 2, lb 2)	8				
Total (7 wickets, 50 overs)	337				

Fall of wickets

1-160 (J Roy, 22.1 ov), 2-205 (J Bairstow, 31.4 ov), 3-207 (E Morgan, 33.4 ov), 4-277 (J Root, 44.1 ov), 5-310 (J Buttler, 46.6 ov), 6-319 (C Woakes, 48.1 ov), 7-336 (B Stokes, 49.4 ov)

Bowling	O	M	R	W	Econ
Mohammed Shami	10	1	69	5	6.90
Jasprit Bumrah	10	1	44	1	4.40
Yuzvendra Chahal	10	0	88	0	8.80
Hardik Pandya	10	0	60	0	6.00
Kuldeep Yadav	10	0	72	1	7.20

INDIA	R	B	4s	6s	SR
KL Rahul c & b Chris Woakes	0	9	0	0	0.00
Rohit Sharma c Jos Buttler b Chris Woakes	102	109	15	0	93.57
Virat Kohli (capt) c sub (James Vince) b Liam Plunkett	66	76	7	0	86.84
Rishabh Pant c Chris Woakes b Liam Plunkett	32	29	4	0	110.34
Hardik Pandya c sub (James Vince) b Liam Plunkett	45	33	4	0	136.36
MS Dhoni (wk) not out	42	31	4	1	135.48
Kedar Jadhav not out	12	13	1	0	92.30
Extras (w 6, lb 1)	7				
Total (5 wickets, 50 overs)	306				

Fall of wickets

1-8 (KL Rahul, 2.3 ov), 2-146 (V Kohli, 28.2 ov), 3-198 (R Sharma, 36.1 ov), 4-226 (R Pant, 39.1 ov), 5-267 (H Pandya, 44.5 ov)

Bowling	O	M	R	W	Econ
Chris Woakes	10	3	58	2	5.80
Jofra Archer	10	0	45	0	4.50
Liam Plunkett	10	0	55	3	5.50
Mark Wood	10	0	73	0	7.30
Adil Rashid	6	0	40	0	6.66
Ben Stokes	4	0	34	0	8.50

England v New Zealand,
Chester-le-Street, 3 July 2019, *Match 41 of 48*

What we had managed to do was adapt to the conditions better than India. We had played smarter and more aggressively when the contest dictated it was necessary.

Thankfully, we were also able to assess and adapt in our final group fixture, at sunny Chester-le-Street, in what was effectively a quarter-final against New Zealand. For us at least, if not them; they had more breathing space. Generally, over a period of time we had responded to such pressure well, and this was to be no different.

Again, it was Jonny Bairstow who raced us out of the blocks and Jason wasn't far behind him. Only this time, the way that they played, after another toss had been won, disguised the fact that this was not necessarily an easy wicket to bat on.

Shortly before J-Roy became the first wicket of the day at 123 in the 19th over, Eoin Morgan said to a few of us in the changing room: 'This isn't going to be easy. It's just that these two are making it look like that right now. Just bear that in mind.'

He was spot on. As the ball got a little softer it began to grip in the pitch a bit more, and we soon found that the surface was not as true as our openers had made it look and was slightly two-paced.

So urging the other batsmen to give themselves time to

assess what the ball was doing proved to be prudent advice. In contrast to the new ball, which had come on nicely, it did become harder to bat on and Eoin practised what he preached with a very clever innings of 42 to make sure that we got another 300-plus total to defend.

This kind of application displayed a different side to his batting than his innings against Afghanistan when he showered Old Trafford with more than 100 runs in sixes. This was a much tougher challenge on a hot day, the high temperature making the pitch drier and drier as time went on and making stroke play increasingly difficult. To scramble above 300 was another indication of how the team had learned from similar situations in the past and the value of being able to judge a score.

Sometimes matches are settled by the finest of margins. In this particular one, we were thankful to Mark Wood's fingertips for the dismissal of the prolific Kane Williamson, after Ross Taylor's return drive deflected into the stumps at the bowler's end to secure a fortuitous run out. Woody reckoned Kane was unlucky there because he has the smallest hands in the world.

To be fair, those kinds of dismissals do not happen very often and rarely can this have been the case for such an influential player. However, having been reduced to 14–2 against the new ball, New Zealand's tactics had already become fairly obvious. They were trying to protect their net run rate, focusing on posting a reasonable score rather than chasing hard at the 306-run target. They knew that with the cushion of their early wins in the group stage that they could lose and still go through to the last four. Only a miraculous, landslide win for Pakistan against Bangladesh in the final group match would see them eliminated.

Not that New Zealand's agenda was going to distract us from our goal of bowling them out and securing the win that would seal our own passage to the semis. Admittedly, when you are used to two teams always playing to win, this was an unusual situation, but when you get to the back end of a tournament you have to be smart about things.

New Zealand were aware that net run rate could come into the equation when attempting to separate two teams finishing level on points. In that scenario, it can be the difference between progressing and being knocked out, so I totally understand why teams do factor that in. Any other team in the same position would have done exactly the same thing. It didn't make any difference how they made the semi-finals, they just had to get there.

Equally, the desperation of our players to book our semi spot at Edgbaston – where we anticipated a re-match with India – revealed itself in the cases of Jofra Archer and Jason Roy. Jofra's side strain wasn't a massive talking point in our changing room but just like with Jason's hamstring, if it hadn't been the World Cup, he wouldn't have played those games against India and New Zealand. Both of them would have been given periods of time to rest properly.

But in a World Cup, players are going to do anything and everything to make sure they are on that field if at all possible. Here were two guys trying to win games for their country, playing through injuries that could have got a lot worse. The chance for glory far outweighed any concerns about their own well-being.

One ball too many for Jofra and he could have ripped his side. That's the kind of injury that would leave you out for six months. For Jason, a slip on the outfield and he would potentially tear his hamstring. That would have seen him on the sidelines for five to six weeks. It had got to a point in terms of our qualification fight where we needed Jason back in the team even if he was only 80–85 per cent fit.

We knew we were off to Edgbaston, a ground where we had won all 10 of our previous matches across all formats. What we didn't know for sure until three days later was the identity of our opponents.

ENGLAND	R	B	4s	6s	SR
Jason Roy c Mitchell Santner b Jimmy Neesham	60	61	8	0	98.36
Jonny Bairstow b Matt Henry	106	99	15	1	107.07
Joe Root c Tom Latham b Trent Boult	24	25	1	0	96.00
Jos Buttler (wk) c Kane Williamson b Trent Boult	11	12	1	0	91.66
Eoin Morgan (capt) c Mitchell Santner b Matt Henry	42	40	5	0	105.00
Ben Stokes c Matt Henry b Mitchell Santner	11	27	0	0	40.74
Chris Woakes c Kane Williamson b Jimmy Neesham	4	11	0	0	36.36
Liam Plunkett not out	15	12	1	0	125.00
Adil Rashid b Tim Southee	16	12	1	0	133.33
Jofra Archer not out	1	1	0	0	100.00
Extras (w 7, b 4, lb 4)	15				
Total (8 wickets, 50 overs)	305				

Fall of wickets

1-123 (J Roy, 18.4 ov), 2-194 (J Root, 30.1 ov), 3-206 (J Bairstow, 31.4 ov), 4-214 (J Buttler, 34.2 ov), 5-248 (B Stokes, 41.6 ov), 6-259 (C Woakes, 44.5 ov), 7-272 (E Morgan, 46.1 ov), 8-301 (A Rashid, 49.3 ov)

Bowling	O	M	R	W	Econ
Mitchell Santner	10	0	65	1	6.50
Trent Boult	10	0	56	2	5.60
Tim Southee	9	0	70	1	7.77
Matt Henry	10	0	54	2	5.40
Colin de Grandhomme	1	0	11	0	11.00
Jimmy Neesham	10	1	41	2	4.10

NEW ZEALAND	R	B	4s	6s	SR
Martin Guptill c Jos Buttler b Jofra Archer	8	16	1	0	50.00
Henry Nicholls lbw b Chris Woakes	0	1	0	0	0.00
Kane Williamson (capt) run out (Mark Wood)	27	40	3	0	67.50
Ross Taylor run out (Adil Rashid)	28	42	2	0	66.66
Tom Latham (wk) c Jos Buttler b Liam Plunkett	57	65	5	0	87.69
Jimmy Neesham b Mark Wood	19	27	1	0	70.37
Colin de Grandhomme c Joe Root b Ben Stokes	3	13	0	0	23.07
Mitchell Santner lbw b Mark Wood	12	30	1	0	40.00
Tim Southee not out	7	16	0	0	43.75
Matt Henry b Mark Wood	7	13	0	0	53.84
Trent Boult st Jos Buttler b Adil Rashid	4	7	1	0	57.14
Extras (w 6, b 2, lb 6)	14				
Total (all out, 45 overs)	186				

Fall of wickets

1-2 (H Nicholls, 0.5 ov), 2-14 (M Guptill, 5.2 ov), 3-61 (K Williamson, 15.1 ov), 4-69 (R Taylor, 16.4 ov), 5-123 (J Neesham, 25.1 ov), 6-128 (C de Grandhomme, 28.1 ov), 7-164 (T Latham, 38.3 ov), 8-166 (M Santner, 39.2 ov), 9-181 (M Henry, 43.4 ov), 10-186 (T Boult, 44.6 ov)

Bowling	O	M	R	W	Econ
Chris Woakes	8	0	44	1	5.50
Jofra Archer	7	1	17	1	2.42
Liam Plunkett	8	0	28	1	3.50
Mark Wood	9	0	34	3	3.77
Joe Root	3	0	15	0	5.00
Adil Rashid	5	0	30	1	6.00
Ben Stokes	5	0	10	1	2.00

Australia v England,
Edgbaston, 11 July 2019, Semi-Final, *Match 47 of 48*

Australia's surprise 10-run defeat to South Africa at Old Trafford changed the make-up of the semi-finals and triggered
chaotic scenes in Manchester and also in Birmingham, where
there were so many Indian fans milling around our hotel.

Everybody in the world shared the expectation that Australia would win that match on 6 July, top the points table, and
therefore stay put and be nice and relaxed to take on New
Zealand at the same venue 72 hours later. Meanwhile, we
would face Virat Kohli's India at a ground we had silenced in
the corresponding group match-up. Once again, Indian supporters had taken the majority of tickets for the match.
Suddenly, however, everything had switched round.

For a semi-final match of a major tournament, I don't think
it matters either where you play or who you are playing, nor
what has gone on between the two teams previously. Forget
what had happened against Australia in the group game, or the
warm-up match in Southampton in late May for that matter,
the results for which went against us. All that counted was this
last-four meeting in Birmingham on 11 July.

What a stunning start we made, too. Jofra Archer's first ball
from the city end will live long in the memory. Aaron Finch
had enjoyed a sensational tournament with the bat up until this
point, so for Jofra to get one to nip back on off-stump to secure

the lbw was a big gee-up for the lads in the field. Early wickets obviously set the tone for any match and when one of them is Finch and another is David Warner, nicked off by Chris Woakes soon afterwards, there is no doubting where the momentum lies. Australia were never going to recover from 14–3. To be truthful, we completely blew them away.

This was soon turning into the kind of comprehensive 50-over performance that England supporters had become accustomed to seeing: knocking a team over for a below-par score, in this case 223, and then knocking those off with eight wickets and 107 balls in hand.

Watching the run chase was so exciting. Jason Roy was simply crunching the ball. He was so authoritative in his striking from the start but then just went berserk. That was the bit I enjoyed the most, particularly the three big sixes in a row off Steve Smith's leg-spin. He was hitting them as high as he was far.

He was playing so well that it was no wonder he was spewing as he left the field not long afterwards, given out wrongly caught behind by Kumar Dharmasena for 85, when he was nowhere near a bouncer from Pat Cummins. Jason signalled for the review and was left in disbelief when he was reminded by Marais Erasmus from square-leg that Jonny Bairstow had already burned it challenging a leg-before decision just a handful of overs earlier. The perceived dissent he showed in refusing to accept the decision cost him 30 per cent of his match fee but also what was looking like a 10th one-day international hundred.

The way he had dealt with Mitchell Starc, Australia's main threat with the ball and with 27 wickets the most prolific bowler at the World Cup by a distance, was masterful. I have never seen Starc treated like that before in a one-day game. The one shot that stuck in my head was the audacious flick of the wrists that sent the ball sailing into the stand at fine-leg during the first powerplay. That was the stroke that people latched on to as evidence that J-Roy could perhaps make a successful transition to Test cricket.

Meanwhile, Starc's World Cup had panned out similarly to that of his captain Finch. The pair of them had been absolutely phenomenal up until the semi-final stage when Finch got out first ball and Starc well and truly went the journey. In sport, you can never predict what is round the corner.

When you can halt two of the opposition's biggest players, and two in-form players at that, you stand yourselves in good stead to win a game of limited-overs cricket. Starc was the leading wicket-taker and Finch one of the leading run-getters, having struck in excess of 500. If neither are contributing anything to the game you are generally winning with ease against Australia.

Contrast this to the unbelievable bowling display from New Zealand that had settled a nip-and-tuck semi against India 24 hours earlier. You could see the way the pitch was playing in the first innings of a game played over two days that it was going to be tight, but the fact that it went into the reserve day swung the balance of power towards New Zealand.

I would much rather have been in the Kiwi camp than in India's, because the match situation would have dictated that India had more stresses overnight. A one-day international is what it says on the tin, a match played in a day, so when you are asked to go back the following day and start all over again it can be a lot more disruptive if you are the team set to do most of the batting. It's genuinely hard to get into the right frame of mind.

Despite our dominance in the other semi, it wasn't until we got the required runs down into the teens in Birmingham that our dressing room began getting giddy. Once the finishing line appeared, it became like that of an Under-15s team: 'We're going to Lord's. We're going to Lord's.' It had been so tense during the chase but now we were like kids again, hugging each other and jumping up and down.

As I'd alluded to in that pre-match team meeting, when you are on the eve of a match like this, the kind that you've dreamed of playing in since childhood, you can't help but think the worst at times. You are close to achieving your goals, yet there is a little voice in the back of your head saying: 'What if Starc comes on for another spell, bowls five yorkers and gets five wickets in as many balls?'

It felt euphoric when Eoin powered a pull over the top of mid-on and to the boundary off Behrendorff for the winning runs. However, we were soon brought down a peg or two by the first words that Trevor Bayliss said to us when the team came together in the dressing room after the match.

'You know why England have never won a World Cup? Because they win the semi-final and think they've already won the damn thing!'

With that, our Australian coach told us that as the final was only three days away we should enjoy relatively muted celebrations, not go overboard, and prepare to have an almighty knees-up if we completed the job at Lord's.

Australia v England Edgbaston, 11 July 2019, Semi-Final, Match 47 of 48

Result: England won by 8 wickets

AUSTRALIA	R	B	4s	6s	SR
David Warner c Jonny Bairstow b Chris Woakes	9	11	2	0	81.81
Aaron Finch (capt) lbw Jofra Archer	0	1	0	0	0.00
Steve Smith run out (Jos Buttler)	85	119	6	0	71.42
Peter Handscomb b Chris Woakes	4	12	0	0	33.33
Alex Carey (wk) c Sub (James Vince) b Adil Rashid	46	70	4	0	65.71
Marcus Stoinis lbw Adil Rashid	0	2	0	0	0.00
Glenn Maxwell c Eoin Morgan b Jofra Archer	22	23	2	1	95.65
Pat Cummins c Joe Root b Adil Rashid	6	10	0	0	60.00
Mitchell Starc c Jos Buttler b Chris Woakes	29	36	1	1	80.55
Jason Behrendorff b Mark Wood	1	4	0	0	25.00
Nathan Lyon not out	5	6	0	0	83.33
Extras (w 10, lb 6)	16				
Total (all out, 49 overs)	223				

Fall of wickets:
1-4 (A Finch, 1.1 ov), 2-10 (D Warner, 2.4 ov), 3-14 (P Handscomb, 6.1 ov), 4-117 (A Carey, 27.2 ov), 5-118 (M Stoinis, 27.6 ov), 6-157 (G Maxwell, 34.5 ov), 7-166 (P Cummins, 37.4 ov), 8-217 (S Smith, 47.1 ov), 9-217 (M Starc, 47.2 ov), 10-223 (J Behrendorff, 48.6 ov)

Bowling	O	M	R	W	Econ
Chris Woakes	8	0	20	3	2.50
Jofra Archer	10	0	32	2	3.20
Ben Stokes	4	0	22	0	5.50
Mark Wood	9	0	45	1	5.00
Liam Plunkett	8	0	44	0	5.50
Adil Rashid	10	0	54	3	5.40

ENGLAND	R	B	4s	6s	SR
Jason Roy c Alex Carey b Pat Cummins	85	65	9	5	130.76
Jonny Bairstow lbw Mitchell Starc	34	43	5	0	79.06
Joe Root not out	49	46	8	0	106.52
Eoin Morgan (capt) not out	45	39	8	0	115.38
Extras (w 12, lb 1)	13				
Total (2 wickets, 32.1 overs)	226				

Fall of wickets:
1-124 (J Bairstow, 17.2 ov), 2-147 (J Roy, 19.4 ov)

Bowling	O	M	R	W	Econ
Jason Behrendorff	8.1	2	38	0	4.65
Mitchell Starc	9	0	70	1	7.77
Pat Cummins	7	0	34	1	4.85
Nathan Lyon	5	0	49	0	9.80
Steve Smith	1	0	21	0	21.00
Marcus Stoinis	2	0	13	0	6.50

5

ADRENALINE

New Zealand v England,
Lord's, 14 July 2019, World Cup Final, *Match 48 of 48*

So then, to the most spectacularly dramatic World Cup final in history. A game that simply refused to be put to bed. Contested between two countries without a previous win, it meant a new name would be engraved on the silverware.

With my background, there were a few messages winging in from New Zealand when it became clear that they were the team standing between us and the silverware at Lord's on 14 July. My cousin Finn sent me a picture message from one of the pubs in Christchurch, the city in which I was born. He had gone on a night out with one of my shirts on. 'Getting it from all directions at the moment,' he texted. I bet he was.

Let's be honest, though, the Stokes family couldn't really lose this one. It was a win-win. Either I was going to be a world champion or the New Zealand team would be. As my dad Ged says on his Twitter feed: 'I support any team my son Ben is in, unless they are playing against the Black Caps.' He and my mum Deborah are very patriotic.

I have a similar pride but a different loyalty. Kiwi born; English at heart. That's how I feel. In fact, although we were playing New Zealand in the final I wasn't necessarily seeing it in the black and white of my past and present; and to be honest I don't really feel as though games against New Zealand are any different to when we play any other nation. To me they are just another team. Obviously, I remember where I am from, and embrace my family and heritage, as you can see from my Maori tattoos. But I don't get sentimental.

My parents regularly contemplate coming over to the UK to watch big matches but they rarely do it, and I'm not sure they got too far down the road with plans this time despite the importance of the match. So they stayed up all night to watch it with other family members and friends.

Apparently, the vast majority of pubs in New Zealand had failed to apply for a late licence to screen the match into the early hours and beyond, because the Black Caps were not viewed as genuine title contenders.

Yet I had much greater faith. Before a ball was bowled in the tournament, I thought New Zealand would go deep because in this 10-team format, in which every team plays each of the others, the best teams are established for the semi-finals. With the core of the XI that finished as runners-up four years earlier, they had to be in the four for my money.

Not only had they lived up to the expectations I had of them, they entered the final itself with confidence from the fantastic semi-final win against a very powerful Indian team.

Over recent years, we'd played against New Zealand lots and knew only too well where their strengths lie. They like to play their cricket in a similar way to what we do, I think, and so we knew what we were up against both in terms of their players and how they would clearly want to play.

They hadn't changed a great deal over the four years since they'd appeared in the previous final in Australia. Sure, they'd lost Brendon McCullum along the way, but his influence on how New Zealand should play their cricket was still evident in the current team. It's just that Kane Williamson has taken it on in a slightly new direction. In effect, they'd adopted the best attacking values of Brendon and tried to complement that with Kane's guidance. One of their enduring characteristics is that whenever there is an opportunity to decide which way to take a game, they always go for the most positive option.

In terms of their personnel, they have a similar set-up to us in their batting. Kane is their rock, just as Joe Root is for us. In both teams, all the other batters play around those two. At the top of the order, Martin Guptill didn't have a great World Cup but we knew what a dangerous player he could be because we had been on the receiving end of his brilliance in the past. When someone like that is on the opposition side, you have to be wary. The same is true of Ross Taylor, not only one of New Zealand's best one-day batsmen now but right up there with the best they've ever produced.

There are another couple of similarities between the way they play and the way we do. The first is that they are not concerned with who they're playing against, and the second is that they never give up. Both teams had bona fide matchwinners. Pitching us together created a final which can only be described in one word: remarkable.

That morning, as we moved towards the scheduled 10.30 am start, Lord's was overcast and seemed to be getting more and more grey as the seconds ticked by, the conditions delaying the toss and the match itself by a quarter of an hour. New Zealand won the toss, one which Eoin Morgan reckoned was a 50–50 call. As a team we are equally confident of chasing a total, as setting one, and if you don't have a particular preference as a team what you want to do first, sometimes losing the toss is the best thing.

The reason it was a 50–50 was because while the overhead conditions said 'bowl', the dryness of the pitch suggested batting might be the way to go. Scoring would surely become harder later in the day as the surface slowed down.

It is natural on such an occasion for nerves to be a factor, the players gripped by both excitement and anxiety at featuring on such a big stage. As someone who sticks to his guns with what he says in his pre-match talk, World Cup final or not, thankfully Eoin Morgan made it feel like any other game.

He reminded us that we'd got into this position playing a certain way and weren't going to change. That was about it. The warm-ups, and even the national anthems, felt the same as any other World Cup game and the preparation for the match was also like any other. What was different, however, was the atmosphere. The game ebbed and flowed and I had never before seen a crowd at Lord's get involved in the way they did.

It was like we had been transported to Edgbaston. There is always a hum around a Test match at Lord's but this was loud and added to the theatre of it all. There was a lot of talk in the build-up to the match that the tickets had been sold predominantly to Indian supporters, but that certainly didn't detract from the backing we received from the stands. You could tell that we had at least 80 per cent of the support – a bonus of being hosts at a global event – while the neutrals who did attend clearly loved cricket and got fully involved in the occasion.

Martin Guptill had experienced a woeful return of scores in the World Cup but clearly came out with a mindset to attack. He hadn't put together anywhere near the kind of tournament that he would have hoped for, or that he was capable of, having top scored with 547 runs in the 2015 edition of the competition. But a man of his class and standards was always going to come out and play some shots in a match like this and he raised eyebrows when, from the first ball at around 10.45 am, he threw the kitchen sink at a Chris Woakes delivery that was called wide.

He didn't make contact with that booming drive but it was some statement of intent. It was clear we needed to get him early because in that kind of mood, with his ball-striking ability, he could easily hurt you with a hundred off 60 deliveries. That seemed to be his intention too, as he tried to hit himself back into form at the last-chance saloon. I don't know whether this is true or not but it almost felt like he'd proposed a way of playing to Kane Williamson and his captain had given him full backing. Go and get us off to a flying start, that kind of thing.

Aside from an uppercut for six off Jofra Archer early on, though, he didn't hurt us. While the ball wasn't really swinging, there was enough lateral movement available off the pitch and Jofra and Chris Woakes exploited the conditions well in an opening 10 overs that cost just 33 runs.

There could easily have been greater rewards for them in that period too but for the first of many contentious DRS calls. Early on, Woakes got Henry Nicholls out lbw only for it to be overturned. Even now I'm still not sure about that. For my money, that was out. If anything it looked to me like umpire's call on height and I certainly didn't think it was missing as the replays suggested. When he went for it, I thought it was a brave review.

Soon afterwards, Guptill was also given out leg-before and we were really surprised when he too challenged the umpire's decision. If he'd gone into that game with any kind of form, I don't think he would have done it. I know what it feels like when you're scratching around and desperate to get some runs. You don't make clear judgements and can make such calls in hope rather than expectation. Had he come into that final with 400–500 runs, there's no way he'd have done it. It was a piece of scrambled thinking, because with Guptill's dismissal for 19 went New Zealand's review with more than 43 overs remaining in their innings.

What a bonus this was for us became clear when Ross Taylor was unable to challenge his dismissal. Had he done so, the technology would have provided a reprieve. For what it's worth, I actually thought that Taylor was out even though ball-tracking suggested that it was going over the top of leg-stump. In my view, DRS is not always 100 per cent correct. You obviously get a feel for what is out and what's not, and you occasionally have to acknowledge that you've got away with one.

These two interlinked incidents were arguably the first couple of examples of the fine margins in this particular game. If Guptill hadn't reviewed, and simply walked off instead, and Taylor had reviewed his, who knows what would have happened? As it was, we got Ross for 15. Of course, sport is full of ifs and buts, yet there is no doubt that these dismissals were the first two turning points in the game.

Like Kane Williamson, Taylor is someone who can really hurt you, and the pair of them are particularly dangerous if they are able to build a partnership together. When the two of them are set alongside each other, they're very hard to get out.

It wasn't a great pitch for playing your shots, being a bit sticky. On dry surfaces, the ball tends to kiss the pitch a bit more, whereas this one didn't have a lot of pace in it, causing the ball to stop on batsmen a touch, and offered a little bit of sideways movement.

The fact that the ball was moving off the seam made Liam Plunkett especially effective for us. At the age of 34, his tactics are fairly straightforward and he knows his game inside out. So when he gets the white ball in hand, he just keeps banging away at an area just short of a length, with an array of cross-seamers at differing paces, which allows the natural variation in the pitch to take effect.

Liam hadn't been a fixture in the side at the start of the tournament but to have someone like him around, a bowler who gets wickets out of nowhere, is invaluable. His strike rate of 28.8 throughout the team's four-year journey was incredible, really. There is nothing spectacular about it. He just does the donkey work, if you like. There is no science to it. No change in what he does. So he is effectively asking the batsmen: 'Where are you going to hit me?'

Because of the differences in bounce, pace and movement his variations create, he gets a lot of people mishitting him into the deep, and that's what Eoin Morgan wants him to do. He never goes away from it. In the nets, he just spends 40 minutes running in, bowling hard lengths, and it has made him so successful in the middle periods of matches.

Morgan has played a big part in Liam's resurgence as an international. A captain has to think tactically about the game but also the way he conducts himself rubs off on the other 10 players on the field. He is a man of steel in terms of his emotions, never looks annoyed with the bowlers, and that means the other players are never under pressure. He is consistent in his behaviour and so you are never going to ask the question: *What's the captain thinking of me?* Post-match he might express his views if he is unhappy about an aspect of our performance, and that's the best time to do it, but especially in the crunch moments he is cool, calm and collected. That's massively helped players like Liam succeed in big moments in the game.

So when Liam switched to the Nursery End after an initial burst of three overs, his two wickets in the space of four overs reinforced the strong position we found ourselves in. Any time you get Williamson out is important, as the rest of the New Zealand team take their lead from him, and the reaction of the close fielders when Pudsey scratched his outside edge with a delivery that kicked off the pitch told you as much.

Although the decision was sent upstairs, after Kumar Dharmasena originally gave it not out, everyone on the field knew we had got him. I was out at deep square-leg but I could tell by the celebrations of Jos Buttler behind the stumps, and those positioned in the inner ring, that he was gone. The elation was reflective of the fact that Williamson sets out to bat all the way through to the end of an innings, exploding in the final 10 overs. He had done so pretty much for the entire World Cup and done it very successfully, scoring 578 runs, so to get him when he was going through the lower gears was a massive boost.

He was building things alongside Henry Nicholls, and got New Zealand into three figures, though they weren't hurting us. The run rate was under control and the chat among us on the field was that they were leaving themselves with quite a lot of work to do at the back end of the innings. When the scoreboard isn't rattling along in a 50-over match, even if a team is only one wicket down, it's not that scary to look at. So although we hadn't taken wickets as quickly as we normally do, waiting until the 23rd over for our second, we had contained them really well.

For a guy who hasn't been on the international scene that long, Nicholls has made quite an impression. He stands out as someone who knows his game, and that includes his limitations. He's very strong square of the wicket and he picks up length very well – but Pudsey seemed to do him with one that swerved back into the left-hander from around the wicket and ricocheted off the inside edge into leg-stump.

When you're bowling first you are trying to stop the other team getting away from you at any point during the innings, and they didn't manage that even at the death when they had the power-hitters like Colin de Grandhomme at the crease. De Grandhomme is a seriously clean striker of a cricket ball, someone very capable of hitting a 50 off 28 balls, but he simply didn't know what to do against the variations of Jofra Archer and Chris Woakes. They neutered him with all the variations they bowled and so instead he had to settle for 16 off 28. In fact, only once, when my former Durham academy teammate Tom Latham picked up Mark Wood for a six, did they get a big shot away during the latter stages of their innings of 241–8.

Jofra bowled five overs at the death and they didn't hit a single boundary off him. His versatility as a bowler is truly remarkable. He challenges the outside edge and top of off-stump at genuine pace with the new ball at the start of an innings, and is one of the world's best death bowlers as well. It's some combination for one player to send down five quality overs at the start and five quality overs at the end.

To be fair, having someone as reliable as Liam in our team allows the death-bowling experts to concentrate on delivering their skills rather than having to come back ahead of schedule. If he bowls two solid blocks of overs in the middle, it allows Jofra, Mark Wood and Chris Woakes to take charge towards the back end.

•

Personally, I was jittery as we started our chase. In situations like this, all you can think of is the worst. I sat there in the dressing room, praying for a good start.

And what a start it was. From the first ball of our innings, Trent Boult produced a beautiful swinging delivery that defeated Jason Roy's drive on the inside edge and crashed into his pad. Not out, said umpire Marais Erasmus to New Zealand appeals.

To be quite honest, I have no idea how he didn't give it. For those of us tucked away watching the action on the TV in the dressing room, we heard the commotion on the field first and then lifted our heads to see the same delivery live due to the few seconds' delay on the transmission. With the naked eye, it just looked so out, and my immediate thoughts were 'oh, no, today's not going to happen.'

Jason is such a massive player for us, setting the tone for

our batting, and that was a real heart-in-the-mouth moment. I know that an umpire's call reprieve saved him following a New Zealand challenge of the decision but the ball would have gone on to hit leg-stump and it just looked like the kind of lbw that should be given to a left-armer. In my mind, he was out and if Erasmus' finger had gone up we could have had no complaints.

Every team needs a slice of luck from time to time, though. That was ours, and only served to highlight how the application of DRS can involve massive swings in fortune. At one end of the spectrum, if Marais had given it out and Jason had reviewed, he would have remained out as the ball was shown to be hitting some of the stumps. Yet the exact same delivery led to a very different decision.

I know that the reason that umpire's call is factored into the decision review system is because they cannot say with 100 per cent accuracy whether the ball will strike the target area or not – but to my mind this was out. If the ball's shown to be hitting the stumps, it should be decisive.

The way the two New Zealand new-ball bowlers Boult and Matt Henry bowled it could have been an opening six overs in which we scored six runs. They combined to produce a brilliant opening spell: Trent swinging it beautifully and Henry hitting the seam and inducing so many plays and misses.

But if opponents are bowling well, Jonny Bairstow and Jason Roy don't just allow them to sit in. They put them under pressure by counter-attacking and therefore we managed to get into the twenties before New Zealand broke through, when Henry's tendency to angle the ball in and then get it to straighten did for Jason.

That put a dent in our batting but what really started to drag New Zealand back into the game was the introduction of Colin de Grandhomme into the attack. No more than a medium-pace dobber, not much to write home about, but on a surface devoid of pace he is a batsman's worse nightmare.

He operates at 75 mph, you get a good look at the seam as the ball comes down the pitch towards you, and you know which way it's wobbling, but it does just enough to prevent you taking liberties and, as you have no pace to work with, you end up hitting the ball straight to the inner-ring field.

Another of the Kiwis, Lockie Ferguson, cranks it up at 90 mph throughout a spell and gives you a completely different kind of challenge, but I would take him seven days a week over de Grandhomme on a pitch like that. De Grandhomme just puts the ball in a good area and challenges you to play shots that invite risk. He also did something in this match that no-one else seemed able to do in one-day cricket – he dried up Joe Root.

Your typical Root innings will see him progress to 30 off as many balls without playing a shot in anger but unfortunately, on this occasion, de Grandhomme had his number. Kane Williamson sniffed it very early that he was the guy who could restrict our run rate, and build some pressure, because he was going to be so hard to get away, and so brought him on in place of Henry from the Pavilion End as soon as the over was up. With no pace to work with, Joe could not play his release shot of running the ball down to third man to get off strike, or take advantage of any balls on his pads by clipping them into gaps.

As the runs dried up it triggered a change of tack from Joe, and when he ran down the wicket and had a swipe across the line at de Grandhomme during the 17th over, I was like: 'Woah, Jesus Christ, Joe.'

After he had survived that aberration, you would have thought that he might have made the most of his chance to reassess, but de Grandhomme bowled his worst ball of the day next up, wide outside off-stump, and Joe followed it and nicked it. That kind of dismissal is never about the delivery itself but the result of building pressure as a bowler. If a batsman has been given nothing to hit previously, when a ball like that comes down his eyes tend to light up.

You'd never have thought that someone like de Grandhomme would ever get one over on Joe Root, who had got to 50 easily several times in the tournament. He certainly would not have been the bowler expected to be troubling him had you considered the key match-ups before the final. New Zealand have plenty of X-factor bowlers to worry opponents but he's not generally one of them.

Joe's departure during a de Grandhomme spell of 10–2–25–1, the second most economical in a World Cup final behind Derek Pringle's 10–2–22–3 for England versus Pakistan in 1992, followed soon afterwards by that of Jonny Bairstow, meant things were far from ideal for us.

Yet any nerves for me had dissipated when I arrived out in the middle. I have always been someone who's a better doer than a watcher. Those nerves went with me when I stepped out of the changing room door and down the steps towards the Long Room but disappeared once I crossed the boundary and heard my name read out over the tannoy. That's the point at which I tend to get into game mode.

So, although the required run rate was going up during the

first half of our innings, I didn't really panic. Yes, when Eoin Morgan got out to a rank delivery, somehow picking out the only bloke in the deep on the off-side from a bit of a tennis smash – it was 80 yards from third man to deep cover – it made me question what was happening.

Even at 86–4 in the 24th over, though, the rate was not an issue to us. It was touching a run a ball from then on, but in my head I knew that if Jos Buttler and I were still there at the end, and we needed nine an over from the final five, all would be fine. The fact that we had restricted New Zealand to 241–8 meant we never had to deal with the issue of scoreboard pressure.

The only pressure was in the wickets column, which meant we had to get something going. It was a totally different situation to being asked to score at eight an over from a standing start; our goal was to build a partnership, there were no other worries, and the longer we were there together the more nervous New Zealand would feel.

We reminded each other of that throughout our hundred partnership. Not that we said too much to each other than 'keep building'. Out of habit, I like to glance up at the scoreboard regularly to see where we are – how many overs are left, what runs are required – unlike Jos. However, there was a point deep into my partnership with him, in which we ran three consecutive twos as Henry began a new spell, and for each one the cheers from the crowd got louder and louder. On the third of them, as we came back for the second run, the place was going berserk. So, when we got together at the end of the over, the conversation turned not to how many runs we were targeting over the next few deliveries but how good it felt to be out there soaking up the atmosphere. It was insane. Real shivers down the spine stuff.

When a knowledgeable crowd senses something is about to happen – that you are about to step on the accelerator – they also get going. There is a real relationship between the not-out batsmen and those people sitting in the stands. The danger with this is that it can draw you out of your bubble at a time when you need to keep calm.

Lord's is very posh and traditional. There's no music – the only ground at the tournament that didn't have any. No guitar player. Even the trumpeter from the Barmy Army, Billy Cooper, is prevented from bringing his instrument into the ground. Yet this day was special for the noise in the big moments.

As we went deeper into the innings, I began to plan how I was going to make the runs we needed to win. In run chases like this one, you sometimes might look to target one particular bowler and on this occasion Jimmy Neesham was in my sights. This wasn't a pre-match plan but something I thought about in the moment. I've always felt that Neesham is quite a similar bowler to me, and fulfils a similar role to the one I do in the England team, filling in overs rather than bowling a full allocation.

So I was looking to attack him and put the pressure back on their team by forcing Kane Williamson to bring back one of his main bowlers earlier than he wanted. I started running down the wicket to him, using my feet to shorten the pitch and try to generate my own pace on the ball.

From 22 yards away, I sensed by the way Jos was moving around the crease, pulling the scoops out of his repertoire, and using his wrists to lift low full tosses over extra cover, that he was about to go for the kill. I sensed he was looking to win it with a couple of overs to spare, when he struck a couple of boundaries in consecutive overs from Boult and Ferguson inside the final 10 overs – a period in which he is without peer when it comes to ball striking. As his batting partner, you have to recognise when he is in the zone like this and get the singles to get him on strike as often as possible.

No-one could have a go at him for skying another big shot to deep extra cover from a well-disguised Lockie Ferguson slower ball, with 46 needed from 32, because he takes on those shots and nails them more often than anyone else in the world. He does so much good for England's limited-overs teams. Just a couple of overs of Jos in full flow and we would have eased to victory that evening. This time, though, not long after reaching a 50 at a tad under a run a ball, he didn't quite get it right – credit Ferguson for taking some of the pace off the ball to draw the mishit – and his departure put another twist in the tale.

At that stage, there was still no need for panic, although it was easier to score as a set batsman than a new one on a pitch like this. Having managed to whittle another seven runs off the tally, I walked down to new batsman Chris Woakes before the start of Ferguson's next over, and, attempting to settle him, said: 'Look. We're not far off here. If Ferguson bowls it short, smack him into the mound stand.'

Some players like to hear that kind of positive chat when they get out into the middle, Chris being one, and I find that it is often better to say something short and sharp rather than laying on a load of instructions on how we are going to get over the line. Too much detail can be counter-productive.

Unfortunately, this advice didn't have a positive conclusion. Woakes is a proper batter, a man with a Test hundred to his name at Lord's, but this was a bad situation for him to come into and although Ferguson did drop short, he top-edged the ball straight up in the air.

At this point, with 39 runs now required off the final 23 deliveries, I knew a lot depended on me. The atmosphere was tense, and becoming more so, but I didn't lack any self-belief that I could do it. That I could win the World Cup for England. The question I kept asking myself was: 'Who will be more nervous at the end if I am still at the crease? Me or the New Zealand bowlers?' Even if we needed teens from the 50th over, I kept telling myself that the answer was them.

As I knew only too well from my own experience as a bowler tasked with sending down the last over in high-pressure matches, when a batter is in, on runs, you are always thinking that he can find the boundary. The modern game tends to favour the chasing team.

My head remained very clear until the penultimate over when Liam Plunkett was outfoxed by a slower ball from Neesham that he clopped to long-off. The equation was now 22 off nine balls. This was not how I had visualised the 49th over. It was meant to go for loads. I had seen it as break or bust time. I was going to win it for England, or Neesham was doing the same for New Zealand. There wasn't going to be anything in between. I'd seen it in very black-and-white terms. And I'd backed myself.

Yet I'd lost the strike to new batsman Jofra Archer and we'd taken just two off the first three when I got it back and sized up the boundary in front of the Warner Stand. I calculated that

I had no other option but to go for a big hit as we needed fours and sixes. But for an errant foot from Trent Boult on the rope, Neesham would have been that hero not me.

Of course, I realised that Boult was positioned at long-on but I backed myself to clear him. It was the area of the ground I targeted to clear the boundary as I guessed Neesham was going to bowl a leg-cutter, and I could therefore use the angle of the delivery, try to hit it as hard as I possibly could, and get enough bat on it to take the fielder out of the equation.

It was not going to be an easy shot to pull off: the ball was at its softest, in its 25th and final over from the Pavilion End, the pitch was sluggish, and Neesham was taking pace off rather than hurling the ball down as fast as he could. I knew that in order to guarantee pulling this off, I would have to strike the ball with power and timing.

As a batter, you know when you have got enough on a shot like that and my look gave it away in an instant. The contact was not clean. I'd toe-ended it. That was it. The game was over. Or so I thought, as I tracked the ball through the golden evening sky. We weren't getting 22 from the final eight deliveries with two new batsmen at the crease.

As the ball tumbled down, my eyes were fixed on Trent. *Go, go, go!* I urged the ball on. I still thought I was going to be out, though.

Even from 80 yards away, I could see clearly that Boult had stood on the rope before he relayed it to Martin Guptill, a handful of yards inside the field of play – and for some reason that I cannot fathom, I started signalling six, my arms raised above my head as though I was the umpire.

What the hell am I doing?

Pressure, eh? It does strange things to you. In that moment I had become like a fan. In subsequent days, when I watched the replays, I noticed an old chap in the crowd behind Boult gesturing in exactly the same way I had.

This was a real let-off because somewhat unusually for a fast bowler, Trent Boult is normally an excellent fielder. He moves really well, has great agility and safe hands. His mistake here, as the crowd held its breath, was that he got too far underneath the ball. It meant he had to take a step back, his momentum carrying him towards the rope.

I simply couldn't believe what had just happened. In the space of half a dozen seconds, I had gone from the deflation of seeing the World Cup disappear from our grasp to a renewed hope that we might get our hands on the trophy after all.

Having got myself back down to the non-striker's end with a ball in the over remaining, I told Jofra that his first ball was effectively a free hit. If he could find the rope it would be a huge bonus. If not, I would settle for getting 15 runs off the last over. He missed; Neesham castled him. But it simply guaranteed the worst-case scenario. I remained on strike, the game's destiny in my hands.

Negative thoughts came into my head again when the first two balls of the final over from Trent Boult were dots. At the start of it, I'd told Adil Rashid: 'I need to take all six balls – so no running, unless we can get two.'

The off-side fielders were all up, so I set myself to clear my leg and hit over the top of them. The first ball was a perfect yorker which I couldn't do a thing with. The second, I missed out on big time. I should have hit it for four over cover as Trent just missed his mark, but I didn't get the contact I wanted and for the second time in the over the ball went to Kane Williamson at extra cover.

With four balls to go, having not knocked anything off the required tally of 15, it was time for some premeditation. Sweeping a fast bowler was not something I had tried before, and I don't know what I was thinking, but my plan was to get my front foot down as far as I could without letting on to Boult in advance of him releasing the ball. I stood in the same position for as long as possible, denying him time to adjust, knowing he would try to bowl a yorker. My intention was to turn it into a full toss, get under it, and help it on its way aerially behind square.

As he released it, I am not sure whether it was hand–eye co-ordination or just because I had been in for so many balls, but I managed to make the adjustment to a ball outside off-stump, closing myself off in the stroke in the process. Despite hedging my bets that it would be a lot straighter than that, I managed to get all my body weight towards the ball and into the shot, using my wrists to gain the elevation and power necessary.

Even though I had to fetch it, and get my body and hands into unusual positions for trying to hit a fast bowler, as soon as I connected, in contrast to the heart-in-mouth moment of the previous over, it felt good. Down the famous Lord's slope, Martin Guptill lined up the catch but I knew it was carrying over him comfortably and plenty of rows back into a delirious crowd.

Then came the most unconventional of 'sixes' through a moment of fortune that I would rather not have happened.

Just as for the previous delivery, I tried to second-guess

what Boult would do. Because I had advanced to take the ball on the sweep for the previous one, I reckoned his follow-up would be a bumper. In anticipation of this, I had gone deeper in my crease, and stayed a bit leg-side.

As it turned out, had I set up as for the previous one it would have been precisely in the slot. But in this game of bluff and double bluff, I received a full toss on the hip and scuffed the hell out of it, luckily the contact unclean enough for it not to go straight to Guptill at midwicket but into a gap. It meant he had work to do to get to the ball, and we had the chance to hare for two.

I knew it was to his right, so I just put my head down and ran, in and out of the crease at the Nursery End as quickly as I could. Not once did I turn to look at him after I had set off, knowing that this was going to be tight.

As I sprinted to make the second run, I kept my eyes firmly fixed on Tom Latham, the New Zealand wicketkeeper, stood at the stumps, to gauge how accurate the throw was. He didn't move a muscle, his gloves remaining over the top of the bails, so I knew it was a good one and that I would have to get a dive in to give myself a chance of making my ground.

I couldn't believe it when I felt the ball strike my outstretched bat on the full. As I looked up, I could see the MCC members in front of the pavilion on their feet, yellow and red ties bouncing up and down, willing it to go for four extra runs. Part of me was willing it on too, but one thought went through my mind as I rose to my knees.

You're kidding me.

As fortunate as it was that it had happened to our advantage, it was definitely not something I'd want to happen in such circumstances. It was such a freakish occurrence: Guptill had thrown the ball from so far away and it had made a perfect connection with my outstretched bat – at just the right angle for it to bisect the fielders backing up and have enough legs on it to beat de Grandhomme's pursuit to the rope.

As I saw the ball rolling further and further away from me, all I could think was: *How the hell has that happened?*

One of the stories that emerged in the aftermath of the game was that I asked Kumar Dharmasena – who signalled to the scorers that six runs should be awarded – to overlook the fortuitous four from the deflection and just count the two runs for the stroke.

Nice story that, but it's simply not true. Remaining on my knees, I held my hands up and apologised to Tom Latham and Kane Williamson. Typical of the blokes they are, there was not one grumble from them. They seemed to accept that while the intervention was a cruel blow to them it was also an inadvertent one as I had not at any point altered course or looked at the ball as I raced to beat its path towards the Pavilion End. In fact, the only conversation I had with the officials, Dharmasena and Erasmus, during that final over was to double-check whether we would head to a Super Over in the event of a tie.

There was another aspect that would raise its head regarding the gifted six, although it did not do so until hours after the match. It was a debate over whether we should have been awarded six runs or five, as the laws state that the only runs counted in an overthrow situation are those for which the batsmen have crossed, at the time of the throwing fielder releasing the ball.

That call, according to the ICC's playing conditions, has to be made on the field of play by the standing umpires, and they conversed before coming to their conclusion. TV slow-motion grabs might have shown that the ball was on its way before we crossed, but it all happened so quickly and so unexpectedly that I found it amazing that people criticised Kumar and Marais afterwards. Remember, they had to make such a judgement without the use of technology.

Those picking faults, as if to discredit the legitimacy of the position we subsequently found ourselves in, were also overlooking one important thing. Even if it had been five, we could still have won the game. We'd just have had to play the situation differently.

As things stood, with three required from two balls, I vowed to play the remaining two deliveries in a calm manner.

From the penultimate ball, I tried to go over the off-side but scuffed my shot once more. Luckily, it was straight down the ground and Rash, who was under instructions to come back for a second run, was left short at the non-striker's end.

Momentarily, as I surveyed where the ball had gone, I considered shouting 'no' and not running at all. Perhaps because of that delay, I was not as far through the second run as I should have been when Mitchell Santner swooped on the ball – had his throw been to my end, I would have been miles out. But Rash's own stutter seemed to attract Santner's attention and the ninth dismissal limited us to one run.

So here we were. The last ball of the World Cup final. Needing two for glory. And out walks my old mate Mark Wood, daft as a brush at the best of times and clearly not thinking straight at this particular moment. Being the last scheduled ball, Woody was not going to take strike in the match so there was no need for any protective gear other than pads, helmet and box. Yet here he was clad in more armour than a *Game of Thrones* extra: arm guard, chest guard, thigh pad and an inner thigh pad were all strapped on.

As he approached me, I was already in conversation with our 12th man James Vince, who had come out with a towel and a drink.

'I think we win if we get a single,' Vincey told me.

He wasn't 100 per cent certain. I wanted to be. So I wandered over to square-leg, where Marais Erasmus was standing.

'What's the craic here then?' I asked him.

With a nod of his head, Marais said: 'Super Over.'

He was confirming what would happen if we only managed to score a single off the last ball. In that scenario, the game would be going into extra time.

Addressing my 10th-wicket partner, I told Woody to get his running shoes on, having made the decision not to try to hit the final ball for four or six.

My calculations ahead of the last legitimate delivery of the innings were simple. I knew we needed at least one run to take us into the extra time of six balls more per side. So if I kept the ball on the floor, we were guaranteed to still be in the game. That was not something that could be guaranteed if, in choosing to go the aerial route, there was miscue.

If I had been caught trying to hit a six I would never have forgiven myself. I didn't want to make the mistake of picking out a fielder in trying to hit a four either, so I tried to select an area in the outfield and hit the ball just hard enough to get two. Basically, I did exactly what I wanted to do, hitting it to long-on's left hand but I just didn't get the pace of the stroke right.

A bit more of a bunt would have been better. With Woody weighed down by all his clobber, no wonder he was only half-way home on the second run when Boult took in Neesham's throw to remove the bails.

Some people might ask why I didn't go for the boundary. Quite simply, I didn't want to do what Bangladesh did in the World Twenty20 against India back in 2016. They should have won that game in Bangalore and thought they had done so when they reduced the ratio to two runs off three balls to win. Despite having players of the ilk of Mushfiqur Rahim and Mahmudullah out there in the middle, both succumbed in consecutive balls going for glory shots and they somehow lost by one run.

Here at Lord's, I knew I had the chance to win the game but it was equally important not to lose it. In that situation, in the middle of all the commotion in the stands, I felt it was import-ant to try to keep my head. Looking at the last over as a whole, after the first two balls, anyone would have taken a scenario of a single to take the contest to a Super Over, and I was pleased that I was able to maintain clinical thinking.

Don't get me wrong, it still led to mixed emotions. The plan had been to finish it off, to claim outright victory, from the 600th and last ball of the day. I just didn't complete my plan correctly.

As I walked off, I booted my bat in frustration. Physically, I felt absolutely cooked. I was angry that I couldn't manipulate that ball for a two.

My thoughts had been to take the game to its end, believing that if I was still batting it would be decisive. I had done that, and trudged off 84 not out, yet there was still work to be done.

6

DESTINY

'Whatever happens, this will not define you as a cricketer.'

I thought it was important for Jofra Archer to hear these words from me as we walked back onto the field as a team. Our task was clear: to defend the 15 runs that Jos Buttler and I had posted in the first half of the first Super Over in World Cup history.

I had been undecided whether to say something to him or not as we prepared for the over that would decide the destiny of this England team. On the one hand, taking into consideration his skill level with the ball and the calmness he had shown throughout the competition, did he need me to say anything? On the other, we were on the verge of the biggest moment of this great young talent's life and it might act as reassurance to know that he had support.

Ultimately, though, it came down to skewed logic. I thought that if I didn't talk to him and we lost, I would blame myself for not doing so. So out came that simple message. Short and sweet.

If there was one man among his England teammates who knew about the pressure he would feel at this particular juncture it was me, given my own experiences versus West Indies at the World Twenty20 final in 2016.

Sure, if things went well it would indeed be a career-defining moment for him. But after being on the receiving end of Carlos Brathwaite's final-over hitting in Kolkata, I knew how things could go wrong. And if they went wrong for Jofra too, I didn't want him to feel that it would be decisive. It was his first summer on the biggest stage of all and he had England's World Cup hopes in his hands. All this at the age of 24.

He'd enjoyed a great start in the sky blue England shirt, an unbelievable tournament from a personal perspective, and yet his reputation had all come down to him delivering six more balls. It's a pretty tough gig, that.

From experience, disappointment really hurts you in the short term. When something goes bad like it did for me in that final three years earlier, it feels like it's something that's going to live with you for ever. Something you are going to have to bear for the rest of your career.

Time says different. That it doesn't have to be like that, and so whatever kind of performance Jofra came up with in the space of those next five minutes or so, it wouldn't necessarily be like that for him either. What I have learned through the highs and lows of my career is that good performances can be forgotten as quickly as bad ones. So there is no point holding on to either for too long.

Jofra asked me about my final over to Brathwaite some

weeks earlier and I didn't really know what to say at the time. This was effectively my reply. It was designed to settle any nerves that he might have. I was glad to get it off my chest.

•

When a match is as tight and tense as this one, your emotions are all over the place. I was still angry that I had not been able to finish the job when I entered the changing room after the tie in regulation time.

I spoke to Eoin Morgan about what we were going to be doing for the Super Over, and said that I thought Jason and Jos should be the two players to bat for us because of the way they had played throughout the tournament.

Immediately, he told me that he wanted me to go back out there with Jos as he wanted a left-hand, right-hand combination. Eoin himself would be the other nominated batsman.

'Sweet,' I said.

I accepted it was a good point and therefore I had to get my head back on for the next few minutes. What had gone had gone. It could not be changed. There was now a new challenge.

So I went out the back into the toilets to separate myself from being out on the field and get into a different place, mentally. To get rid of the feelings that had built up over a crazy last couple of hours. I had carried them all with me as I'd walked off the field. I wanted to be on my own for a few minutes. To experience a bit of solitude. I needed some 'me' time.

No point in looking back, I thought. Only at what lay ahead. If I was going to face just two balls in the Super Over, they would be the most important two balls of my career. I couldn't be carrying any baggage with me. I needed to be in a place completely by myself to get ready to deliver, to get rid of any lingering anger and disappointment that despite dragging us to the brink of victory, I had fallen short.

It might not be viewed as a conventional way for an international sportsman to prepare but it worked for me, massively.

The other lads in the dressing room were witnessing Jos's own unusual preparation. Tournament rules stated that the team batting second in the match automatically batted first in the six-ball shootout, so there was no need for a toss. Normally so calm and collected, he was hammering his bag with his gloved fist to get psyched up before we made our way back into what had become by this stage a cauldron of noise.

As we did so, we discussed which of the two of us would take strike. Jos suggested me – with Trent Boult bowling from the Nursery End of the ground, I would be hitting with the wind towards the Tavern and Mound stands on the leg-side.

If ever there was a ball to hit for a six in a Super Over, the first ball was the one. It was straight in the slot. I wound up but totally mishit it. Luckily, I managed to get enough wood on it to get it up and over short third man. We scrambled back for three but, to be honest, I am not sure how it didn't go for four. Normally at Lord's, if a ball gets through the outfield, even if it is going uphill it gets to the rope, but this one almost plugged due to the backspin on the ball as it hit the turf.

Next up, Jos also got one that he would arguably have hit for six several times out of ten, but in pressure moments things become a lot harder to pull off. Instead of striking it cleanly, he scuffed it to deep square for one and so we had four runs off two deliveries.

Boundaries are key in a situation like this and getting one

away early not only increases your confidence, it puts the opposition under pressure. Thankfully, I managed to get a good connection on the third ball of the over, getting down to sweep off middle-stump to deep square-leg, bisecting the two New Zealand boundary riders on that side of the ground.

Yet another opportunity to find the rope presented itself from the next ball, but unfortunately I hit a full toss straight to Lockie Ferguson at point. The entire off-side field was up inside the circle and if I had manipulated the ball into the gap it would have been four. Instead, we had to settle for a single.

It handed things back over to Jos. I knew when we got to the crease that, despite it being the end of a very physically demanding day, I'd potentially have to run my arse off for every single one of these six balls. So as soon as he made contact with a perfect, dipping yorker, I got my head down and sprinted.

Henry Nicholls, the fielder at deep extra cover, appeared to lose the path of the ball momentarily in the sun which potentially bought us a couple of seconds, but I would have backed us to get home regardless.

When Jos then worked the last one – a full bunger on his knee roll – over midwicket for our second boundary of the over, it was another one of those moments for me on a see-saw day of emotions. The world's most famous cricket ground was bouncing.

That's it, we've won the World Cup, I thought.

I jumped up in the air, arms aloft in celebration. Before New Zealand's batsmen had even faced a ball, I was going nuts. Hand on heart, I no longer thought we could get beat. In my mind, there was no way that they could knock off 16 from one over from Jofra Archer, who had spent our six-ball innings warming up with our bowling coach Chris Silverwood by the dug-outs.

In contrast, Jos didn't react at all. There was no alteration in his facial expression. He just walked off.

•

No-one in our dressing room was surprised when Eoin Morgan asked Jofra to be the bowler to close out the victory for us. When it came to selecting the man to deliver the last half-dozen balls of the 48th and final match of the tournament, it was only ever going to be him. You don't look beyond someone who can bowl as fast as he can and deliver pinpoint yorkers at will. There were no discussions, it was just a case of a nod of the head for each of them apparently. I had not been present at the time as I had been clearing my thoughts out back.

If the umpire had been a fast bowler in his playing days, the opening delivery of New Zealand's reply would have been a dot ball. Unfortunately, Kumar Dharmasena was a spinner. He reckoned it was a wide. It was a big call.

Jofra had sent down the perfect yorker to the left-handed Jimmy Neesham, right on the tramlines, just as he had planned to. I looked up at the big-screen replay and considered it was a bit harsh. It hit the chalk, though, and therefore I guess it was a 50–50 that could have gone either way. As I say, it was a big call.

All Neesham could do with the next one, another of a per-fectly delivered full length, was dig it out through mid-off and hurry back for two, meaning that like us they had effectively scored three runs off one ball at this point.

Then, with a huge jolt, this ridiculous match took a turn in another direction. Jofra got another one from around the wicket to angle in at off-stump and Neesham got under it to haul it miles over square-leg.

I turned my head to watch it fly halfway up the rows of seats in the Tavern stand and burst out laughing. Not that I thought it was funny. I just wondered: *What else is the game going to produce?* Surely, there was no more drama possible. Thankfully, I was wrong.

I was stood at long-on. I would have been at deep mid-wicket in normal circumstances as it is myself, Jonny Bairstow and Jason Roy who patrol the leg-side boundaries in our 50-overs team. But as I was pretty sore and tired, I had asked Jason whether he would switch with me.

But for this request it would have been me and not Jason in the thick of the incidents that were about to unfold.

With four balls left, New Zealand were cruising and, at this point, their dressing room would have been a lot calmer place than ours.

But Jofra is a gutsy guy. That had been shown by the fact that he even contemplated bowling a knuckle ball only two months in the making. He only began developing it after his maiden England call-up two months earlier. Now here he was using it in a match situation.

Not just any match situation either: this was a World Cup final heading right to the wire. It was absolutely awesome that he decided to bowl it. Yes, it got hit for six but you have to be gutsy to even try it. And it showed his confidence in delivering new skills under such pressure, highlighting exactly why he has become one of the world's leading bowlers in such a short space of time.

Jofra's confidence did not buckle and he came back brilliantly, not allowing the New Zealanders any room for manoeuvre despite them only requiring seven off the final four balls.

From the third legitimate delivery of the over, the ball went out to J-Roy at deep midwicket and it was obvious they were going to run two. Make no mistake, he is one of the best fielders in our team but he fumbled it, something you wouldn't expect him to do. That's what pressure does to the best. It makes simple things so much harder. On this occasion, the ball came straight to him and to see him run at it and fail to gather was a bit of a shock. It left New Zealand needing five off three.

I ran over to Jason, tapped him on the back, and simply said: 'Next one.'

When something like that happens, you have to put it to the back of your mind and concentrate not on what has gone but on what is to come. Sod's law, I guess, but the next one ended up going to him as well.

This time, he picked the ball up cleanly but unfortunately threw it to the wrong end. Martin Guptill made his ground easily at the non-striker's – at 6 ft 3 in with long strides, and one of the fastest men between the wickets in international cricket, he had a head start knowing he just had to put his head down and run – but Neesham would arguably have been struggling by a yard or two at the other end, as he was on the back foot when playing the stroke.

So, although it was an absolute missile of a throw, had he been thinking clearly, Jason would have sent it to the keeper's end instead. Another example of how the tension was making people do things they wouldn't normally do.

As soon as he opted for the bowler's end, I think Jason

would have been questioning himself as to why he'd done it. But clarity of thought does not come easily in this kind of situation. In the middle of a run-of-the-mill one-day international, his cricket sense would have kicked in and the ball would have been launched in a different direction. I believe that 100 per cent.

Then from the penultimate ball, with three runs required by our opponents, we received a stroke of luck that might not have been apparent in the heat of the battle.

Jofra bowled a bumper – probably the delivery you least expected him to send down at this point when, as a batsman, you would almost certainly be thinking that he would be trying to jam in a yorker. At the time, I thought Neesham had mistimed it so badly that he had clunked the ball from an attempted pull straight into the floor.

Only later, when we watched TV replays of the match, did it become apparent to the majority of our team, that it had redirected into the off-side from an under-edge. The ball crashed into his boot and dribbled to the off-side of the cut strip. Had it taken its normal course, it would have leaked out in the opposite direction into a huge no man's land behind square on the leg-side, just beyond the 30-yard circle, at a speed which – with all our leg-side fielders on the boundary – would have allowed them to collect another two.

Fortunately, it deflected in Jofra's direction so he was able to pick up in his follow-through instead. In a contest of so many twists and turns, this one was barely noticed but it was arguably as significant as any of the others. Without the deflection, it would have been pretty much game over for us. Yet another knife-edge, 50–50 moment had gone our way.

Seconds earlier, Neesham and Guptill had checked the rules with the two standing match officials Kumar Dharmasena and Marais Erasmus. They were told mid-pitch that if the scores finished level once again then New Zealand would lose out on boundary count, which stood at 24–14 in our favour. Eoin Morgan had informed us of this during the change-over.

This changed the look of the last ball, and the complexion of the game as it headed right to the death. It also required a change in the field from us, as we switched from a left-hander to a right-handed batsman, causing me to scream at Jonny and Jason to re-position themselves on the other side of the field. In normal circumstances, we might have pushed the guys back on the off-side for the left-hander, but I knew it could be important to have our very best fielders in that on-side hitting arc.

One thing we've been good at during the development of this team has been to allow Eoin Morgan to concentrate on communicating with the bowler and delivering tactical aspects of his captaincy by taking responsibility for stuff like this. There was never any need for him to worry about who was fielding where. He just needed to know that everyone was ready and in position for every single ball.

Everyone knows where they need to be at certain times in an innings and so at critical moments like these, guys who aren't as agile or who don't have strong arms are always in the circle. That's just self-management. Equally, we all know who our preferred boundary riders are and it was important to get the three of us in the hotspots for this most crucial of moments.

So, four years of effort had all come down to this moment. Each and every one of us had to be ready to produce a catch, a diving stop, a sprint in a heartbeat.

As Jofra entered his delivery stride, I was 15 yards off the boundary, having been walking in to put pressure on the batsmen should the ball be struck towards me at long-on.

As I saw the ball come out of his hand, I knew he had got it exactly where he was aiming to bowl. It was right in the blockhole. My walk turned into a run as I tried to pre-empt where it was headed off the bat as Guptill made contact.

My head start was not necessary, though, as the ball headed out to Jason, who was pelting towards it. He picked the ball up and threw it to Jos's end. Another one of those suspended animation moments. For those involved everything speeds up under the pressure, but for onlookers it kind of slows down.

The rest of us couldn't do a thing. It was all in Jason's hands. In that moment the 27,000 crowd had swelled in number by nine. That being the nine other England players on the playing area as the throw was relayed from Jason to Jos. We were all fans temporarily, having no influence on the outcome from this moment forward.

By this stage I was not in a great position to know how good the throw was, and whether it would beat Guptill's attempts to claim the crucial second run. The only way I was going to get an indication was from the reactions of Jos and the fielders square of the wicket.

The ball skipped off the turf, the bounce taking it to Jos's right at shoulder height, meaning he had to get back across his body to break the stumps and remove the bails. He did so with a thrust of his left arm, and when he started on a celebratory run, throwing his gloves off on the journey, followed by some of the lads, it sank in that the ball had beaten Guptill in this particular race.

As I pushed off to join my teammates, I lost my footing, the slip flipping me onto my back on the hallowed turf. Almost simultaneously, something weird happened to me. I started crying. I just lost it.

I had Mark Wood's sunglasses on my cap because the light at 7.30 pm was not great – half of Lord's soaked in sunshine and the rest cast in shadows from the stands. Vision-wise it was horrible. To the extent that even with the glasses on I couldn't see as I would have wished. If anything, it was actually even worse, so I had taken them off.

I got back to my feet, the sense of achievement overwhelming, threw my cap onto the floor, smashing Woody's shades in the process, and ran over from one side of the ground to the other. Eighty yards to join the bouncing mass of teammates wheeling away in front of the famous Lord's pavilion. Everyone was going absolutely crazy. There were hugs, screams, shouts. So this was what it was like to complete what we had set out to do four years earlier. It felt bloody good.

It was also unexpectedly emotional for someone like me. I am not a crier but the more I tried to stop the flow, the more the tears leaked. The old jaw was going too. I was overcome by happiness. I guess you can never plan for a moment like this. You never know how your emotions will reveal themselves.

To be together with all my teammates in celebration was incredible. That excitement was something else. Everyone made a point of congratulating Jofra for what he'd done. Then, everyone turned to me and told me how well I'd played in the game.

It didn't last long but I will remember that flash of time we spent in the immediate aftermath for ever.

Obviously, we still had a duty to shake our opponents' hands. In contrast to our feelings of elation, Martin was distraught at being run out. I went up to him and Jimmy to say what needed to be said.

'Well played. What a great game that was.'

I am not sure I could have put it any other way. England and New Zealand had battled it out to put a new name on the trophy 44 years after the inaugural World Cup final was contested at the same venue, and both teams had given their all.

As we walked off the field, I found myself alongside Martin once more and said exactly the same thing.

'What a game.'

There were more tears as the coaching staff and other squad players made their way onto the field. This had been such a collective effort and every one of them was buzzing. We'd spent such a long period of time together and some of their congratulatory words sparked the tears again.

I never thought I would cry on a cricket field. Now I had done it two or even three times in the space of five minutes.

I couldn't have cared less, of course.

NEW ZEALAND	R	B	4s	6s	SR
Martin Guptill lbw Chris Woakes	19	18	2	1	105.55
Henry Nicholls b Liam Plunkett	55	77	4	0	71.42
Kane Williamson (capt) c Jos Buttler b Liam Plunkett	30	53	2	0	56.60
Ross Taylor lbw Mark Wood	15	31	0	0	48.38
Tom Latham (wk) c Sub (Vince) b Chris Woakes	47	56	2	1	83.92
Jimmy Neesham c Joe Root b Liam Plunkett	19	25	3	0	76.00
Colin de Grandhomme c Sub (Vince) b Chris Woakes	16	28	0	0	57.14
Mitchell Santner not out	5	9	0	0	55.55
Matt Henry b Jofra Archer	4	2	1	0	200.00
Trent Boult not out	1	2	0	0	50.00
Extras (nb 1, w 17, lb 12)	30				
Total (8 wickets, 50 overs)	241				

Fall of wickets

1-29 (M Guptill, 6.2 ov), 2-103 (K Williamson, 22.4 ov), 3-118 (H Nicholls, 26.5 ov), 4-141 (R Taylor, 33.1 ov), 5-173 (J Neesham, 38.6 ov), 6-219 (C de Grandhomme, 46.5 ov), 7-232 (T Latham, 48.3 ov), 8-240 (M Henry, 49.3 ov)

Bowling	O	M	R	W	Econ
Chris Woakes	9	0	37	3	4.11
Jofra Archer	10	0	42	1	4.20
Liam Plunkett	10	0	42	3	4.20
Mark Wood	10	1	49	1	4.90
Adil Rashid	8	0	39	0	4.87
Ben Stokes	3	0	20	0	6.66

ENGLAND	R	B	4s	6s	SR
Jason Roy c Tom Latham b Matt Henry	17	20	3	0	85.00
Jonny Bairstow b Lockie Ferguson	36	55	7	0	65.45
Joe Root c Tom Latham b Colin de Grandhomme	7	30	0	0	23.33
Eoin Morgan (capt) c Lockie Ferguson b Jimmy Neesham	9	22	0	0	40.90
Ben Stokes not out	84	98	5	2	85.71
Jos Buttler (wk) c Sub b Lockie Ferguson	59	60	6	0	98.33
Chris Woakes c Tom Latham b Lockie Ferguson	2	4	0	0	50.00
Liam Plunkett c Trent Boult b Jimmy Neesham	10	10	1	0	100.00
Jofra Archer b Jimmy Neesham	0	1	0	0	0.00
Adil Rashid run out (Mitchell Santner/Trent Boult)	0	0	0	0	0.00
Mark Wood run out (Jimmy Neesham/Trent Boult)	0	0	0	0	0.00
Extras (w 12, b 2, lb 3)	17				
Total (all out, 50 overs)	241				

Fall of wickets

1-28 (J Roy, 5.4 ov), 2-59 (J Root, 16.3 ov), 3-71 (J Bairstow, 19.3 ov), 4-86 (E Morgan, 23.1 ov), 5-196 (J Buttler, 44.5 ov), 6-203 (C Woakes, 46.1 ov), 7-220 (L Plunkett, 48.3 ov), 8-227 (J Archer, 48.6 ov), 9-240 (A Rashid, 49.5 ov), 10-241 (M Wood, 49.6 ov)

Bowling	O	M	R	W	Econ
Trent Boult	10	0	67	0	6.70
Matt Henry	10	2	40	1	4.00
Colin de Grandhomme	10	2	25	1	2.50
Lockie Ferguson	10	0	50	3	5.00
Jimmy Neesham	7	0	43	3	6.14
Mitchell Santner	3	0	11	0	3.66

7

CARNAGE

To be named man of the match in the World Cup final was not something I coveted, although I confess it was an amazing feeling when my name was announced over the tannoy to confirm my award.

The huge eruption from the crowd was something I will never forget. That was probably the best bit for me: not receiving the award itself, or speaking about my performance on live television, but the reaction as I stepped onto the podium. It was approaching eight o'clock in the evening but it felt like every spectator was still there as I hit this wall of noise. It was spine-tingling stuff.

The downside to all this was that in the immediate minutes after the conclusion of this incredible match – this historic success for an England cricket team – I just wanted to be in among my teammates. Yet at every twist and turn people were trying to separate me from them.

When you win the man-of-the-match award in an international, you are asked to stand away from the other players slightly, so as to have a clear walk up as you approach the stage. On this occasion, when asked to come out of the group, I declined, telling the officials that I would go up when summoned.

I wanted someone to come and get me just before they started the spiel about player performances. Not before. I didn't want to stand by myself. This was a moment for me to stand shoulder to shoulder with the rest of this team. A team that had shown great togetherness over such a long period of time. Unity had been a key ingredient to our success.

Being part of such a diverse group of people has been so special to each and every one of us. We are teammates but have also become the closest of friends. Yes, we came together from different backgrounds and cultures – my own New Zealand heritage included – but we were so proud to pull on that England shirt. And we all like to celebrate together. So it really grinded my gears when some keyboard warriors on social media made a thing of Moeen Ali and Adil Rashid dashing out of the team line-up for the champagne-spray moment.

For those that don't know us, I can tell you that as a group we know all about the religious beliefs of Mo and Rash, and the non-Muslims in the squad have the deepest respect for them, just as they respect us and our behaviours.

Let's be clear here. We know they do not want to be around alcohol or come into contact with it. They never ask us to refrain from popping the champagne. And they never would. All they do ask is that we have a team picture first. This is something that has come as second nature whenever we win a series, and let's face it we have won a few together over the years.

They then rush stage left to avoid the spray. We have no problems, they have no problems. The only problem, I would say, belongs to the people that tried to make a big deal of this. We ask Mo and Rash all the time about certain aspects of their religion that we might be ignorant about and they happily inform us. We are proud to have Muslim players in our team and have a genuine curiosity about their lifestyles and routines. To even question our relationships is a complete insult. To suggest a lack of respect could not have been further from the truth. There is full respect going both ways.

As our Dublin-raised captain Eoin Morgan said in the post-match press conferences, when asked whether England had enjoyed the luck of the Irish: we also had Allah on our side. As I say, this team has taken a bit from lots of places far and wide.

As if to emphasise how important inclusiveness is to us, everyone got a turn to hold the trophy on our lap of honour. Only Trevor Bayliss, our Australian coach, declined, not wanting anything to do with it. His response when Jofra tried to pass it to him was to palm it straight off, saying: 'I don't want it. I didn't win it.' That's typical Trev.

Halfway round our Lord's lap, we got to where the Barmy Army were gathered in the Compton Stand of the Nursery End. This was a big part of our celebrations and I missed most of it because I was taken away to fulfil some more media duties. It is no exaggeration to say that I was gutted.

Why? Because these folk are quite simply the best supporters in the world. In any sport. They follow us all over, through thick and thin, never giving up on us, and are so loud even when we are getting mashed in Test matches. That, to me, is the definition of a true fan. Someone whose support is unconditional. This was one of those chances to pay them back in some small way. To show them that this was a day for them and us to share together.

Ever since the Ashes trip of 2013–14 when I made my

debut, I have been aware that they are everywhere we go. They make such sacrifices to be there in the stands and we all appreciate the backing they have given us over the years, and so when I was watching the other lads having selfies with them on the boundary edge, I was desperate for the interview that I was engaged in to be cut short.

Frustratingly, I was dragged away from the celebrations several times during the course of that hour or so immediately after the match. Now I get that in the modern world of sport every media organisation wants a reaction there and then. An instantaneous summary of your feelings and a reflection on the big moments of the game. Obviously, after I had done well in the game, everybody wanted to speak to me. I understood that. But quite honestly, it's the last thing you want to do. You just want to be with your team, all together sharing the experience. Making memories.

These moments don't come around too often in your career. This was a fresh feeling of joy and the interruptions were mildly annoying. I totally get the reasons why I was being asked to fulfil my media duties, and I have no issue doing these at all. It was just in the timing.

This was the time to savour our success as a group, to be with our pals, and so I was less accommodating to the organising team from the ICC, who were handing out GoPro cameras on sticks to capture footage of our celebrations to post on their website, than some of my colleagues like Adil Rashid and Liam Plunkett. They were too nice to say no. I declined, using the most polite of terms, or at least no more than one term beginning with F.

It was also a time to share with our families, who sacrifice lots for our careers. I had already carried the trophy once on our lap when we approached the Allen Stand, in which our families were situated. Jonny Bairstow had asked Joe Root for it moments earlier, but Joe told him no and passed it to me instead. It was the first time I had raised it up and it felt great to do so in front of my wife Clare, and my kids Layton and Libby.

By this point, the revelry was in full swing and I managed to grab a beer after making a deal with Elma Smit, a television reporter working for the ICC, that I would only do an interview in exchange for one. That first one after a win always tastes so nice. As we completed our wander, some of the other players chugged back bubbly and the songs were in full flow.

As we got back to the pavilion end of the ground, our loved ones meandered down to us from their upper-tier retreat. To have Clare, my mother-in-law Jane, plus Layton and Libby out there on the Lord's turf with me was pretty special.

There were also a group of guys I'd invited down from Durham. Chris Youldon, Libby's godfather, is the soppiest sod I have ever known. I have been quite up front about my own blubbering in these pages, but this guy cries more than a baby teething.

To be fair, Chris and I go back a long way. We first played against each other as 13-year-olds in a Cumbria *v* Durham fixture in 2004 and were teammates, alongside Joe Root, for the North of England at the Bunbury Festival two years later. So he got quite emotional as soon as he got near me. You could see the eyes getting wet and the top lip started curling over.

Michael Turns, another lad I played alongside for the North as well as in Durham's academy, was there to witness this momentous occasion. He'd had one or two by this stage, declaring that it had been the 'best day of my life'.

'Aye, decent wan' it?' I agreed.

We commit a lot to get to play for England, and there are always people behind the scenes making commitments too, so to be able to cut them in on some of the good times feels very rewarding. I know that inviting friends and family into the middle of the ground to be with us was important to the entire squad and backroom staff. As the sun sank over the ground, it was some start to the after-party. It was so nice to have everyone enjoying each other's success and welcoming the team's wider circle of friends and family.

Michael's dad Frank also joined us out there after we negotiated his entrance – he had been stuck in the crowd round the back of the pavilion trying to get through it and onto the playing area. I stayed at the Turns family house when I first joined Durham as an academy player and I could see Frank moved by the nostalgia of the little ginger kid they'd put up during the summer months turning into a world champion.

•

From there we took things into the home dressing room, where we would get the chance to reflect on our achievement and allow it to sink in. Within two minutes of leaving the hallowed turf to re-locate, however, I was asked to speak to the written press by Danny Reuben, the England team's media manager.

Bear in mind, I have always been one to enjoy toasting the team's successes, let alone a World Cup final win, so I got Andy, one of our security guys, in on a plan to get out of this request.

'I am going to act like I've had a few,' I told him.

Truth was that I was only on my second beer, but I reckoned there was no way Danny would let me do it if I was slurring my words.

Thankfully, Andy is a Leeds lad and pretty chilled: 'I'll do whatever you want, mate.'

So I went down from the second-floor dressing room to the ground with Andy, wearing no shoes or socks, swaying from side to side, eyes rolling around their sockets.

'Reubs, am I really doing more media in this state? Are you, the England media manager, going to put me in front of cameras like this?'

Sam Dickason, one of our senior security team, was with him. He didn't know I was putting it on either and the pair of them fell for it.

'You're off the hook, get back upstairs,' Sam instructed me.

Undoubtedly, that was one of the best moves I'd pulled off throughout the entire World Cup.

There was all sorts going on in that changing room. Laughs, jokes and sing-songs. In our team every player has a song about him penned by Jos Buttler and Mark Wood. Those two take well-known tunes and change the words, making them relevant to each individual within our group. So everyone was given a rendition of his song from the rest of the lads. It was an absolutely class half-hour.

The guests and families milled about and as the night drew on we got rowdier and rowdier. The trophy, sat on the table in the middle of the room, received the occasional pat, slap or rub and everyone had his medal hanging around his neck. Our kits remained on for the duration. And when I say duration, I mean when we finally pulled up stumps between five and six o'clock the next morning.

There were a few formalities thrown in during our time up in the dressing room. Eoin Morgan had his say on our achievement, namely that what we had managed to pull off was amazing and that we should all enjoy it. That we should all be proud of setting a target at the start of our World Cup journey and hitting that target.

Then it was the turn of Phil Neale, our team operations manager, to speak. He broke the news to us that we were required to report for duty at the Oval the following morning for a public parade. On reflection, I wouldn't have wanted to have been in his shoes. That's not the kind of thing you want to break to a room full of giddy blokes intent on letting their hair down after two months of intense focus.

Now Phil is a very logistical man and takes his duties very seriously wherever we are around the globe. Whenever it's his time to speak he wants everyone to listen, and to be fair to him there was no other time to address us given that we had to report for duty in the lobby of our hotel, the Landmark in Marylebone, at 9 am, approximately 11 hours later.

He told us the finer detail of the schedule and that TM Lewin were providing shoes and pants for us because we didn't have spares. After a few beers, though, we were all in playful mood and only too willing to wind him up.

'How many pieces of laundry can we put in?' I asked him.

Then, pointing to the World Cup trophy parked in the centre of the room, Jos Buttler chirped in with: 'Can we bring that?'

Cue collective 'wa-hey'.

It was all in good fun. Just boys being boys. Let's face it, walking into a changing room full of guys on cloud nine and intoxicated, this was not a good time to be serious. But Phil's blood was rising. So, having already taken a few smart comments, he completely lost it with Graham Thorpe, our batting coach, when he chipped in.

'Will you lot stop being so bloody immature,' he told us, turned on his heels and walked out.

During several hours of drinking, we kept wandering in and out of our own changing room and the committee room adjacent, also taking in the Long Room in joyous laps of the pavilion. One of the images of the night for me came at around 10.45 pm, when my four-year-old daughter Libby was being cradled by Mark Wood's mother while drinking a full bottle of blue Powerade. She was absolutely cooked but the Powerade clearly gave her a second wind. Layton, our six-year-old son, was still going nuts. I don't know where he gets it from.

The New Zealand lads also shared drinks with us. They are a brilliant team to play against, led by not just an amazing player but an amazing person – and someone who is an absolute credit to the game – in Kane Williamson. He hates speaking about himself, tries to deflect any plaudits he gets towards the team, and is such a grounded player. He is the epitome of a normal bloke who happens to play cricket for a living. He's so natural, so chilled and so likeable.

The class of the man revealed itself in the way that he spoke to Sky Sports' Nasser Hussain immediately after the game when he had to deal with the disappointment of losing in such cruel circumstances and did so with such grace and good sportsmanship.

'Both sides showed a lot of heart, a lot of fight. You can nitpick, but perhaps it just wasn't meant to be for us,' he said.

And the image of him when it was announced at the post-match presentations that he was man of the tournament will stick with me. Unaware that the cameras were on him, he was like 'who, me?' Almost in disbelief that he should be considered. He has such grace, such humility.

For my money, though, it was hard to look past Rohit Sharma for that particular award given the amount of runs he scored, and how he scored them. To hit five hundreds in nine completed appearances, under pressure to guide India's innings and meet the weight of expectation placed on someone in such a position, was a phenomenal effort. In contrast, Kane was clearly recognised for not only his own batting contributions – finishing 70 runs behind Rohit's tally of 648 – but also the influence of his captaincy.

Personally, I also spent some time that evening with Ish Sodhi, a legend of a bloke I played with for two years at Rajasthan in the Indian Premier League. He was obviously experiencing emotions at the other end of the spectrum to me but he is another typical of that New Zealand team.

They always play the game in the right spirit and are never less than ultra-competitive when they get on the field. Yet they are not a team that people tend to fear or speak about as potential champions whenever a global event comes around. Perhaps after making the last two World Cup finals, and pushing us so close at Lord's, they should no longer be thought of as underdogs for anything.

If there had been another team I'd wanted to win the World Cup – if we were unable to reach our goal – it would have been

New Zealand. That's not because of my background or any-thing to do with my parents. Putting all that family stuff aside, I just love what the Black Caps stand for as an international sports-team. They play in such a positive manner and make the most out of all of their undoubted skills. They are a team never to be underestimated.

•

As we clambered onto the bus to leave Lord's, midnight approaching fast, Eoin Morgan shouted to us all: 'Get your game faces on.'

He was reminding us that there would be news photo-graphers and TV crews awaiting when we disembarked a mile down the road at our hotel and that we should be ready for such an eventuality. So I spent the next few minutes making my best efforts to freeze my face, like I was in a stare-off contest.

Bare-footed, because my white socks were filthy by this time, I stepped off to the rattle of clickety-clicks. The flashes of photographers' cameras tend to send you into a blinking frenzy, meaning that when they catch you between frames you can look absolutely blotto. Not that I think anyone in the coun-try would have denied us this night of controlled excess after delivering a first 50-overs success in 44 years, or minded what state we were in as Sunday turned to Monday, but it's not the most flattering of circumstances in which to have your pic-ture taken.

The downstairs bar at the Landmark, where we held a private party, was absolutely rammed. The champagne was flowing, people were pouring their own drinks, and everyone was having a great time. The most enjoyable bit for me, though, was when the pizzas turned up. Given my poor record at eating on match days, I was famished. And so, nestled in the middle of three small tables, so I could get pieces from the boxes in front of me, as well as the ones to my left and to my right, I got stuck in.

We stayed in our kits throughout the night, medals dangling around our necks. At the bar, we were being stupid, asking each other whether our medals were real gold and biting them as if that was the test to prove whether they were or not. We were so giddy that occasionally one of us would just stop and ask the rest of the group: 'Oh, what's this? Where's it come from?'

We'd talked about winning these medals for months on end, never afraid to express our confidence or our ambition. But we also knew that it was one thing saying it and another thing doing it. So to be sat there on the other side of these pledges as a World Cup winner felt totally surreal. We always knew we were good, but you have to be the very best to win a World Cup.

We wanted to enjoy these moments as much as we could because we knew it wouldn't be long before the sun came up and they'd all be gone.

Typical of most London hotels, the majority of the staff were Europeans. They seemed to be loving the whole atmosphere too. Although they might not have got cricket they clearly knew what had happened, that we had just been crowned world champions. It felt like that kind of weekend: we'd brought the game of cricket to the attention of people who had not previously given it a second thought.

It remained carnage in that bar until the last revellers left. I went to bed eventually at around 5.30 am. Clare had gone up to our room at about 3 am and I found her in bed with the curtains open, fully clothed, asleep on top of the bed covers. When she woke up later that morning, she found that the curtains had been closed but all the lights were on, with me fast asleep in bed. Yep, it had been a great night.

When mornings follow great nights so swiftly, they're not so great. While I was getting showered ahead of our 9 am departure to the Oval, Clare took a call on the room phone from Danny, the England team media manager, who greeted her by saying: 'Morning. Just checking Ben's alright. I'm ringing rounds all the lads just to see that everybody's on time to report for duty.'

Clare suspected, contrary to Danny's claims, that he was just making sure I was where I was supposed to be . . . and conscious. As it happens, I arrived early for the resumption of our official duties as England's first 50-overs champion team.

•

I have never known our team bus as quiet as it was on the hour-long journey from Marylebone across the Thames to the Oval. We got off on time, bang on 9 o'clock for a 10 o'clock start, and for the first part of the journey it was obvious that everybody was suffering. The only one who appeared to have any sense about him was James Vince, who prepared by bringing along sunglasses. Not because it was a glorious summer's day, but rather so he could hide his sins of the night before. Every single player was armed with a bottle of water. But Vince was fully prepared. Exactly why he went a step further than the rest of us would become apparent later.

Even feeling as dusty as hell it felt pretty cool to see the excitement of the hundred or so school children at the Oval as we showed off the trophy and posed for selfies and autographs. I am used to handling kids at unearthly hours, although I have to confess that I lost my rag with at least one parent. I watched a mother push her way through the queue so that her son could get to me, moving kids who had been waiting patiently out of the way, and so she ended up getting a piece of my mind rather than any signatures. What kind of example was she setting?

Later that day, being called to 10 Downing Street for a reception hosted by the Prime Minister Theresa May reflected the significance of our achievement. That's not really my scene, to be honest, being a northern lad. The people there, very well-educated and sophisticated, were not what I was used to but they served us good wine to be fair and we gave a good rendition of 'Allez, allez, allez' before beating our retreat.

I have to say our behaviour was considerably less raucous than when the 2005 Ashes-winning team paid their visit. Not that we held back particularly. There was a cooler full of beer waiting for us up in the home dressing room at the Oval that was cracked open before we made it back across the capital that lunchtime. Admittedly, drinking the first couple of beers felt like swallowing nails, but once through that we all began to feel normal again. All apart from my great mate Vince, that is.

He copped it that day because after returning to the hotel to shower and change before our date with the Prime Minister he did not re-emerge, sending his wife-to-be in his place when everyone met up again in the bar around 2 pm. With him tucked up in bed, it all became clear exactly why he had been the one with the shades that morning.

A day like this also provided time for reflection. My own wife Clare has always stood by me and I love being able to share moments like this with her. She didn't seem overly emotional immediately after the game, but she did get so when listening to Joe Root speak about me in a television interview. Hearing Joe say that it was destiny for me to be there at the end, after all I had been through off the field in the previous couple of years, got to her. Joe and I go back a long way, and he knows me as well as anyone in professional cricket.

From a personal performance perspective, I felt that when situations dictated, particularly with the bat, I handled them as well as I possibly could have done. Obviously, there were some low scores within my runs tally of 465, but I was able to perform as the tournament got to its business end. Understanding how I play when I am at my best definitely helped me to do that; to be more consistent and to be the reliable guy still standing at the end when games were up for grabs.

There is a big difference between being that guy and one who passes over the responsibility to others when things are still in the balance. As we got deeper into games, when it counted most, I was able to stick my hand up and deliver.

Cricket is a statistics-driven sport and a batting average of 66.42 across 10 innings represented a really healthy return for me. It's not what I am focused on, though. I have never been into numbers other than number of wins, and my feelings about my influence and ability as a cricketer are totally dependent on the results of games.

My post-match analysis tends to focus on the part I have played in relation to whether we have won or lost. An example of this came in the Sri Lanka defeat at Headingley. In the immediate aftermath, I said I would have done exactly the same given the chance again, but later I questioned myself privately. Had I done the right thing in terms of pacing my innings? Did I leave it too long, or waste too many balls, before looking to get us towards the finish line?

My unbeaten 84 at Lord's went according to the plans I made, and although we only made it by that 26–17 boundary count in the end, I was proud to have played a part in what had undoubtedly been a great day for cricket in this country. The overall television viewing figures of in excess of eight million people showed the national appeal of the drama we provided, and due to my leading role in the win, there were several offers to appear in the public eye outside of the usual sports environment.

When Neil Fairbrother, my manager, called to tell me that Piers Morgan had made contact requesting that I appear on ITV's flagship breakfast programme *Good Morning Britain*, I knew I couldn't say no, even though I initially stalled for time by telling him I'd think about it.

I am only too aware of the responsibility I have to promote the sport, but this was more than that. This was a chance to reach another audience entirely and show the real me to the British public. There is nowhere to hide when the cameras are on you for an hour.

The night before the show, which was three days after the final, I realised I didn't have anything appropriate to wear at my hotel. I thought I should be in a shirt, a nice pair of trousers and smart shoes. So I messaged Piers to say so, warning him that all I had was a black polo shirt. It was late notice but was there anything he could do? Did they have any spare shirts in the studio?

He told me not to worry, that something would be sorted, and upon arrival I discovered that he had sent someone out to get some shirts for me. No joke, they couldn't have picked any worse than the three options on offer. I didn't like the look of the blue shirt and the other two were purple and pink. It was like they'd completely ignored the fact I am ginger.

I didn't want to be dismissive, yet at the same time I was desperate for one of the production crew to say: 'Actually, you look absolutely fine as you are.' So when one did, I jumped into a reply as polite as I could muster: 'Really? Do you reckon?'

To be honest, doing this kind of stuff is completely out of my comfort zone and being comfortable in what I was wearing was only going to help. I know what a big cricket fan Piers is and it was a comfort that he was so welcoming when I was there. The producers of the show told me they had never seen him as excited about a guest before. But I was so conscious of not making a fool of myself.

In trying to be as natural as I could, I felt I came across shy and a little bit more timid than I would have liked. Later, when I watched it back, I thought I was bordering on bland. But part of that was nerves, I reckon. Not the kind you get in a match situation. Put me in front of the biggest crowds on the planet and I am in my element. Here, though, all I could think of was: *How many people are watching this?*

Everywhere you look in that studio, you can see yourself on one TV monitor or another. I felt more comfortable as time wore on, although the producer had initially told me I would be on for about 15 minutes, so to still be sat there 45 minutes later was a surprise.

So was being presented with the certificate to confirm that

I had joined the nobility as Lord of Sealand by my fellow guest Brian Blessed. I thought it was all just a joke. But it's legitimate. And if I want to put Lord on my postal address I can do. So there.

As long as Clare doesn't find out. A few days later, I had to fill out an online form. It had the full-on drop-down list of titles. There, below Mr, Mrs and Dr was Lord. I called her over and showed her, just to get her approval. Safe to say she didn't grant it.

'Don't you bloody dare,' she told me.

For the uninformed, Sealand is a tiny self-proclaimed principality seven miles off the Suffolk coast. It is actually a former war-time fort originally called Roughs Tower, built in 1942, which is a platform of 932 square yards in area supported by two 'legs', which look like huge oil drums. Inside them is accommodation for around 160 people. And it has its own constitution, flag, currency, stamps and passports. Other countries recognise it as a separate state to the UK.

It was all a bit of fun. My only concern in being in a situation like this, on daytime television 72 hours on, is that the achievement was not a personal one but one from the collective efforts of a squad and sizeable support staff. A small part of me wished there had been a bit more focus on the team. The last thing I wanted was to come across like Billy Big Bollocks.

One recognition that I was not comfortable with was my nomination for New Zealander of the Year, an award all Kiwis over 15 are eligible to be nominated for. Others put forward for this year included former rugby league player and *Dancing with the Stars* winner Manu Vatuvei, Christchurch shootings hero Abdul Aziz and hepatitis C treatment pioneer Professor Ed

Gane. The shortlist of 10 candidates was due to be announced in December 2019, with the 2020 winner revealed at a gala dinner in February.

So I withdrew my name, explaining my reasoning in a public statement: 'I am flattered to be nominated for New Zealander of the Year. I am proud of my New Zealand and Maori heritage but it would not sit right with me to be nominated for this prestigious award. There are people who deserve this recognition more and have done a lot more for the country of New Zealand.

'I have helped England lift a World Cup and my life is firmly established in the UK – it has been since I was 12 years old.

'I feel the whole country should align their support to New Zealand captain Kane Williamson. He should be revered as a Kiwi legend. He led his team in this World Cup with distinction and honour. He was the player of the tournament and an inspirational leader of men. He shows humility and empathy to every situation and is an all-round good bloke. He typifies what it is to be a New Zealander. He would be a worthy recipient of this accolade. So New Zealand, fully support him. He deserves it and gets my vote.'

My mind was on an altogether different position as thoughts turned from cricket played in coloured clothing with a white ball to a more traditional form. Its most traditional form, in fact, and the series with the most entrenched tradition: the Ashes.

THE
ASHES
2019

8

TRANSITIONS

England v Ireland,
Lord's, 24–27 July 2019

The date was 24 July. Ten days had passed since the World Cup final. It was the opening day of the one-off Test versus Ireland at Lord's.

I was so pleased that I had been able to contribute to the success of a team that means so much to me, but I was not involved in this match. There was just over a week until the second part of our dual mission of 2019 was scheduled to begin.

As we prepared to face Australia at Edgbaston, however, I could not help feeling that there was something missing for me. Of the punishments I'd received in the aftermath of the Bristol incident, losing the Test vice-captaincy was what hurt me most. So I decided I would take the plunge. I sent a text message to Tom Harrison, the ECB chief executive, to inform him that I wanted to be Joe Root's deputy once more. It certainly left him in no doubt how much I wanted things to revert to how they were previously:

Hi Tom. I've been thinking of how to ask this in different ways. But there is only one way and this is how I want to put it, I began.

Am I getting my vice-captaincy back? I understand the reasoning it was taken off me and the politics that didn't allow me to have it, even with how hard Joe has pushed for me to have it back.

We're about to play in the Ashes and without sounding arrogant Joe needs me as his right-hand man.

I want it back desperately and I want to help Joe through all the highs and lows for the rest of the summer and his career as England captain.

I don't beg for anything but this is as close as I will ever come to doing so.

Stokesy.

It was not something that I had spoken about previously to anyone other than my manager Neil Fairbrother, and Joe Root, the man who had selected me as his deputy when he took over from Alastair Cook in early 2017. Having the honour returned to me – and I consider it a *huge* honour – was not something I had particularly pushed for outside of this relationship.

However, I was aware for some time that Joe had been lobbying for me, pressing people on my behalf about a possible reinstatement. There were a couple of occasions when he'd had a few drinks that he told me of his intentions. I had been quite relaxed about it, as there was nothing else I could do.

Perhaps the powers that be were resistant for a while. Now, however, I changed tack and chose to reiterate my desire to get it back.

Some people will ask why it is important. What does a vice-captain really do? And I guess it's no more than a status symbol. A status symbol that I hold dearly, though.

If you put my whole career in chronological order, the day I was told I was being made vice-captain of England's Test team was a major landmark. There are some amazing highlights on the journey of an international cricketer's career – making your debut, scoring your first hundred, taking your first five-wicket haul. As you pass through each stage of this journey, you are gaining more and more experience, and if you keep performing, keep justifying your selection, you become a more senior player as time passes. The landmarks signify key moments in the transition from junior to senior player.

When there are more guys that have come into the team since you than before you, you start to feel a responsibility for how the team conducts itself and the style in which it plays. You no longer just feel like one of the foot soldiers. You take on responsibility for making each new member of the squad welcome, to alleviate the pressure on them, so that they don't feel any extra to that which goes with representing England.

I guess, after a period of time of being like this, the next step is something like the vice-captaincy. It suggests that the transitions for your career have gone well over the first four to five years and that the team management view you as being a fixture for a few more years to come. Although I didn't feel my standing within the team had changed, to lose the official title felt devastating.

I had been stripped of the reward that went for showing the qualities required within that England team, for something that I had been caught up in outside of my working environment.

Jos Buttler had taken on the role from the 2018 summer onwards and some people would argue he hadn't done anything wrong to lose it. Then again, I always felt it was mine and I so wanted it back.

Jos had done a great job as Joe's deputy. He has a good cricket brain, is excellent at coming up with tactical suggestions and is a very popular player among the group. He commands the respect of the dressing room so naturally.

Forty-eight hours later, I had Ashley Giles, the England managing director, in contact to offer me the position once more. I was in my garage at home when the phone rang. It was the night before the first Ashes squad was being announced. To be honest, if Ashley Giles rings you late at night like that, you're thinking: *What have I done now?* Especially if your name is Ben Stokes.

Thankfully, it was good news and the nicest of conversations was kept fairly short and sharp. My reaction to being told that I had been reinstated was no more than 'Cool.' But it meant the world to me. Believe me.

Later, in an interview, Jos said that he always envisaged I would be getting the vice-captaincy back at some point and that he was effectively keeping the position warm for a while. That he felt like a stand-in.

•

Neither he nor I played against Ireland in the four-day Test match. Decisions on whether senior players would do so came after we had concluded our World Cup campaign.

Trevor Bayliss asked me at the bar before we went to Downing Street on that Monday lunchtime whether or not I felt I needed the game or could do with some time off. It wasn't even something to which I gave a second thought.

My response was something like: 'Nah, I'm done.'

Post-World Cup, my body was telling me that I'd had enough. I needed a break. I just wanted to get home, away from cricket for a bit and recharge the body before the Ashes. The best thing for me, and for my cricket, at that time was to go and spend some time with my family. To be in my own house and relaxing. I certainly didn't feel in the cricket bubble at that moment in time, and if I'd played that Test match I'm not sure it would have done anything for me, or that I'd have contributed much. Drained by the demands of the previous couple of months, I couldn't have faced five days of Test cricket.

I know some people would kill to be in my position and would never turn down a Test appearance, but there is more to such decisions than just a physical side, or just a short-term view. There is a mental side to playing at the highest level, and you have to look after yourself, to make sure you are fresh when called upon. My head certainly wasn't in the right place and I think you only understand those types of feelings when you are in that position, particularly as an all-rounder.

Given his own dual role, it surprised me that Jonny Bairstow opted to play when given the chance for a week off. I didn't understand why he thought it necessary. All the decisions were left to the individual and, although I am sure he had his reasons, he had put in a hard shift at the World Cup and we were all informed it would not be frowned upon whatever we decided.

Of course, Joe Root felt obliged to play as captain, and someone like Chris Woakes wanted to get established again in the Test team following a great World Cup, but Jos Buttler felt the same way as I did, that he needed some time off to chill.

Observing from a distance, the best thing about this particular Test match against Ireland was that we were dismissed so cheaply on the opening day. Bowled out for 85, it clearly wasn't an indication of how good the England team were on paper but more to do with the extreme challenges thrown up through a combination of the pitch and atmospheric conditions.

It went without saying that England were a far superior side to Ireland, so the examination from the end of that first innings onwards was more of a mental one. They possessed all the necessary skill and overall quality to out-perform Ireland. The question was: could they produce this on any given day?

The fact that they overcame that mental challenge would have been good for everyone involved within that team. No, the match shouldn't have turned out like it did, England shouldn't have been dismissed for 85 by a new Test-playing nation on the first day of a match, but it happened and they then had to deal with it.

From then on, they coped with things really well. Psychologically, they did so well to come back from such a vulnerable position to win the game. It was easy in the end, as Ireland succumbed for 38 under sustained pressure with the new ball from Stuart Broad and Chris Woakes, but it had taken quite some resolve and no little skill to get back into a position where they could take the upper hand once more.

Part of the challenge was adapting to the different tempo required in the longest form of the game. It is quite an adjustment to make to change from playing against the white ball in a 50-over World Cup to the red one of Test cricket, where it not only moves through the air but off the seam as well. I know from experience, particularly in the first couple of net sessions in Birmingham that following week, that I felt absolutely nowhere ahead of the first match of the Ashes series.

I turned up buzzing to go but then started questioning how on earth I was going to get a run that week when the match began. I was being beaten outside off-stump, then getting rapped on the inner thigh pad when the ball nipped back the other way. It literally felt like I'd never picked up a bat before, as balls were jagging past either edge of my bat. And I was only practising against throw-downs with the dog stick!

In the World Cup the ball had not done a great deal, and you could find a release of the pressure on occasion by running down the wicket and hitting the ball over the bowler's head. No such option exists in the more traditional form of the game. Try it in a Test match and you are likely to be in trouble, given the movement bowlers are able to get through the air and off the pitch.

England v Australia,
First Test, Edgbaston, 1–5 August 2019

Edgbaston has been a great ground for us over recent years but I have no idea as to why from a cricket perspective. In fact, the only thing I can say about the ground which might give us an advantage over opponents is that of all our home venues it has the best atmosphere.

Personally, I never walk out thinking that we have a better chance of winning a match because we are at a certain ground – even though recent history told us we had won 11 straight games in Birmingham and Australia had not done so in 18 years. I walk out believing that we can win every match.

On an individual basis, I tend to do well whenever I turn up at Southampton. Again, I have absolutely no idea why. My record is good, I know that, and I am confident at that particular ground, even though it doesn't necessarily show in our team results.

The feelgood factor on this occasion in the Midlands was enhanced when we turned up for our first net practice and the scoreboard was still showing the final score of the semi-final match between England and Australia at the ground a few weeks earlier, with Joe Root and Eoin Morgan as the not-out batsmen. I am not sure it was done on purpose, but it was a reminder of our most recent success.

Alongside Joe's name was 'No. 3', the position in which he decided to bat in this series, one place higher than had become customary for him in Test cricket. There is no doubt he is our premier batsman, as well as being our captain, and in that particular position he can set the tone as early as possible.

There was certainly a lot of attention given to this particular move by the media, I guess because it was made on the eve of the biggest series that we play. Yet it was not something that worried us unduly. Joe is an adaptable player and over time I think he will make this position his own. There's no doubt to me that he's still finding out how to bat at number three, and he wants to lead from the front.

Obviously, his record at number four is phenomenal, as an average of 48.31 shows, and as a world-class player he has shown that once he gets in, it can look to opponents like you'll never get him out. The thing he was trying to work out, during this Ashes summer and ahead of the away series in New Zealand and South Africa, was how to play his first 20–30 balls. The first 20–30 balls at number three are undoubtedly harder to face than they are when you face them at number four, when, generally, the ball is just that little bit older and slightly less likely to move about. If those above you have done their jobs, some of the dangerous elements to batting will have worn off a bit by this stage. The lacquer may have gone and the ball might not be as hard. The bowlers also tend to be that slight bit fresher when you walk in first wicket down.

For this 2019 Ashes series, Australia's top order was strengthened by the trio of Steve Smith, David Warner and Cameron Bancroft returning from their Cricket Australia-imposed bans for their roles in the ball-tampering scandal of spring 2018. With the three of them back in the fold, Australia looked a lot stronger.

On the eve of the series, I actually believed that Warner would be the big wicket for us to take. Of course, statistics will say that Smith was the big wicket but his consistency has been such over the last few years that he always looked destined to score heavily. Imagine if Smith had experienced the series he did and Warner also produced something that he was evidently capable of. Then, we really would have been in trouble.

In dismissing Warner so cheaply on all but one occasion, we managed to negate one of their huge threats. The way that he plays at the top of the batting order is just so dangerous for opponents. Just a few hours of him at the crease really ruins your day. There aren't many players on the world scene that you can say that about. For this reason, I viewed him as the one we needed to get rid of as early as possible.

Without a doubt it would have been a different series but for the misfortune that befell Jimmy Anderson on the opening morning of the series. It might not be universally accepted that one man's presence could swing the balance between two teams so significantly the other way, but when that man is a bowler with 575 Test wickets, and is the best in the world at exploiting the conditions we were being pitched into, I think it's a justifiable claim.

When Jimmy pulled up with a recurrence of a calf injury after bowling just four metronomic overs, it was a huge blow. Just two days earlier, on his 37th birthday, he was bowling fine, and had done everything he needed to in terms of fitness tests. Yet four overs into his Ashes campaign, he was walking out of the attack. As we would later discover, he would not return that summer.

Jofra Archer had reported 'excruciating pain' between the World Cup and the start of this series and wasn't fit enough to get through this Test even though he would have argued that he was. He'd played quite a few games not fully fit during the tournament and it is a different challenge when you are playing a five-day match compared to an ODI.

When Jimmy returned to the field later that first morning, we weren't sure what his mood was going to be like. While he was off the field, it had been decided among us that no-one should go up to him with sympathy. It was the last thing he would want. Let's face it, who wants to hear: 'I'm gutted for you.' You have to be sensitive when a bowler goes down like that and Stuart Broad – his long-term new-ball partner, who knows him really well – agreed.

•

What with our main strike bowler on and off the field, plus the extensive use of the decision review system, it was a cha-otic start to the Test match. Then there was the moment that Warner nicked one down the leg-side off Stuart Broad – and nobody appealed. There wasn't one of us among the close catchers that had any inkling of a connection between bat and ball. It was only when they showed the replay back on the screens that it became apparent. *He's hit that.*

Warner was leading a charmed life. We reviewed for leg-before unsuccessfully, then he had an lbw decision against him overturned. This set the tone for the match in terms of the use of technology. Later in the series, I posed the question in our dressing room: 'Has the umpiring got worse? Or is it that umpires have always made bad decisions for years and that now we've got the technology it's getting highlighted more?'

No-one seemed to have a definitive answer, but you do see some decisions and cannot fathom how the standing official has arrived at his conclusion. To be fair, the benefits of slow-motion replays, Snicko and Hotspot can turn them into terrible calls, whereas back in the day the same decisions would have been under less scrutiny. It would certainly not have been as forensic in its assessment of the umpires' performances as it is nowadays.

From my experience, what I will say about the officiating is that if an umpire gets overturned from 'out' to 'not out' by his TV colleague, a reluctance to give more 'outs' usually follows. That's human nature perhaps, not wanting to make mistakes.

We did a good job of taking back-to-back wickets through-out the first session and a half but during subsequent spells we realised we'd done well to get them into such a position. It certainly wasn't a pitch on which a team should be reduced to 122–8, as the scorecard read.

You can be guilty of chasing things a bit in this kind of situation when your opponent has lost wickets in clusters and the tail has to redress the balance. It's easy to go away from your disciplined lines and lengths in such scenarios, searching for the outside edge in the belief that they will nick off eventually. We weren't really guilty of that here. It was just that Peter Siddle had a game plan to bat for as long as he possibly could. He can certainly bat, as a 2019 County Championship average in excess of 32 attested.

What I would say is that if we'd had Jimmy, the situation

would have taken on a different complexion. Steve Smith might have still got runs but personally I don't think the late-order pair of Siddle and Nathan Lyon would have lasted as long. I don't want to take anything away from anyone else within our group, but Jimmy is a standout in that he is so relentlessly accurate as a bowler.

Smith's 144 was a great hundred and while we set really defensive fields to him, as he opened up and played a few more shots, and some big shots at that, we knew we could afford the odd boundary if we bowled the other guys out. His efforts changed the dynamic, though, partly aided by Siddle and Lyon playing and missing so many balls.

While it was frustrating that they were able to put on 88 and 74 for the final two wickets respectively, it was important for us to remember where we were as a team at the end of the first day of the series: Ashes cricket, day one, lose the toss and bowl the opposition out before the close. You're happy with that and you'd take that regardless of the route taken to get there.

Yes, they managed to build a total much larger than we should have allowed but we were batting before the end of day one, and that was a positive result.

The next day showed the credentials of Rory Burns as a Test batsman. He'd started the county season really well in terms of runs, but the closer the Ashes got for some reason the flow stopped. So to come out and get a hundred in his first innings was a huge boost confidence-wise.

One thing I have thought about Burnsy since I saw his first Test match is that although he hasn't set the world alight yet, I have confidence that he will. Some individuals have something about them that tells you they're more than just your run-of-the-mill player. That the statistics they carry around with them in the first few months as an international cricketer are nowhere near where they will end up. He had that something that said: 'This guy is a Test match player.'

He's tough, and he doesn't care about how he looks because he is focused on the end product – for an opening batsman, that is runs. Not always pretty but effective. Those qualities served him well in Sri Lanka at the start of the 2018–19 winter, maybe not in terms of overall runs but in combating some pretty tricky conditions. He battled and battled, and then battled some more.

The thing with people like him, those that have something about them beyond the currency of wickets and runs, is that if you stick with them long enough you will get a return on that investment. He started paying that faith back with this good hundred and would follow up with a couple of other fifties later in the series.

The class he showed in hitting 1,000 runs five times in as many County Championship seasons between 2014 and 2018 was starting to come through at a higher level. His return of 390 for the series was far superior to any other opener on either side of the Ashes divide.

With people like Rory coming through and succeeding at Test level, against a high-quality Australian bowling attack, you might as well get that MCC coaching manual and throw it in the bin. It shows that when it comes to technique it's all very much down to the individual. As long as you can leave the ball well, hit the ball and score runs, who cares what you look like?

When he made two scores of six against Ireland I have no

doubt he would have felt like he was short of form heading into the big series of 2019. But he is not the sort of person to go away and make changes. He has always been determined to succeed in his own way. By this stage, at the age of 28, he had played a lot of first-class cricket, captained Surrey, had a good head on his shoulders and got lots of experience under his belt. He's very confident in his process of playing. He stuck to his guns, knowing what has worked for him in the past, and it paid off.

I have a habit of being at the crease when other people get hundreds. I guess that goes with the territory of batting at numbers five or six. And it often occurs not long after I have arrived at the crease.

On this occasion, my fifth-wicket partner was on 92 and he seemed pretty relaxed at the prospect of getting to three figures. But he found himself stuck on 99 for nine balls, and to be fair Nathan Lyon bowled a really good maiden to him. All I kept thinking was: *Don't sweep.* In my head I was talking to him, saying: *Keep calm, you'll get one.* In other words, he will bowl a loose one or allow you a tuck for a single.

Lyon didn't really let up – everything was in tight to off-stump and some were going on with the arm, others turned away from the bat – and so when we dashed through for a single, I turned my head to look over my shoulder and watch the ball travel to the bowler's end. The bails came off, and the Australians launched into a mass appeal.

'You good?' I asked him as I met Rory mid-pitch.

'Yeah, yeah.'

A run-out chance like that does ruin the spontaneity of the moment somewhat. But these are still precious seconds in an international career. In this kind of situation, I am always keen to congratulate my partner and then step back and watch them enjoy their time. First hundreds are always so good to witness. I recall with fondness the Test match in Cape Town in 2016 and the emotion that Jonny Bairstow showed that day in getting to 100 for the first time.

Rory's signature celebration for the century was not to look skywards as Jonny did but to remove his helmet and place his hands together in a prayer motion. The second-wicket stand between him and Joe Root had laid a foundation for the innings, and we were intent on capitalising. Our own partnership spanned into the next morning, and to within two runs of Australia's 284 – when I felt we'd reached a point where I could impose myself on the game.

I had just reached 50 and envisaged that for the next 45 minutes I would expand my way of playing. The situation in the game dictates to me how I feel I need to play. When I walked to the crease I assessed that consolidation of our position was necessary. Now I sensed it was time to really open up.

This would work for me later in the series, as it had done in the World Cup previously, but it didn't go to plan here. The second evening had been about survival. I just wanted to get through to the close. Once that had been accomplished, however, I knew the new ball was just around the corner.

Of course, this tends to be a period in which the pace bowlers attack but I sensed the chance to put the pressure back onto the bowlers with a counter of my own. It has worked for me in the past and when I looked at the scoreboard, we were four wickets down and level pegging. I recognised that we had a chance to blow Australia away if I played well.

You can always nick one against a quality fast bowler like

Pat Cummins with a new rock in his hand, and although it was disappointing to throw away some of the momentum we had built, we remained on top.

The lead of 90 runs, which we eventually managed following a slump from 282–4 to 300–8, was a significant one. Mainly because it takes a full session for the opposition to wipe out the deficit before they can start thinking about dictating terms. The talk in our dressing room was positive: Australia were effectively in the red, starting on minus, meaning they had a lot of work to do despite us being a man down.

One thing none of us could escape was that in addition to Jimmy's injury absence, Moeen Ali was struggling. He had said as much in a frank newspaper column on the eve of the series.

Mo is an extremely honest person. An honesty that stems from his beliefs. He is not someone that is going to lie about his feelings. It is not the way he lives his life. His religion allows him to be very open in his assessments and he shared his struggles for form with the readers of the *Guardian*.

After I read his words, the day before the series began, I sent him a text message. It was not ideal for it to be out there that one of our A-list players was feeling this way, but I wasn't overly disturbed by his openness. He's a good friend and I know what he is like. Instead, I focused on the part of the column I enjoyed: that he was going to go out and express himself, to enjoy his cricket once more.

I so wanted him to go out and play like he did in 2015, a summer in which he took contests away from Australia. When he is at his destructive best, I don't care if he gets out caught at deep square-leg pulling, or if he nicks off trying to play a huge drive on the up, or if he holes out trying to hit the spinner for a straight six. I told him all this in the message. Why? Because I have also seen him pull fours and sixes, crash the ball through the covers without anybody moving and effortlessly lift the ball over the bowlers head and into the stand – and that can be devastating for us.

He's an amazing player who can score hundreds at a run a ball and better, and I so wanted him to snap out of how he felt at that moment. I told him I wanted to see the confident player of the previous home Ashes. Not carefree but the Moeen cricket fans in this country had come to love. He's capable of such special things and I had the feeling that he could turn on one of those performances here in his home city of Birmingham.

Mo is a big personality, and a popular guy within the dressing room, so I was not alone in being keen for him to snap out of the poor form he was experiencing. The structure of the team is so much easier when he's involved and playing well, and I know at times Joe Root has found it so much easier to pick an XI when Mo has been available.

He just needed a breakthrough innings either with bat or with ball. Unfortunately, though, Nathan Lyon, who had turned the ball prodigiously throughout his spell, produced one that didn't spin at all and Moeen watched it straight onto the top of off-stump. It was a dismissal that highlighted how difficult things had got for him.

•

Stuart Broad is brilliant at bowling to left-handers and so David Warner was always going to be given the sternest of tests at the start of Australia's second innings, even in the absence of Anderson. He had thrown down a marker in the first innings when Warner walked off for an lbw which was clearly missing not only leg-stump but another set of stumps too.

This was an indication of how things were going to go for him throughout the entire five-match series. He just couldn't get his game in order against Broad and that meant we always found ourselves in a decent place at the start of an Australian innings.

What makes Broad so effective to left-handers is the perfect combination he produces from that around-the-wicket angle. He has the ability to swing the ball away from them but also, just by changing the way he holds the ball, make the exact same-looking delivery cut back in towards the stumps. As a batsman, I can tell you it's particularly tough work against a bowler when you know you can get beaten on the outside edge just as easily as the inside one. You can get an outside edge, struck on the pads or bowled.

Dismissing Warner for a second time in the contest gave Broad his customary start to an innings for the series – no-one has dismissed Warner as often in Test cricket and Broad has not dismissed a batsman as regularly either. It also gave us a situation whereby we were effectively one wicket away from breaking Australia open at the equivalent of 34–3 in their second innings as the game resumed on day four.

At this point, however, the pitch had lost all of its pace and we felt as a pace bowling attack that we became quite ineffective with our original plans. We just weren't getting what we needed to out of the surface. It became a dull pitch for the seamers – there was no swing on offer, no seam movement. Then there was Mo, who was struggling for confidence as our frontline spinner. With only three seamers rather than four, fatigue was also a contributing factor in our struggles as the day progressed.

Jimmy's injury hadn't affected us in the first innings but here it came back to hurt us. Put it this way, it clearly wasn't in our game plan for Joe Root and Joe Denly to bowl 26 overs between them.

One of the things that we say in the field is that a pitch shouldn't change our energy levels, or our enthusiasm. We changed field settings, the way that we bowled – we tried bowling to a 7–2 split and hung the ball outside off-stump, then went for short balls, followed by a period of leg-cutters. We literally tried everything. That's something you have to do when you are faced with an unresponsive surface.

This was not the kind of pitch on which you want to be bowling to a guy in the kind of form that Steve Smith was in. Let's face it, he had been this prolific for two years, a period in which he took his career average to an extraordinary 65. Take out the slow start to his career – he was picked by Australia as a leg-spinning all-rounder for the majority of his first 11 appearances, when his average sat below 30 – and it is 73.

Quite simply, Smith has an obsession with batsmanship. I have got to witness this as a teammate at both Pune and Rajasthan during spells at the Indian Premier League. When you are in India, there is not a lot to do outside the match days, so you tend to spend a lot of time as a team together, particularly the overseas players, hanging out in the team room at hotels, stuff like that. It's fair to say that he and I are at opposite ends of the spectrum when it comes to cricket. Yes, we both love the game but we have contrasting ways of going about our preparation for it.

For me personally, I could not indulge cricket as he does. The full-on attitude towards his batting works for him. I cannot invest my time like he does. Put it this way, I can't imagine asking Clare to throw me balls like he does with his partner Dani. I'm someone who loves playing. I give my all when I am on the ground and switch off when I leave.

For Steve, it's just cricket, cricket, cricket. That's just too much for me. I couldn't let it consume me like that. For him everything has to be just so. Nothing out of place. Everything in sync. It's the way he believes he gets the most out of his batting. Everything is taken to such extremes in a bid to get the best out of himself. The attention to detail is seriously obsessive – he has elastic tied around his ankles to ensure his laces do not protrude under his pads – but it works for him.

Along with Matthew Wade, who also hit a second-innings hundred, Smith helped Australia bat us out of range and set a notional 398-run target. That's not the kind of total you can chase on the final day plus seven overs on the penultimate evening. With only two results possible – a win for Australia or a draw – the dynamic of the match had undergone a serious makeover.

The positive difference for Australia was that they now only had one last effort to give with the ball. Psychologically, they didn't have to worry about getting up physically and mentally for another day. It was a finite amount of time remaining – after Rory Burns and Jason Roy negotiated a tricky half-hour spell on the fourth evening.

Sometimes, when you're not sure where the game's going, and you know there is cricket left, you tell yourself: *I could still be bowling tomorrow*. It's not as though you are conserving energy, it's just that the stakes are clear when you know you are into the fifth day, knowing you have one shot and then it will all be over. Not that you put any less work in. It's just that you are aware of the presence of a finishing line.

Also, you can't compare batting in the fourth innings on the fifth day of a Test match to batting on its first. If you win the toss, you are disappointed if you don't get through a full day's batting. But if you negotiate a full day at the other end of the spectrum to save a Test match, it's a real sense of achievement. That's how much a game changes over its duration. There is also so much more pressure to handle on the last day.

The way Australia operated throughout the first four Test matches was to have three seamers and then the off-spinner in Nathan Lyon. He often came on to bowl early in an innings and that allowed their big men to rest. He doesn't always produce spells heavy with wickets but he more often than not contains because he is such an accurate bowler.

Here, he didn't necessarily bowl any better in the second innings but the pitch had dried out, it started spinning a lot more, and that made him more dangerous. Bowling in exactly the same manner in more favourable conditions meant he got greater rewards.

To be honest, Lyon is a hard bowler to get on top of and in this particular series the frustration was that the first four pitches of the series were conducive to spin. He puts so much over-spin and revolutions on each delivery he sends down, and that increases the amount of bounce he gets.

Back in 2015, when the pitches didn't really spin, we took advantage of it against him. This year, the pitches offered far more turn and that wasn't ideal because my pre-series thinking was that if they were going to maintain a policy of three seamers and a spinner, we could really take on Lyon. If you can take the controlling spinner for four to five runs per over and reduce his threat, the other three have to bowl a hell of a lot more. Unfortunately, we couldn't force this issue, he found surfaces to his liking and our game plan was out of the window.

This was certainly not how we wanted to play Lyon as a team. At 60–1, after an hour of that final morning, things were going okay for us. Rory Burns and Jason Roy had fought hard, with the former the only casualty. Then, things took a turn for the worse.

Everyone will look back at the end of their career and not be very proud of certain shots. The one in the second innings of this match will be one of Jason's. That's probably a good way of putting it. He ran down, missed the ball and then continued running. You could see him thinking: *What have I done?* But he knows. We have all played a bad shot before.

Cricket is a sport which is judged on the outcome of what someone does, the outcome of a certain shot or delivery, not the process. If he had run down, struck the ball high and handsome and cleared the rope with a straight six, you could imagine the conversations about the confidence and ability he possesses. Of the natural talent. Of the disregard for the game situation.

I admired his bravery in a way. Attacking Lyon was the way of putting pressure back on Australia. As always in these kinds of situations, newly arrived batsmen found the conditions the trickiest and Lyon was in his element as the seamers rotated from the other end.

Yes, he's an orthodox off-spinner: there is no mystery in his armoury, he's just so accurate. You can see from slow-motion replays how much energy he puts on the ball. He doesn't have a doosra, or anything equally exotic, but on a surface like that he's hard work because he gets spin, bounce from the over-spin he imparts and drift because he puts so much energy on each delivery. He's not a Saqlain Mushtaq or a Shane Warne, bowlers with lots of tricks up their sleeves.

But he knows what he's doing, and how he will use subtle changes of pace – the stock ball tends to come out from a higher delivery point – plus the natural variations of a pitch's turn and bounce to outfox a batsman.

He was always going to be the danger to us and he exploited the favourable conditions brilliantly – the extra bounce he was extracting accounted for me, the ball just flicking my glove as it rose up.

His six for 49 was chiefly responsible for us only negotiating half the final day's 90-over allocation. It also left us with the challenge of becoming the first team to come from 1–0 down to win an Ashes series since Michael Vaughan's team in 2005. Despite the 251-run defeat we were not despondent, and we were certainly up for the challenge as we moved on to Lord's.

England v Australia First Test, Edgbaston, 1–5 August 2019

Result: Australia won by 251 runs

AUSTRALIA First Innings

	R	B	4s	6s
Cameron Bancroft c Joe Root b Stuart Broad	8	25	2	0
David Warner lbw Stuart Broad	2	14	0	0
Usman Khawaja c Jonny Bairstow b Chris Woakes	13	23	2	0
Steve Smith b Stuart Broad	144	219	16	2
Travis Head lbw Chris Woakes	35	61	5	0
Matthew Wade lbw Chris Woakes	1	5	0	0
Tim Paine (capt) (wk) c Rory Burns b Stuart Broad	5	14	0	0
James Pattinson lbw Stuart Broad	0	2	0	0
Pat Cummins lbw Ben Stokes	5	10	1	0
Peter Siddle c Jos Buttler b Moeen Ali	44	85	4	0
Nathan Lyon not out	12	26	3	0
Extras (w 2, lb 13)	15			
Total (all out, 80.4 overs)	**284**			

Fall of wickets

1-2 (D Warner, 3.5 ov), 2-17 (C Bancroft, 7.3 ov), 3-35 (U Khawaja, 14.2 ov), 4-99 (T Head, 32.4 ov), 5-105 (M Wade, 34.6 ov), 6-112 (T Paine, 39.4 ov), 7-112 (J Pattinson, 39.6 ov), 8-122 (P Cummins, 43.6 ov), 9-210 (P Siddle, 67.2 ov), 10-284 (S Smith, 80.4 ov)

Bowling

	O	M	R	W
James Anderson	4	3	1	0
Stuart Broad	22.4	4	86	5
Chris Woakes	21	2	58	3
Ben Stokes	18	1	77	1
Moeen Ali	13	3	42	1
Joe Denly	2	1	7	0

ENGLAND First Innings

	R	B	4s	6s
Rory Burns c Tim Paine b Nathan Lyon	133	312	17	0
Jason Roy c Steve Smith b James Pattinson	10	22	2	0
Joe Root (capt) c & b Peter Siddle	57	119	6	0
Joe Denly lbw James Pattinson	18	36	3	0
Jos Buttler c Cameron Bancroft b Pat Cummins	5	10	1	0
Ben Stokes c Tim Paine b Pat Cummins	50	96	8	0
Jonny Bairstow (wk) c David Warner b Peter Siddle	8	35	1	0
Moeen Ali b Nathan Lyon	0	5	0	0
Chris Woakes not out	37	95	1	1
Stuart Broad c James Pattinson b Pat Cummins	29	67	2	0
James Anderson c Pat Cummins b Nathan Lyon	3	19	0	0
Extras (nb 1, w 2, b 10, lb 11)	24			
Total (all out, 135.5 overs)	**374**			

Fall of wickets

1-22 (J Roy, 7.2 ov), 2-154 (J Root, 49.6 ov), 3-189 (J Denly, 62.1 ov), 4-194 (J Buttler, 65.4 ov), 5-282 (B Stokes, 97.1 ov), 6-296 (R Burns, 104.1 ov), 7-300 (M Ali, 104.6 ov), 8-300 (J Bairstow, 105.5 ov), 9-365 (S Broad, 129.6 ov), 10-374 (J Anderson, 135.5 ov)

Bowling

	O	M	R	W
Pat Cummins	33	9	84	3
James Pattinson	27	3	82	2
Peter Siddle	27	8	52	2
Nathan Lyon	43.5	8	112	3
Matthew Wade	1	0	7	0
Travis Head	2	1	7	0
Steve Smith	2	0	9	0

AUSTRALIA Second Innings

	R	B	4s	6s
Cameron Bancroft c Jos Buttler b Moeen Ali	7	31	1	0
David Warner c Jonny Bairstow b Stuart Broad	8	8	2	0
Usman Khawaja c Jonny Bairstow b Ben Stokes	40	48	6	0
Steve Smith c Jonny Bairstow b Chris Woakes	142	207	14	0
Travis Head c Jonny Bairstow b Ben Stokes	51	116	6	0
Matthew Wade c Joe Denly b Ben Stokes	110	143	17	0
Tim Paine (capt) (wk) b Moeen Ali	34	44	2	1
James Pattinson not out	47	48	2	4
Pat Cummins not out	26	33	2	0
Extras (nb 6, w 3, b 11, lb 2)	22			
Total (7 wickets, 112 overs)	487			

Fall of wickets

1-13 (D Warner, 2.6 ov), 2-27 (C Bancroft, 9.1 ov), 3-75 (U Khawaja, 18.2 ov), 4-205 (T Head, 52.6 ov), 5-331 (S Smith, 85.1 ov), 6-407 (M Wade, 98.2 ov), 7-409 (T Paine, 99.4 ov)

Bowling

	O	M	R	W
Stuart Broad	22	2	91	1
Chris Woakes	13	1	46	1
Moeen Ali	29	1	130	2
Joe Root	12	1	50	0
Ben Stokes	22	5	85	3
Joe Denly	14	1	72	0

ENGLAND Second Innings

	R	B	4s	6s
Rory Burns c Nathan Lyon b Pat Cummins	11	33	1	0
Jason Roy b Nathan Lyon	28	58	4	0
Joe Root (capt) c Cameron Bancroft b Nathan Lyon	28	57	3	0
Joe Denly c Cameron Bancroft b Nathan Lyon	11	16	2	0
Jos Buttler b Pat Cummins	1	25	0	0
Ben Stokes c Tim Paine b Nathan Lyon	6	28	1	0
Jonny Bairstow (wk) c Cameron Bancroft b Pat Cummins	6	8	1	0
Moeen Ali c David Warner b Nathan Lyon	4	28	0	0
Chris Woakes c Steve Smith b Pat Cummins	37	54	7	0
Stuart Broad c Steve Smith b Nathan Lyon	0	1	0	0
James Anderson not out	4	9	1	0
Extras (nb 2, b 4, lb 4)	10			
Total (all out, 52.3 overs)	146			

Fall of wickets

1-19 (R Burns, 9.5 ov), 2-60 (J Roy, 21.2 ov), 3-80 (J Denly, 25.5 ov), 4-85 (J Root, 29.1 ov), 5-85 (J Buttler, 32.6 ov), 6-97 (J Bairstow, 36.6 ov), 7-97 (B Stokes, 37.1 ov), 8-136 (M Ali, 47.3 ov), 9-136 (S Broad, 47.4 ov), 10-146 (C Woakes, 52.3 ov)

Bowling

	O	M	R	W
Peter Siddle	12	2	28	0
Nathan Lyon	20	5	49	6
James Pattinson	8	1	29	0
Pat Cummins	11.3	3	32	4
Steve Smith	1	1	0	0

9

BELIEF

I am not going to lie. This one meant so much more to me than my other hundreds. Not just because this was the Ashes.

It really had been a long time since I'd got a hundred for England, stretching back to August 2017 against West Indies at Headingley – 15 Test matches had passed since, plus 36 ODIs and a couple of Twenty20 internationals.

I am not normally one for looking at my personal score when I am in a match situation. Yes, there is always ongoing assessment of where you are, but this is generally an observation of the team position and the general state of the game when you are out in the middle. Only this second innings of the second Ashes Test at Lord's was different.

I was willing myself to three figures to break that sequence of 53 matches. Of course, there had been some near misses and some match-defining contributions from me with the bat along the way, but on this occasion, when I started to play more aggressive shots, to swing harder, and progressed to within sight of those three figures, I got a bit more emotional about things.

When I eventually got there it felt like a relief. People who follow the England team will know by now, I hope, that I am not in this sport for individual accolades. But when I knocked the ball to square-leg to get to 100, it was the first moment of the summer that I'd experienced any selfish feelings. This was something I really wanted for me.

There was a culmination of everything in my celebration as I hurried through for a single to the leg-side off Nathan Lyon. I leapt in the air during the dozen strides that took me along the 22-yard journey, clenched my fist and screamed 'yes'. This was my seventh century in Test cricket but there was so much feeling in it. A hundred for England is always a moment to cherish, but I cherished this one even more because of that gap without one.

My first instinct was to look straight up to the England team's family box. I struggled to see if my wife Clare was there, to be honest. It's quite a small box and that day there were a fair few wives and partners in it. But I wanted to acknowledge her first as she is the one that always stands by me and has been so supportive throughout the years. Your family go through everything with you, good and bad, so it is great to be able to show your appreciation at times like this.

Then I swung my glance to the changing rooms, and around the crowd. It felt like a huge release for me, even though I had done some really good things in the World Cup and played my part in that exhilarating final on the same ground just a month earlier.

There was another aspect to my unbeaten 115 too, as it

helped set up the possibility of beating Australia to level the series at 1–1 despite almost the equivalent of two full days being lost to rain, and we had been so keen to hit back at the first opportunity possible following that defeat in Birmingham.

There were eight days between the first and second Tests of this series, which was unusual for series of similar length in recent years. It has been customary to start with back-to-back matches with the slightly bigger breaks tending to come half-way through.

As it turned out, the schedule gave us time for reflection. Not that we needed a great deal of it as a team. It was pretty obvious that we were up against it, having been forced to play with 10 men in the first Test. So it was more of a chance for individuals to reflect. When you lose you tend to ask more questions than you do when you win. *What could I have done better? What could we have done better as a team?*

Steve Smith had played two unbelievable innings in the first Test to hold Australia together when they were vulnerable, and although Matthew Wade got a hundred as well he piggy-backed off Smith a little bit. It had been Smith who had got them to an impregnable position. Sometimes you have to hold your hand up to opponents and say: 'Well done.'

During our pre-series team meetings, we came up with a plan for Smith: we set out to post a leg-slip to him, and we would go on to do so for periods throughout all five matches. If you bowl anything straight to him he doesn't miss it, he's really that good, but equally we felt a lot of balls would there-fore go off his bat in the air in that area behind square on the leg-side – it's actually a fairly wide arc. So while we weren't bowling deliveries in an attempt to lure him into strokes off his pads, to get him caught at leg-slip, we did feel that he might offer some chances there if we got a bit too straight with our lines and he worked the ball off the stumps.

Sometimes, when you have funky field placings like that you might ditch the plan after an hour or so in the belief that it's not working. But we stuck with it. On occasions, if we'd had the fielder in a slightly different position, it might have gone straight to him at catchable height, because it's a total guessing game on where to stand with that particular position. You need the ball to go straight to you, as it comes from a deflection and is therefore travelling fast. It's not a gap-picking shot to pierce the field, made with the full face of the bat, so you're not in full control as a batsman of where it's going to go.

The one change for England for this second Test was the inclusion of Jofra Archer, now fully recovered from an inter-costal muscle injury, in place of Jimmy Anderson. It added a different dimension to the England bowling attack which we hadn't seen in a long time. Top-end pace.

Generally, I tend to watch the county cricket highlights on Twitter while I am sat on the toilet. It's ideal bathroom viewing and it meant I had seen a lot of Jofra playing for Sussex – albeit in condensed chunks. The end-of-day videos compress every-thing into four or five minutes and for these small reels he would look like the best bowler in the world. He always seemed to be taking wickets.

Obviously, we saw how special he was throughout the World Cup, but I was really excited to see what impact he would have with the red ball because of the exaggerated movement you get from the Dukes version used in Test cricket in this country.

Not that I wanted people to get carried away. If anything, I was warning everyone to temper their expectations as it was not realistic for Jofra to come into Test cricket and blow a high-quality team like Australia away. The only thing I expected of him was to show the same attitude, the same commitment, the same desire that he showed during his first couple of months in one-day international cricket. Those are the qualities you can transfer into a Test match, although it involves doing so for much longer periods and therefore makes it much harder on the body.

Justin Langer, the Australia coach, had suggested on the eve of the match that our opponents might be able to wear him down by making him bowl for long periods. I could understand where he was coming from in one sense because one-day internationals limit you to 10 overs, whereas in a Test match you might have to withstand a full day's effort in the field, bowling your first spell at 11 o'clock in the morning and your last at around 6 pm. I don't think this was necessarily a mind-games tactic from Langer. It was a reasonable question to pose – could Jofra do the same things, have the same impact, and maintain the same pace he managed over two or three spells with the white ball, in one and a half to two days of Test cricket?

Could he meet the challenge of backing up for spell after spell without losing pace, hostility and accuracy? Well, it was certainly an exhilarating watch as we discovered the answer was an emphatic yes.

During what would become the most talked-about spell of bowling in the match, and indeed the series, in which his duel with Steve Smith had everyone gripped, Jos Buttler was fielding at short-leg. He came up to me at the end of one over and said: 'Jofra's not even finished his first game but he's the best bowler in the world. He is number one.' That's pretty awesome to put such a strong impression into a colleague's mind after just one Test.

The frustration was that there was a delay to letting Jofra loose, as incessant drizzle descended over north London on the first day soon after Chris Jordan, the man who played such a big part in helping him relocate from Barbados to launch his career in England as a teenager, led the cap presentation to him on the Lord's outfield.

Yet four days still represented a lot of cricket and, when it's the first day that has been washed out, the way you approach the match is not really any different. The changes to tactics and tempo tend to come on the second and third days on the field – so what would, in permanent dryness, have been days three and four in this case. More often than not that tends to cover the period when whoever is on top has the chance to take control, alter their mentality and play a bit differently.

Whenever an England team walks onto the field, we are always playing to win, always thinking of ways to do so, but you have to pace yourself in Test cricket, calculating when it is your time to press home an advantage. If you misjudge the position you are in and push hard too soon, you can leave yourself exposed against high-quality opponents like Australia. So it's about trying to play as naturally as possible when things get underway.

We lost the toss on what I would say was a fair wicket – one that provided an even contest between bat and ball. There was a bit in it for the bowlers but Lord's is such a fast-scoring ground for a batsman who is *in*, no matter what the pitch is like, because the outfield is so quick. It really can give you

20 per cent more value for your shots than other grounds. Equally, there was enough in it for the bowlers that day to get the ball full and make use of the overcast conditions and challenge the batters.

By putting 258 runs on the board in what had become a four-day match, it gave us something to work with, and allowed us to apply some pressure when the Australians went out to bat. Obviously, we would have liked more but we knew there was an opportunity to dismiss them for a total that would give us another chance to dictate terms. That's how things would work out, but few could have scripted the drama that followed as a slender first-innings advantage of eight runs opened up for us.

Initially, Jofra was searching for the ball to do more, especially through the air, during his first spell. What we found out throughout the series with this particular batch of Dukes balls was that it took about 15 overs for them to start swinging. In some years, like in 2018, they tended to move around from the off, but these ones only hinted at swing early on, and would only hoop once the lacquer had come off one side of the ball. You could tell from Jofra's early reactions that he was searching for the big inswingers to the right-handers which is the stock delivery for him. He was getting the balls exactly where he wanted them, starting in the corridor just outside off-stump, but the frustration for him was that they were not coming back into the batsman.

The odd thing was that the 2018 and 2019 balls were effectively the same batch, or at least made to the same specification following the ECB's decision to continue using balls with fewer strands in the seam for the summer's Test cricket. What's more, Lord's is a place where the ball does generally swing.

This was Jofra's first spell as an England Test cricketer; he wanted to come in and make an impression by bowling quickly but he just wasn't getting the movement he envisaged with the new ball. The impressive thing about his first spell, however, was his discipline. Of course, although they are rare breeds, there have been plenty of bowlers over the years who have had the kind of pace Jofra is blessed with, but there have been very few that have been able to control it as well as he did on his debut.

Mitchell Johnson, at his very best in the 2013–14 Ashes, did something similar. He was bowling as quickly as Jofra and as accurately. What we saw with Johnson, though, was that he had other periods in which he was just as fast but the ball went everywhere, providing batsmen with the loose stuff that could be put away. Jofra has this ability to generate high speed while maintaining an unbelievable range of skills when it comes to swing and bowling wobble seam. In sending down his first 17 overs in Test cricket for 30 runs, Jofra provided Joe Root and the England team with great control.

During his initial overs, the frustration for us was being forced off the field for showers, the most significant and sustained one coming when Australia were 80–4. It really felt like we were on top in the game and so an interruption that came in at lunch and did not allow play for the remainder of the third day took pressure off them. As a batting side, it's better to take refuge in the changing room in that situation in order to take some sting out of the situation. Every time we got momentum with the ball, the weather seemed to intervene and that meant starting again.

The most intriguing period of cricket in the series in one

way was the ridiculously brilliant spell Jofra bowled to Steve Smith in particular on the fourth afternoon. Australia had played well to take their overnight position to 155–5 by lunch, but we changed our plans after lunch and did so spontaneously because of how well Jofra was bowling his bouncers.

It was obvious that Smith was uncomfortable against this mode of attack and with a field set for sustained short-pitched stuff. This has been a tactic we have used when I have been bowling over the years, but not in this sustained, hostile manner.

Fielders are posted in the deep to protect the boundary but are also there to seize on a chance to take a catch when batters don't play the shot well. If the bowler is bowling well, it is also quite a hard field to penetrate for runs because even a good shot is only for one unless it's perfectly struck into the gap or is top-edged over the wicketkeeper. We took to placing a very fine fine-leg, almost like a backstop, as we felt we needed someone down there to either stop the edges going for four or be there for a catch should the ball go straight up in the air.

Smith tried to take a few on, and I totally get why – it's fine to let someone like Jofra bowl bouncers at you, and just keep ducking, but you also need to score at some point, especially if you can play the pull shot because it's a huge opportunity to get some runs. As someone who feels that he plays the pull shot well, regardless of the field set, I will always look to strike the ball, to play an aggressive shot, and if I feel I can't, I then adjust. Not the other way around.

I feel that we got on top of Smith here when he did try to sway out of the way for a while. To be fair, I am not sure he would have faced anything like that over such a sustained period of time. It was a rare kind of spell. A couple of aggressive strokes ended up flying over wicketkeeper Jonny Bairstow's head, and another mis-controlled shot plugged in no man's land between leg-gully and deep square-leg, just a yard or two short of where I was positioned. It's a bit of pot luck when you are setting fields for short-pitched stuff like this.

The atmosphere throughout this great theatre was amazing. The crowd sensed the battle going on between a cricketer, at the start of his career destined for the top, and another already there as the best batsman in the world.

Jofra was being carried to the crease on a hand-clap beat from the stands and releasing thunderbolts that were making the seemingly unflappable Smith flap. It's that kind of gladiatorial cricket that gets the real purists engaged. The crowd knew they were witnessing a special passage of play and were excited about what the outcome might be. It felt equally exciting to be experiencing this duel at close quarters on the field.

Twice Smith was struck on the body and it was clear that Jofra's hostility had highlighted a potential weakness, if indeed one exists, in his game. One blow drew a huge egg-shaped swelling on his forearm, resulting in him being bandaged up by the physio in the first of the delays to play. Unless you have broken a bone, you don't go off the field as a batsman and you could see immediately that he wanted to carry on. Smith, though, is not the kind of cricketer who likes to change his attire while batting, so it really was needs-must for him to have protection over the damaged area.

When he took the blow to the unprotected area at the back of the neck from Jofra's next heat-seeking missile, it was a real concern. I was stood at leg-slip and when you see someone get hit like that and fall straight to the ground, everyone close to the batsman has the same instinct. You want to make sure he is alright.

Jos Buttler was the first one in there, being closest at short-leg. There was genuine concern for Smith's well-being as he lay sprawled on the turf, face down. In these situations, what you must avoid is 11 guys gathering around because that can make the batsman feel claustrophobic. He was a bit spaced out in the immediate aftermath of the blow and he needed reassurance and most importantly space, not a group of people surrounding him, in that minute-long wait for the professionals to come out and deal with the matter.

Head and neck strikes are taken very seriously in the modern game and it has become commonplace for stoppages to take lengthy chunks of time out of the game. This one was seven minutes in length.

Several minutes into this interval there was a TV picture of Jos and Jofra laughing and social media rather typically and rather ludicrously was soon awash with accusations that they somehow found Smith's predicament funny. How on earth do people make issues out of these things? It was three to four minutes after Smith had been struck; Jos was the one who rolled Smith over, showing concern for his welfare, and once he saw that he was okay he walked away. In turning to Jofra, Jos was undoubtedly trying to change the mood of the bowler.

It's easy to overlook the fact that a bowler does not feel nice when he puts another player's health in jeopardy with a strike like that. As a senior player, Jos would have been trying to get Jofra to relax a bit. So the fact that it was even hinted that any of the England team would laugh at Smith in that disturbing situation was an absolute joke. Later that evening, Jofra got a few messages off the back of it that weren't very nice, and that hacked me off.

We know that top-level cricket is a dangerous game. It's a five-and-a-half-ounce ball and when it's coming at you at 90 mph it's going to hurt. Taking a blow in certain areas of the body can also prove fatal and so seeing Smith get back to his feet and be able to walk off of his own accord (he obviously wasn't best pleased to be told to leave the field) was very reassuring, because we knew just how grave a situation this could have been and, as a team, one of the things we talked about out in the middle was how lucky he was because it was such a similar area of the body to where Phil Hughes had been hit.

No international team wants to see an opponent floored in this way, and for me it also brought back memories of Mitchell Starc delivering a thudding clunk to Eoin Morgan's helmet in an ODI at Old Trafford in 2015. I remember standing at the non-striker's end. Hughes' passing was still very fresh in Australian minds and it was immediately obvious how hard the ball had struck Eoin. Clearly for them this hefty impact brought back what had happened to their mate. A few of them became very shaken up and emotional, Starc in particular.

The fact is that a bouncer remains a bone fide weapon for a fast bowler, often in a wider-ranging strategy for dismissing batsmen, and the target for a good one is always the head. Not to inflict physical injury; it just happens to be the ideal place to be aiming because it is very uncomfortable to have to play a shot from that position. You have a split second to react and it is an unnerving prospect to be faced with a situation where the ball is hurtling towards your eyes at breakneck speed. No matter what people say to the contrary, no one really likes it.

If delivered accurately it means you have to be so decisive and that can be stressful – if it's at your body, human nature is to do anything possible for it not to hit you first and foremost. So you are either trying to sway, duck or hit it with risk involved. The risk being you play a shot without full control and jeopardise your stay at the crease.

Being aggressive, not letting batsmen settle, is a huge part of Jofra's armoury as a fast bowler, and that bouncer of his is a huge asset. When someone takes a nasty blow, no bowler is going to say: 'I'm not going to bowl that again because I don't want to hit them again.' That shouldn't even come into your thinking.

What makes Jofra's bumper so effective is that he doesn't have any *tells* – there are no signs that he is about to bowl one. Because everything is so rhythmical when he is approaching the crease and entering into his delivery stride, there are no noticeable changes in his body shape or the way he releases the ball from his hand. He's very tight to the stumps as well. Everything looks just so languid too. Everything is so well disguised.

Yes, Smith scored plenty of runs from the pull shot against us across the 2019 summer, but I know from my personal contributions that some were from drag-downs. It's a lot easier to make good contact with nothing deliveries like that than with testing bouncers. Proper, testing ones in the right target area were definitely a different proposition and proved disconcerting to him.

Smith was not wearing stem guards on the back of his helmet, and the fact that he was struck on the neck drew attention to this. He says they feel uncomfortable. He's quirky in this regard and even after this episode rejected wearing them in subsequent net practices (though he did end up wearing them later in the series).

My excuse for not wearing them in the early part of the summer was not that I had made a conscious decision to stop doing so. It wasn't that I had taken them off my helmet, rather that I'd never put them on in the first place. My most recent one didn't have the stem guards clipped to it when I pulled it out of the box. Some do, others come with the stems in a polythene bag inside the packaging for you to clip on yourself. This was one of the latter examples.

I clipped mine on not long after this when Jason Roy received a blow during the practice days of the next Test at Headingley. Jason was struck on the stem guard itself and still sported a huge bruise underneath.

'Jesus, weren't you wearing the stem guards?' I asked, when I saw him in the changing rooms afterwards, and that persuaded me. To discover he was came as a shock.

That Saturday evening, I texted Steve Smith: 'Hey mate, hope all's well. It was a nasty knock. Good to see you walk off the field.'

His response was: 'Yeah, just a bit of a headache now.'

Knowing things were okay, I couldn't resist following up with: 'Jofra must have a really good shot to hit you in the head.'

The running joke between teammates of Steve from all over the globe is that he's got a pea head. When he replied with the laughing emoji, I knew he was as good as he possibly could be.

He had not looked great at the time of the incident. Having been escorted from the field by the Australia team doctor Richard Saw, he must have passed the concussion protocol otherwise he would not have come back on the field. He resumed his innings at the fall of the next wicket and hacked at his first ball. We were like: 'Bloody hell, he is concussed.'

We'd not seen him play like this before. It was a combination of the ridiculous and the sublime. Next came a beautiful back-foot drive, which was more like his old self. Then, he wiped one which went a million miles in the air, came down, plugged and rolled into the boundary rope, before finishing off by missing a straight one from Chris Woakes that was so out that he literally walked yet then decided to review the lbw decision. It all suggested he hadn't been thinking straight.

My theory is that even if you feel fine in that situation, if you come out with a sore head you are not going to play in a normal manner. It's like when you are physically exhausted. It can make you a bit light-headed, or dehydrated, as though you are almost having an out-of-body experience. Yes, he was playing with the tail for company, but I am not sure if he would have done those things under normal circumstances.

We knew he had gone for a scan on his forearm during the evening session, as we began our second innings, and although that showed no break, he struggled with concussion symptoms when he awoke the next morning.

I was batting during a delayed opening session of the fifth day when Cricket Australia announced that he had been withdrawn from the game:

Steve has been closely monitored by medical staff overnight and this morning reported that after sleeping well, he woke with 'a bit of a headache and a feeling of grogginess'. As part of the Cricket Australia concussion protocol, repeat concussion testing of Steve Smith was also performed this morning and demonstrated some deterioration from his testing which is consistent with the emergence of the symptoms he was reporting. On that basis Steve has been withdrawn from the match by team doctor Richard Saw and the Australia team will lodge an application for a concussion substitute with the ICC match referee in line with the ICC protocol.

On the field, we had resumed on what was effectively 104–4 some 70 minutes late due to further rain. The game was delicately poised and my partnership with Jos Buttler didn't exactly possess the kind of tempo usually associated with us batting together. There was no flamboyance to our efforts; this was an exercise in crease occupation because what the England team needed was to build something over a period of time. Yes, you always need to be scoring runs but the objective of the first half of this final day was to get something going, to take the game deeper and deeper – a tactic designed to move us into a position from where our team could only win or draw.

When we had come together the previous evening, initially we had to avoid the innings turning from the equivalent of 79–4 to not many more for five. Had that happened, we really would have been struggling.

It was a straightforward situation in that the longer we stayed together, the more chance we had of getting out of range of a potential Australia run chase – and the time factor would also be key in our bid to win because it allowed us to set attacking fields. We had to reduce the fourth innings to a period which would rule out realistic chances for an Australian victory while giving us enough time to bowl them out.

Beginning just after noon with a lead of three figures, we knew it was one and a half hours of normal batting, putting a high price on our wickets, so that if Australia were to dismiss us during the period it would be from really good deliveries. They'd have to work hard to get us out.

The bowling conditions had been favourable to Australia the previous evening when I arrived at the crease at 64–3, 72 runs in front, after Joe Root had asked me bat at five, in a switch of positions with Jos. The floodlights were on and the ball was nipping about as it often does when conditions are like that.

To be fair, Australia bowled well to me and I led a charmed life. Put it this way, if you wrote out my seventh Test hundred as a scorecard it would have read 115–4 because of the luck that went my way out in the middle. But I knew I had to play according to the situation, to apply myself and bat on, and as they say: 'You have to buy a ticket if you want to win the lottery.'

I had faced just one ball when Nathan Lyon was reintroduced to the attack by Tim Paine. Within my first handful of deliveries from the off-spinner, I inside-edged past leg-stump, nicked one past David Warner at slip for four and was then dropped by Warner.

I might have been run out on six, too. Soon after Rory Burns was dismissed, I was out of my ground at the non-striker's end when Jos miscued one to mid-on. I had not added to that tally when the Australians opted not to go for an lbw review after Aleem Dar gave me not out. Replays showed it would have hit leg-stump. Australia had already made a mess of a couple of reviews against Burns in that elongated evening session. I wasn't out of single figures when I spooned one over square-leg off Peter Siddle.

But the most important thing? I was still there. I hadn't let any of these incidents affect me.

As my career has developed, I have been so much better at taking the responsibility on as an individual and recognising how important certain phases of a game are. As I have got older I have been able to place a higher value on my wicket. In my younger days, I would have the attitude of win some, lose some. I could be devastating but I could also get out cheaply.

Where has the maturity come from? When did I change? It's a question I often get asked. The answer is I am not sure, other than saying a volume of games and the experience of a variety of game situations shapes you as a player. There's no better place to learn than on the job.

I was in the fifties when Jos top-edged one to fine-leg off Pat Cummins shortly after lunch, but at 161–5 it was a time to change the tempo. There were 64 overs remaining, and before the final day's play we had discussed wanting 45–48 overs to bowl at Australia in a bid to secure victory.

When as a batter you get to a point in the game where you lose your inhibitions, when you no longer have to consider the consequences of getting out, having worked that position for yourself by getting through tougher periods, it is fun.

Once again, Nathan Lyon had bowled well, getting the ball to grip and turn past the outside edge regularly, but I finally managed to get a couple out of the middle of the bat, with consecutive slog sweeps for six taking me to 80.

With Jonny Bairstow also given licence to play some shots, things were happening fast out in the middle. Jonny had struck a half-century in our first-innings 258, and was transferring his eye-catching World Cup ball striking into the longer form of the game effectively. As for me, my second 50 only took up 54 deliveries.

I was forever looking up at the board to see where we were. Not long after I progressed into the nineties with a crunched square drive off Josh Hazlewood, I looked up at the balcony. Graham Thorpe, one of our assistant coaches, was up there and I signalled three overs and got a thumbs up. We knew the declaration was coming quickly then.

In addition to slog-sweeping the off-spinner Lyon, I walked down the pitch to the fast bowlers, and improvised wherever I could to deflect deliveries into gaps. After I took 15 off a Siddle over that cost 16, Joe Root called us in.

Australia would require 267 runs in 48 overs to double their advantage in the series. However, while five runs per over is straightforward enough in one-day cricket, it is a totally different challenge in Test match conditions and on a fifth-day pitch (even one that only had the equivalent of three days' play).

Any thoughts the Australians might have formed with regard to having a crack at the target disappeared after they lost David Warner cheaply once again – this time to a flirt outside off-stump at Jofra Archer. When Usman Khawaja became Jofra's second victim within half a dozen overs of the start of the innings, we were buzzing.

There were mutters of 'we're winning this'. Positivity was everywhere on the field. In contrast, Australia must have been feeling the strain. The pressure on you as a batter when you are trying to save a game is huge.

In came Marnus Labuschagne, Test cricket's first concussion substitute, at number four and we gave him a bit of a welcome. Jack Leach mentioned as he made his way down the Lord's steps that, during his time with Glamorgan in county cricket, he had taken exception to being called Lambshank by an opposing team.

Not being a shy lad, I tested this observation as soon as he arrived at the crease and, from the death stare I received, I can confirm that he definitely doesn't like it.

Fair play, though, to Marcus Lambshank, as we referred to him throughout the next two and a quarter hours. He stood firm and showed himself to be a very organised player. When he got struck on the helmet second ball by Jofra, he sprang straight back to his feet: 'I know where I am, what Test it is, I am on zero, and it was a fast bouncer.' He punched his gloves together. It didn't faze him. We knew he was fine.

Better than fine from an Australian perspective, actually. It's amazing how things can sometimes work out in a Test series. If Smith had not been hit, and forced out of the match, Labuschagne probably wouldn't have played in the series and yet he turned out to be their second-best batter.

In fact, the way we eventually dismissed him was uncharacteristic of what had gone before in a very well-constructed 50. Jack Leach started bowling his slow left-arm over the wicket, into the rough outside the right-hander's leg-stump, and Labuschagne responded by playing a few sweeps.

'You ain't playing for Australia again if you get out, trying to save a Test match, sweeping,' muttered the close-field chorus. It was the typically stupid stuff that opponents always say.

Unperturbed, he kept on with it, the angle of attack not seeming to have him in any particular difficulty. If anything, it seemed to me that we as the fielding team were being restricted.

So I had a word with Joe Root, suggesting he ask Leach to revert to round the wicket.

'Look, we can't get him out lbw, as Jack's landing the ball outside leg-stump, I don't really feel in the game at slip. Is this working?' I asked.

'No, stick with it. He's going to do something stupid,' Joe insisted.

With that, he moved himself from second slip to in front of square on the leg-side, and two overs later his hunch was proved spectacularly right: Labuschagne creamed one, straight onto Jos Buttler at short-leg and Joe was perfectly positioned to dive and catch the rebound.

What was he thinking? After combating us so well, he had opened the door for us with a dozen overs remaining. Although it wasn't the most remarkable dismissal of that final day, in my opinion. When Tim Paine, the Australia captain, was sixth out, held spectacularly by Joe Denly's goalkeeper-style grab at mid-wicket, trying to pull Jofra Archer, one thought went through my head. *Really? He was supposed to be trying to save a Test match for his country.*

In the end, Australia did get out of it with a draw, and we were left to rue the return of the rain that morning that had cost us 70 minutes of a day in which 98 overs had been sched-uled. With just another half-hour's play who knows what might have happened?

Knowing the possibilities of what can happen often makes the game of cricket easier. In a first innings, not knowing what's a good score, it's hard to dictate what goes on. But at the end of the game, when you have a finite number of overs remaining and are a certain number of runs ahead, it's easier to judge. We knew what we wanted to do on that final day and executed the plans. Only the limit of the timeframe and the weather defeated us.

Yet it felt like a bit of momentum had returned to us in a series that generally had seen advantages swing from one side to another. If you had taken the series at that point, and broken it down into hour-long segments of play, I reckon it would have been 50–50, despite the fact that Australia held a 1–0 lead. There had been parts where we had been so much better than Australia, and others in which Australia had been so much better than us.

Equally, when you nearly pull something off like that it can be hard to take. We just had to channel the pride in the performance rather than dwell on what might have been, so that we could travel to the third Test in Leeds justifiably upbeat.

England v Australia   Second Test, Lord's, 14–18 August 2019

ENGLAND First Innings

	R	B	4s	6s
Rory Burns c Cameron Bancroft b Pat Cummins	53	127	7	0
Jason Roy c Tim Paine b Josh Hazlewood	0	3	0	0
Joe Root (capt) lbw Josh Hazlewood	14	20	3	0
Joe Denly c Tim Paine b Josh Hazlewood	30	67	4	0
Jos Buttler c Tim Paine b Peter Siddle	12	23	1	0
Ben Stokes lbw Nathan Lyon	13	22	3	0
Jonny Bairstow (wk) c Usman Khawaja b Nathan Lyon	52	95	7	0
Chris Woakes c Tim Paine b Pat Cummins	32	62	3	1
Jofra Archer c Usman Khawaja b Pat Cummins	12	20	2	0
Stuart Broad b Nathan Lyon	11	15	2	0
Jack Leach not out	6	9	1	0
Extras (w 6, b 12, lb 5)	23			
Total (all out, 77.1 overs)	258			

Fall of wickets
1-0 (J Roy, 1.3 ov), 2-26 (J Root, 9.1 ov), 3-92 (J Denly, 31.6 ov), 4-116 (R Burns, 38.3 ov), 5-136 (J Buttler, 42.3 ov), 6-138 (B Stokes, 45.2 ov), 7-210 (C Woakes, 64.6 ov), 8-230 (J Archer, 70.2 ov), 9-251 (S Broad, 73.5 ov), 10-258 (J Bairstow, 77.1 ov)

Bowling

	O	M	R	W
Pat Cummins	21	8	61	3
Josh Hazlewood	22	6	58	3
Peter Siddle	13	2	48	1
Nathan Lyon	19.1	2	68	3
Steve Smith	2	0	6	0

AUSTRALIA First Innings

	R	B	4s	6s
Cameron Bancroft lbw Jofra Archer	13	66	1	0
David Warner b Stuart Broad	3	17	0	0
Usman Khawaja c Jonny Bairstow b Chris Woakes	36	56	4	0
Steve Smith lbw Chris Woakes	92	161	14	0
Travis Head lbw Stuart Broad	7	21	1	0
Matthew Wade c Rory Burns b Stuart Broad	6	45	1	0
Tim Paine (capt) (wk) c Jos Buttler b Jofra Archer	23	70	2	0
Pat Cummins c Jonny Bairstow b Stuart Broad	20	80	3	0
Peter Siddle c Jonny Bairstow b Chris Woakes	9	31	1	0
Nathan Lyon lbw Jack Leach	6	17	0	0
Josh Hazlewood not out	3	4	0	0
Extras (nb 1, w 2, b 17, lb 12)	32			
Total (all out, 94.3 overs)	250			

Fall of wickets
1-11 (D Warner, 4.2 ov), 2-60 (C Bancroft, 22.5 ov), 3-60 (U Khawaja, 23.2 ov), 4-71 (T Head, 30.1 ov), 5-102 (M Wade, 44.2 ov), 6-162 (T Paine, 66.6 ov), 7-218 (P Siddle, 85.2 ov), 8-234 (S Smith, 87.5 ov), 9-246 (N Lyon, 93.1 ov), 10-250 (P Cummins, 94.3 ov)

Bowling

	O	M	R	W
Stuart Broad	27.3	7	65	4
Jofra Archer	29	11	59	2
Chris Woakes	19	6	61	3
Ben Stokes	8	1	17	0
Jack Leach	11	3	19	1

ENGLAND Second Innings

	R	B	4s	6s
Rory Burns c Tim Paine b Peter Siddle	29	52	3	0
Jason Roy c & b Pat Cummins	2	13	0	0
Joe Root (capt) c Tim Paine b Pat Cummins	0	1	0	0
Joe Denly c & b Peter Siddle	26	51	4	0
Ben Stokes not out	115	165	11	3
Jos Buttler c Josh Hazlewood b Pat Cummins	31	108	3	0
Jonny Bairstow (wk) not out	30	37	1	2
Extras (nb 1, b 5, lb 19)	25			
Total (5 wickets, 71 overs)	258			

Fall of wickets

1-9 (J Roy, 4.1 ov), 2-9 (J Root, 4.2 ov), 3-64 (J Denly, 18.5 ov), 4-71 (R Burns, 20.2 ov), 5-161 (J Buttler, 56.6 ov)

Bowling

	O	M	R	W
Pat Cummins	17	6	35	3
Josh Hazlewood	13	1	43	0
Peter Siddle	15	4	54	2
Nathan Lyon	26	3	102	0

AUSTRALIA Second Innings

	R	B	4s	6s
Cameron Bancroft lbw b Jack Leach	16	40	2	0
David Warner c Rory Burns b Jofra Archer	5	11	1	0
Usman Khawaja c Jonny Bairstow b Jofra Archer	2	6	0	0
Marnus Labuschagne c Joe Root b Jack Leach	59	100	8	0
Travis Head not out	42	90	9	0
Matthew Wade c Jos Buttler b Jack Leach	1	5	0	0
Tim Paine (capt) c Joe Denly b Jofra Archer	4	17	1	0
Pat Cummins not out	1	17	0	0
Extras (nb 1, w 1, b 4, lb 8)	24			
Total (6 wickets, 47.3 overs)	154			

Fall of wickets

1-13 (D Warner, 3.3 ov), 2-19 (U Khawaja, 5.3 ov), 3-47 (C Bancroft, 13.6 ov), 4-132 (M Labuschagne, 35.6 ov), 5-138 (M Wade, 37.1 ov), 6-149 (T Paine, 40.6 ov)

Bowling

	O	M	R	W
Stuart Broad	7	0	29	0
Jofra Archer	15	2	32	3
Chris Woakes	3	0	11	0
Jack Leach	16.3	5	37	3
Ben Stokes	3	1	16	0
Joe Root	1	0	7	0
Joe Denly	2	2	0	0

First Test: Birmingham, 1-5 August - lost by 251 runs

Stuart Broad was back to his best
and took 5-86 in Australia's
first innings.

It's the end of day two and I'm
congratulating Rory Burns for his fine
innings. He went on to score 133.

It was nice to get three wickets in
Australia's second innings. Here I'm
getting Travis Head caught behind.

Matthew Wade scores an excellent
century and the Aussies draw
first blood.

Bowling to Steve Smith can be a frustrating experience.

A Jofra Archer delivery strikes Smith a sickening blow to the back of the neck. A scary moment.

Jonny Bairstow is the first to congratulate me for my second-innings century.

Concussion replacement Marnus Labuschagne is struck in his helmet grill, courtesy of another Jofra Archer short ball.

A high-five with Jofra, who bowled beautifully to take 6–45 in Australia's first innings.

Josh Hazlewood's bowling also caught the eye. He returned figures of 5–30 as we were skittled out for just 67 in our first innings.

Captain Joe Root leads by example and scores a vital 77 in our second innings.

Day four and a delivery from Josh Hazlewood strikes me on the helmet, sending fragments spinning into the air.

A nonchalant wipe of his spectacles and Jack Leach is ready to continue the battle.

Tim Paine appeals for lbw against me off the bowling of Nathan Lyon. The Aussies had no reviews left.

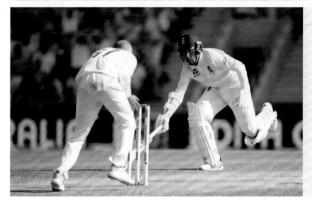

Nathan Lyon fumbles a straightforward run out opportunity and Jack Leach squeaks home.

We've done it! Somehow, we've done it!

The feeling of euphoria was something else.

Limbs everywhere!

Leaving the field after an extraordinary Sunday at the office.

A Player of the Match award. Truth is, it was a brilliant *team* comeback.

Exhausted in the dressing room.

Steve Smith's batting in the series was astonishing. In this Test alone he scored nearly 300 runs: 211 and 82. Outstanding.

Rory Burns cuts behind square in a first-innings knock of 81.

Mitchell Starc takes my scalp in the first innings.

Left. Mitchell Marsh gets the ball swinging on day one and finishes with 5–46.

Right. Jofra Archer gives it right back to the Aussies, returning impressive figures of 6–62.

Joe Denly deserved a century in our second innings: his 94 was pivotal in setting up a strong platform to pressurise the Aussies. Joe even had time earlier in the match to nip off and welcome his baby daughter into the world.

I cling onto one at leg-slip to remove Steve Smith off Stuart Broad. The scent of victory was in our nostrils.

10

ECSTASY

England v Australia,
Third Test, Headingley, 22–26 August 2019

'Hope you see history made today, mate.'

Chris Wilds, my next-door neighbour and recipient of my text message on the morning of 25 August, replied: 'Yes, I'm a believer. Always a believer. Go well!'

I had acquired a couple of tickets for them for the fourth day's play at Headingley. I was unbeaten on two overnight in an England score of 156–3, the weather was glorious (Chris had packed his factor 50) but the forecast for us staying in the series not so bright.

The Ashes were on the line. No England team had ever chased down 359 runs to win a Test match before. But I truly believed this one could, and I wanted to be the one to get us there. I couldn't bear the thought of Australia retaining the urn with two matches unused. The vow I made to myself was to be there at the end no matter what.

An extra motivation, if any were needed, had been provided the previous evening when I had applied myself exactly as I had wanted to despite scoring just those couple of runs off 50 balls. Watching the excellent work of the two Joes, Root and Denly, in repelling Australia's bowling following the loss of two early wickets, I visualised everything I wanted to do out on the field when my turn came and then followed through with the goal I'd set of being undefeated at the close.

It took an eternity for myself and Joe Root – my overnight partner was 75 not out – to get changed that evening, so much so that our teammates had long since returned to our Leeds city hotel.

'The one thing that is going to drive me to win this game, to be there not out at the end, is shaking David Warner's hand before I leave the field,' I told him.

I had extra personal motivation due to some things that were said to me out on the field on the evening of day three when I was trying to get through to stumps. A few of the Aussies were being quite chirpy, but in particular David Warner seemed to have his heart set on disrupting me. He just wouldn't shut up for most of my time out there.

I could accept it from just about any other opponent. Truly. Not from him, though.

Until this match he had not said a bean to anybody on the field, as far as I was aware, since the Australians had arrived on British shores in May for the World Cup. Suddenly, a switch had flicked. He was getting stuck into a number of our lads and getting very vocal. During the first innings, he celebrated catches with snarls and roars rather than cheers. The aggression suggested the old David Warner was back.

The changed man he was adamant he'd become, the one that hardly said boo to a goose and even went as far as claiming he had been re-nicknamed 'Humble' by his Australia teammates, had disappeared. Maybe his lack of form in his new guise had persuaded him that he needed to get the bull back? Although he'd enjoyed a prolific World Cup campaign, he had struggled with the bat at the start of the Ashes and was perhaps turning to his old ways to try to get the best out of himself. The nice-guy act had done nothing for his runs column.

You could see it a little bit with the way he batted in contributing 61 to Australia's first innings here. He looked like the old David Warner when he was hitting the ball and running between the wickets, and he was much more animated fielding in the slips than he'd been previously.

When I am in the zone for batting, it is very difficult to knock me out of it. That's something I have got better at as I have got into my later twenties. When I get out there to bat, even if I speak to opposition players I am really focused on what I am doing. I stay nice and calm.

Warner's words came pretty close to popping my bubble.

To the best of my knowledge, not one of our players had mentioned anything to him or Steve Smith and Cameron Bancroft about the misdemeanours that kept them out for cricket for between nine and twelve months. This hadn't been a team decision. We just didn't do it. *Why go there?*

I muttered 'Bloody Warner' a few times as I was getting changed. The more time passed, the more it spurred me on. All kinds of ideas of what I might say to him at the end of the game went through my head. In the end, I vowed to do nothing other than shake his hand and say 'Well done' if I could manufacture the situation. You always shake the hands of every member of the opposing team at the end of a match. But this one would give me the greatest sense of satisfaction.

•

Time was not an issue with the number of runs we needed to score. We could take the game all the way to day five if we really needed to, so it was a matter of being focused on what we required within the match situation when we walked out to bat on the fourth morning.

The task was to start again, to redevelop the partnership and be better than Australia during the first session. There wasn't too much said between Joe and me because the situation we found ourselves in was a pretty obvious one. With no time-constraint pressure, we just had to settle in and bat.

It was a pitch on which you could feel in for 20 minutes and then, just as you felt settled, one would fly through or nip just to put doubts in your mind and encourage the bowler. It was not a surface on which you could get carried away, even when you felt like you had played yourself into a position from where it ought to have become easier. There was always something there.

But I felt comfortable in absorbing another dozen or so deliveries without adding to my overnight total. My feet were moving as I wanted them to, I was handling everything that Australia had to offer, my defence was solid and I was leaving balls that I needed to leave. Everything felt in tune.

My game plan had been to be stubborn on day three. I knew if I managed to see it through to the close, then there would be time to reassess when play resumed.

My thoughts had not really altered, though. I placed a huge price on my wicket. The number of runs and balls faced were absolutely irrelevant to me. Being there in the middle, 22 yards away from Joe at the other end, was my mind's focus. I felt totally engaged in what I was trying to achieve.

I have to tell you that in this situation I don't care what other people might think. Some observers would no doubt question not trying to make the board tick but, as I have mentioned, when I decide a way I am going to play, I fully commit to it. The only shots I was interested in making were ones that were calculated. I wanted to guarantee a *not out* by my name.

It is not the style of batting with which I might be most associated but this was a needs-must and I didn't consider what anyone else, including our Australian opponents, thought of my method.

My face was expressionless as we entered the fray that morning, and it barely changed throughout the rest of my innings. That's my concentration face and hopefully what I look like more often than not when I bat. It means I have created a batting bubble. The place where I live while I am at the crease.

Australia began with three maidens in a row. Pat Cummins and Josh Hazlewood bowled so well, providing Tim Paine, their captain, with exactly the start he would have been looking for. You don't want any freebies at the beginning of a session, to allow the batsman to settle in with an early boundary or two, and they set the tone brilliantly. As a pair, they are hostile when they want to be, but the thing that makes them so successful is that they dry up the opposition's runs.

The relentless accuracy of their bowling in the corridor outside off-stump was followed by a short ball from Hazlewood, the fifth of the fourth over, which was right on the money too.

I actually have a mental set-up in which I tell myself that every ball a fast bowler is about to send down will be a short one. Having that in my mind helps me play it well when I do receive one, not that I premeditate. I just make sure my weight and balance are ready to play the stroke if necessary, as preparing to play a pull shot every ball is actually a much better method, I have found, than reacting instinctively.

On this occasion, I went to play it and the ball was onto me a lot quicker than I expected. It struck me straight on the helmet, causing the stem guards to explode in spectacular fashion. And the blow hurt. My left ear was ringing, but I was determined not to show it. I told myself not to react, to forget the pain, not let the Australians think it had affected me whatsoever.

Get your stem guards picked up and crack on, I told myself.

As I gathered my thoughts, some of the Australians like Nathan Lyon came up to me to check if I was alright. Marcus Harris handed me the stem guards. They were genuinely checking that I was good. That was nice of them, I guess. But as I explained, when I am in that place for batting, I don't want to be moved out of it. I just wanted to focus on the task in hand. The Australians were doing the right thing by checking I was fine but I didn't acknowledge it, not because I was being mardy, rather that I just wanted the game to continue as quickly as possible.

Unsurprisingly, Warner was keen to mess with my concentration.

'Oh, big tough guy!'

Tough guy? Actually, no. You don't want to be hit and I'd been hit by a good one. Hard. He might have been looking to engage me in a conversation, but as I have matured as a cricketer, I speak less and less on the field. My theory is that if you get involved in chat while you are batting, you never win. If the opposition want to get a bit wordy with you and you go back at them, you are distracting yourself from the task at hand. This applies whether you are on two or 122, so unless I have to speak, I don't bother.

I wanted to get on with the game as soon as possible, but nowadays being struck like this means it stops and medical people come onto the field to carry out the necessary checks before it can resume. Even though it was a flush blow, I didn't want to go through the concussion tests because the longer our team doctor Gurjit Bhogal spent with me, the more chance there was of my bubble popping.

'Come on, let's go, I am absolutely fine. All good.'

Of course he ignored me, insisting on asking the cricket-specific Maddocks questions used in these scenarios – where I was, the date, the day, what I had scored in the game the previous week, that sort of stuff. (Maddocks questions were developed to help medical experts check the cognitive responses of competitors on a sports field in relation to head injuries. They form part of the protocol for concussion assessments – if recall is delayed, it is a sign that a concussion may have occurred.) Full respect to Gurj, he was doing his job with my interests at heart, but my agitation was because my return to batting was being delayed. Equally, our team docs also know we are out there to do a job and are desperate not to lose focus.

In the end, Gurj saved me a bit of time. Until my stem guards flew off in this fashion, I had not realised they needed tying onto the grille of the helmet. There is another clip you have to apply, other than those that attach at the back, only I didn't know. I'd told Gurj to leave as I fumbled about but he insisted that he should secure them properly.

'Yeah, if they come off and hit your stumps you'll look an idiot, won't you?' Joe chipped in, with a smile.

This incident followed the one at Lord's that led to Steve Smith missing this match as part of the concussion protocol. I'd also struck Smith on the grille of the helmet at Edgbaston. Some suggested that batsmen were being hit more than in other corresponding series. Because strikes to the head are now seen as a serious health risk, a lot more time is taken over a player's welfare before a resumption, and it is the delays that bring such episodes to people's attention and which give the impression that bouncers hitting their intended targets are becoming more prevalent. Not so, to my mind; it's just that greater attention is being drawn to such episodes by the broadcasters covering the games.

•

When the first run came from the morning's 26th delivery, from a Joe Root nudge into the off-side, the cheer from the crowd was an ironic one. Don't get me wrong, they were with us all the way, urging us onwards in our pursuit. We could feel from the start that they wanted to get involved, and in cheering for the break in the sequence of dot balls they were simply acknowledging that we were in a tough passage of play. Twenty minutes is a fair wait for something to cheer. Let's say the anticipation had been building.

One thing they might not have anticipated was the way in which Australia were to get their first wicket of the day soon afterwards. It was unexpected to lose Joe in the circumstances we did – a diving David Warner at slip gobbling up an inside edge that had ricocheted off his pad from the bowling of Nathan Lyon. It was pretty unlucky. The ball had looped up and completely missed the wicketkeeper Tim Paine, who did well to dodge it on its journey. It was a good instinctive catch, and the kind of misfortune we didn't need. I fully understood what Joe was trying to do: milk the single down the ground to long-on, a shot that he is good at executing.

Joe is a very good player of spin, they had the field set back and you still have to look to score even on a day four surface that is providing considerable turn. Even though scoring was not a pressing concern, you have to assess where the options are for runs on the field. This was a good option for a right-hander.

The way that Australia celebrated highlighted what a big wicket it was for them, although when you are out in the middle, and fully concentrating, it doesn't have the same impact as it does if you are sat among the rest of the team in the dressing room. That's the bubble for you. It protects you from distraction. It keeps the focus on the task in hand.

Throughout the series, when the ball turned they tended to have Lyon operating at one end and the seamers rotating at the other. On a wicket that helped the off-spinner, it was a particularly good tactic because not only did he remain an attacking option for his side, it also allowed one of the three seam bowlers to rest. Here, he was on for the sixth over of the morning, and 78th of the innings, as Cummins and Hazlewood were given breathers ahead of the second new ball.

My third run of the innings had come the ball before Joe was dismissed, the 67th I'd faced – a clip to deep midwicket. Another off Lyon through that region, off my 74th, represented my first boundary, not that I had been looking to hit the ball for four at this stage. My game plan against a bowler like Lyon, on a wicket that's spinning, is to try to play as straight as I possibly can and not come across the ball unless he has bowled too full. This was one of those rare times he'd overpitched and allowed me to do so. Attempting that shot to a ball that's a good length or slightly shorter carries greater risk because the leading edge comes into play. Seizing on the error, I didn't try to hit it too hard, instead relying on timing and place-ment into the gap, so I was extremely surprised it went for four. As a batsman, that was a good sign, though. Yet to play an attacking shot in the best part of two hours, but my timing was there.

Feeling good about my batting doesn't necessarily mean scoring 40 off 60 balls, to be honest. In this innings, yes, I had played and missed a few times – and you are going to against a good bowling attack – but everything felt in sync. If I had to leave, I left well. If I had to defend, the ball was hitting the middle of the bat and I didn't feel in any trouble at the crease even though I was seven not out, off 76 deliveries, when Aus-tralia took the second new ball – at 166–4 after 80.2 overs.

This was a big moment in the game. The very first delivery with the new cherry from Cummins reared from the back of a length towards the throat of Jonny Bairstow, who did brilliantly to play it so well early in his innings, the impact off the gloves deflecting the ball into the leg-side for a single. Importantly, it was a warning of what the new ball does in comparison to the old one and reiterated that we would be tested whenever they got it into good areas.

I could not fault Jonny's attitude from the moment he joined me. He seemed to relish the challenge. After that snorter, he was beaten outside off-stump and then replied by getting a couple of fours away through the off-side from consecutive deliveries off Josh Hazlewood. It was the start of a partnership that I believed was crucial. Give Jonny credit for this. He not only negated the new-ball threat by the rate at which he scored, he came out from ball one and played in a way that gave Australia something to think about. He wasn't going to allow them to settle into the rhythms they were after.

As a batting pair, we dovetail naturally. Memories of my 257 in Cape Town in early 2016 are mint. As in that match against the South Africans, suddenly we were in the midst of a flurry of boundaries. You get great value from strokes against the new ball because it comes off the pitch quicker and runs across the outfield faster when it's at its hardest. I guided one over the slips off Cummins and Jonny played a glorious straight drive off Hazlewood. The way Jonny applied himself was a reminder that, at a stage in the game like this one, you will get beaten by some really good balls but to be on the lookout for bad ones.

Belief that we would win never left me. Yes, there were a lot of runs left to score, but this partnership of 86 in less than 22 overs was crucial in increasing my confidence. To be honest, I don't think Australia were expecting it to happen. They had got Jonny, a player struggling for a bit of form in the series, to the crease on the eve of that second new ball – just the kind of scenario they would have wanted.

Yet every run was a step closer to our intended destination, we were really sharp between the wickets, and the crowd fed off the urgency with which we played. Then, a bit of a top-edge from me to greet Pat Cummins' first ball of a new spell – a roll-the-wrists pull carrying into the advertising hoardings in front of the western terrace – really seemed to get them going. At this stage, they were so into it that even dot balls were drawing roars of approval. There were still plenty of them, and a fair few plays and misses too. Some, like the one that turned and bounced from Lyon in the 91st over to beat the outside edge, were unplayable. Tim Paine, the wicketkeeper, took this one a stump and a half high. You just have to wipe those kinds of deliveries from your memory.

To an off-spinner bowling in the fourth innings of a match, you play the line of the ball and if it spins, hopefully you miss it as I did this one. Everything has to be played on its merits when some balls are spinning square, because the danger is the one which doesn't spin, skids on and can punish you for over-compensating. It brings your inside edge into play and leaves you vulnerable to lbw if it misses the bat completely. To combat this, I always try to make sure I play the line of the ball and expect it to go straight on, because one of the traps you can fall into when you see it spin is to drag yourself across to the line of the ball. Your hands follow it like a magnet rather than remaining on its original line and that's when you increase the chances of edging one behind.

We'd lost just one wicket during the morning session when the Australian captain Paine introduced Marcus Labuschagne's part-time leg-spin. He's a bowler that changes the dynamic. He's a bit different, can bowl some rubbish but is also capable of the odd beauty, and I just prayed he didn't get me out. When his type of bowler comes on, my standard response is: *Oh, God*. To be honest, everybody feels this way about decent part-timers – ones who carry the ability to make the break-through, not just tread water for six balls before an interval.

The reception we received all around Headingley at the end of his over was simply awesome. Jonny knocked a single to the sweeper on the cover boundary and the noise that greeted the fact we had got through a morning's work for the equivalent of 82–1 was indescribable. My poker face remained as I strode off, and I barely spoke a word, as there was still so much work to do. But the response of the crowd was inspirational. Head down, I had a glance at the western terrace. I liked what I saw, but the job was not yet done. Nowhere near done, in fact.

Had I been more disconnected from the on-field environ-ment that morning than usual? Without a doubt. The Ashes were on the line here. As we entered the dressing room, I broke my silence.

'We've had a great session there, lads. We've only lost one wicket. But I start again and Jonny starts again, on nought, when we go back out. As good as that work was, it literally means sod all now.'

There was a buzz around the place but I knew no-one would look back on that morning favourably if we didn't win. I am sure the mood around the nation, as in the ground, was one of positivity too. The crowd were feeding off what they had seen. We needed 121 more runs for victory with six wickets standing. Easy, right? Certainly not. The ball was doing plenty for Lyon, and was still relatively new for the seamers. It was still a big task.

The Australian camp would also have been feeling the pres-sure, undoubtedly. They needed six more wickets, and they knew they would have to bowl well. But as we knew from the experience of being the bowling team in the final innings of a tight match against India at Edgbaston the previous year, when we successfully defended a target of 194, you can get on a roll if you can hold your nerve. One wicket can so often open the door to others.

•

There was a bizarre review immediately after lunch when Jonny played at one outside off-stump, the Australians went up in unison for a caught behind and the umpire Chris Gaffaney raised his finger. We weren't worried as we met mid-pitch, though. He was nowhere near it.

Generally, you know when you've nicked one, although this isn't always the case as I proved soon afterwards. Playing with bat and pad together against Lyon, the ball flew away through the fingertips of the sprawling David Warner at slip to the boundary at third man. 'Did I hit that?' I said to Jonny, perplexed. I had hit my pad at exactly the same time as I hit the ball and I wasn't able to recognise the distinction between the two.

When a team has been bowling in such a disciplined manner – as Australia had – it's amazing how many times a short, wide delivery accounts for the breakthrough. Unfortunately, it was exactly the type of delivery to which Jonny succumbed. To be fair, the ball jagged away off the wicket and that made a real difference. He was trying to hit the ball hard through the point area and the fact that it left him was crucial in his downfall. People would say it was a poor shot because of the outcome, but it was a genuine chance to score and you can't leave those balls alone. No-one would have given the shot a second thought if he'd cracked it for four as intended.

Ten minutes later, disaster struck. There hadn't been a square-leg in place off Nathan Lyon's bowling throughout the morning session, and as a left-hander facing an off-spinner you know that if you beat short-leg it's a run. Trouble was, Travis Head was now in the square-leg position. I just couldn't see him because he was obscured by the short-leg, Marcus Harris.

By the time I acknowledged his presence, it was too late. I'd clipped the ball and called 'yes', which resulted in Jos Buttler hurtling down the pitch towards me. I knew he was a goner before he turned around. That's why my hands went straight to my head. I was furious with myself as Head's precise underarm throw struck its target at the bowler's end.

What the hell have I done?

Australia's chorus let me know: I'd gifted them a wicket: 'Well done, Stokesy. Well done, mate.'

I had to take it, head bowed. *I've sold Jos down the river there.* I'd sacrificed one of England's real impact players. Someone who can change the course of a game very quickly. That bubble of mine? Let's say it broke for a good few seconds.

A quarter of an hour earlier, the ground had been the most raucous place imaginable. Now, having slipped from 245–4 to 253–6, the silence was deafening. *Great day for a barbecue*, I thought as Jos trudged off. That's right, the weather was absolutely spectacular, and I'd just marinated Jos.

But, at the risk of repeating myself, the Ashes were on the line. I couldn't dwell. I had to let it go. Yes, I felt awful. But we still had the chance of winning this match and the onus was well and truly on me.

The mistake is to let something like this affect you. You

have to separate what has gone and what lies ahead. There was almost a repeat when Chris Woakes scrambled back into his ground in the same Nathan Lyon over that I brought up my slowest Test 50. Not that I was in any mood to celebrate it.

'He's not even raising his bat,' chirped Marnus Labuschagne.

Damn right. What was 50 worth in this situation? Nothing. Sure, cricket is a sport all about milestones and any other time I would acknowledge the applause. It's usually a sweet feeling. This was not one. There was more to worry about than lifting my bat. A lot more within seconds, in fact.

After suffering such a horrendous run out, the last thing we needed was Woakes to smoke one straight to the only fielder on the off-side. It's at times like this when you start thinking things are conspiring against you. I'm sure they were the thoughts of most of the 18,000 people gathered at Headingley that afternoon. But I couldn't go there. I could not embark on any negative theories despite the fact that the pendulum had swung further towards Australia with 98 runs still required and just three England wickets standing.

I don't make a point of talking to players when they come out to bat, but I broke my rule with Jofra Archer because I felt he might need some guidance in such a situation, considering it was only his second Test match.

'You're going to get a lot of short balls here,' I said to Jofra. 'What are you going to do?'

'Get out the way first. Then play it,' he said.

In other words, it was safety to start with for him. Then, once he had a look he might take it on.

'Make sure you do get out the way,' I told him.

At this point, I had to change my whole approach to playing

the off-spinner Lyon. He had settled into a rhythm in which he was bowling ball after ball in the same area. Doing it over and over and over again. I knew I had to expand my options while still being selective. Confident in my ability to get to the pitch of the ball because of the metronomic nature of his spell, I used my feet and struck him powerfully through mid-on for four.

I'd faced dozens of balls from him and this was the first time I'd done it. That can play on a bowler's mind and I wanted it to. I wanted to make him think differently about what he was doing. The calculated decision to leave my crease was made in the hope it might lead him to drag his length a bit shorter and give me the opportunity to cut a few away through the covers. Playing one shot can often open up the chance to play others.

With seven wickets down I also knew that the length of the game needed to be shortened. I had to play a few more shots as I would have to score the majority of the 86 runs left to get. It wouldn't be a grind to the finish line. We needed to pick up the pace.

However, there was no farming of the strike from me because as far as I am concerned, despite not showing it yet at international level, Jofra can bat. After all, he came into the match with a first-class average in excess of 30. I just tried to support him with occasional advice.

At one point, he tried to hit Lyon through the covers. I walked down the wicket for a quiet word.

'Don't play that shot, Jof. It's what he's trying to get you to do. To play against the spin. If you want to go big, hit it that way,' I said, pointing to the expanse of green on the famous west side of the ground.

I didn't want to order him about. I didn't want to tell a

talented batter what to do. Let's call it a gentle nudge. You can see with the shots Jofra is able to play that he is better than what he has shown in an England shirt so far, and when he got his chance, he put a loose one from Cummins through the covers for four.

Following my suggestions on how to tackle Lyon, he swung him into that area of the ground for fours twice in quick succession, the second one causing some hearts in mouths as Josh Hazlewood came forward at long-on. However, I could see he was never getting there as the ball bounced well in front of his dive and over his sprawled body.

'We've got nine off the over,' I said, walking down after he blocked the next one, reminding him, if he was going to hit the off-spinner, to hit him hard. To be honest, I backed him to hit Lyon out of the ground. After all, he was going with the spin.

And so when he chose to do it from the very next ball, I was urging it on through its aerial journey.

'Go, go, go.'

Three quarters of the way, I realised it had not gone. There was just a bit of top-edge on it that meant Travis Head could complete the catch, with a little bit of improvisation, on the rope at deep square-leg. People subsequently asked me why I didn't have firmer words with Jofra about how to play the situation. But that's the last thing I wanted to do. I have always found that teammates respond best when you back them to make their own decisions.

'Stay with me,' I said to Stuart Broad, the next batsman in. Jofra and I had crossed when the ball was in the air and that meant Stuart was on strike immediately to James Pattinson.

Unfortunately, he couldn't. As soon as he was struck on the pad second ball, I was pretty certain about his fate. With two reviews left there was no choice but to use one – just in case. I hoped that the ball was somehow sliding past off-stump. Of course it wasn't.

Again, my facial expression did not change, although being ginger and with the temperature hovering around 30 degrees I was undoubtedly a little ruddier by this point.

•

So here we were, at the start of a partnership I will never forget. The hour of play that I will be able to recall vividly for years to come.

My instructions to Jack Leach upon his arrival at the crease were simple: five and one, or four and two. In other words, I would take the first five balls and he'd take one; or I'd take four and him two. I had to make those two options clear to him. I'd need him to support me. I would take the responsibility for the runs.

I knew it was a tall order. But the Ashes were on the line.

I also knew that I had to change gears from two to five in an instant and that the field would be set back whenever I was on strike. First of all, though, Jack had to face four deliveries. What surprised me was how many short balls Australia bowled at him. Pattinson banged in the first couple. I considered this a bit of a waste.

Jack works on his batting, has a solid technique and puts a high price on his wicket. His job was survival and so he was not going to be flapping at anything they pitched halfway down the track.

From his fourth ball, the last of the over, he squeezed out a yorker and I momentarily lost my mind, charging down the pitch in search of a single. Thankfully, I recovered it just as quickly.

At the start of the next over, I warned Jack that as well as hitting boundaries, I would be looking at manufacturing twos. What I knew in my mind was that I couldn't be trying to hit everything. I had to pick my deliveries. When you need 73 to win in a last-wicket stand, the danger is trying to hit every ball for four or six. But it is a time to try to keep calm. Although we didn't have a great deal of time – because it only takes one ball to get out – I knew that an amount of patience was required in my plan to face four to five balls an over. I would also have to pick and choose which deliveries to go for as the necessary big shots.

On strike against Lyon, I tried a variety of things. A cut, a reverse sweep and a prod into the covers amounted to nothing. Next, I went down the ground – for what I believed was my least risky shot on this pitch. I plinked it, which set a bit of a tone for my other sixes off him, but thankfully it had enough on it to get over the rope at long-off.

With half a dozen wiped off the requirement, we then got into the game within the game – of getting me onto strike for the next over. Unable to get one from the fifth ball, I created the opportunity for the single from the sixth when I walked across my stumps to off, to work the ball off the hip to deep square-leg.

Following a bat change during the next over from James Pattinson – my mishit off Lyon had put a huge crack down my previous one – I immediately stole a two by dropping the fourth legitimate delivery into the covers. In the knowledge that I had to compress the length of the game, I actually went for a big shot off the fifth ball but was happy when a thick edge took it down to third man for one, leaving me at the non-striker's end for the final delivery of Pattinson's over. Had I managed to get the boundary I was seeking off that penultimate ball, I was quite confident of manipulating a single wherever he bowled the final ball of the over. Equally so for Leach to keep out whatever was sent down next, to put me down the other end for the first ball of the next over.

I decided to go straight down the ground off Lyon again at the start of the next over. You know straightaway whether you've got enough on it when you're trying to hit a straight six, and although this was another miscue it did have just enough to clear the diving Hazlewood. To be fair, it was one of my better plinks to clear one of the tallest blokes in the Australian team.

Four balls later, I had a hunch. As the ball was spinning away from me, I knew that a reverse slog-sweep was on. Generally, if you get a decent connection these particular shots go quite far. Even if you don't middle it the ball tends to travel the distance. Some might argue that it was a risky selection in the circumstances. I didn't see it that way. It was much less of a risk than an orthodox slog-sweep as a left-handed batsman. That would have been dangerous, against the turn and extra bounce that Lyon was extracting. The reverse shot meant I was using the bounce and the spin to my advantage.

The consistency of the bowler helped make my decision. I knew he was going to be there or thereabouts, pitching the ball around off-stump, because he was not trying to bowl wonder balls – landing it on the line of leg-stump in an attempt to hit the top of off. He was bowling a good line and length, waiting for me to slog one straight up in the air, or to mishit sufficiently to be caught on the boundary. It was a game of cat and mouse. It was as though he'd conceded I could hit him for a few but he would get me in the end.

This particular hit was a sweet one. The ball before had gripped and gone past my outside edge. This one I nailed. The only way to execute a shot like this in a match situation is plenty of practice, and I have found that the way I feel most comfortable to switch from a left-handed position to a right-handed one is not to jump as some batters do but roll my feet over and back my hands to do the work. Although I fell away after making contact, my balance was just about perfect, as was the timing, and I enjoyed watching it sail several rows into the seating out at deep point.

I was also aware of the increase in volume. This was now like a ground with surround sound. The first couple of sixes I had struck were greeted with 'wa-heys'. Like the crowd were cheering acts of defiance. The celebrations for this one, which reduced the target to 50, felt different.

The Australians were soon acting differently too, as the fans burst into a chant of 'Shoes off, if you love England'. I sensed the tension between their fielders, particularly from the next delivery, the last of the over, when I squeezed a bit of an outside edge to Pat Cummins at mid-off and bolted to the other end. It should never have been a single.

People all around the ground seemed to stay on their feet, some with their shoes above their heads, as though they were anticipating something to happen off every ball.

Something did happen two balls into the next over from the Football Stand end – I made a big mistake. Having taken a blow to the knee from an inside edge previous ball, I struck a low full toss from James Pattinson through extra cover and believed there were two runs to be had. As Usman Khawaja swooped to pick up, however, it was obvious it was only one. I was stuck at the non-striker's end.

Bent over my bat, I admonished myself. *What have you done?* I'd told Jack 'four and two' and now I'd turned it into 'two and four'. As Pattinson steamed in, the crowd remained unperturbed.

'Stand up if you're Eng-er-land,' they boomed.

Thud. The first delivery struck Jack on the gloves, the ball deflecting short of the slip cordon. The wringing of his left hand panicked me. I thought he'd busted his thumb. Thankfully, it soon became apparent it was something else. The impact had simply displaced the protection inside the glove and he just needed to get it back into position.

Jack kept his composure superbly throughout this four-ball period. As for me, I was hunched at the non-striker's end, eyes to the floor. Not because I thought he was going to get out. It was just an inability to cope with watching someone else survive. In this kind of situation, I feel much more settled if it's me taking on the responsibility. If someone was going to get out, I would rather it be me because Jack would have felt terrible. And I'd left him more vulnerable than was necessary.

From that position, I would watch Pattinson run in and then avert my gaze as deliveries in excess of 90 mph were met by sound defensive technique. Each one drew a 'yes' or a clap of my bat towards my partner. Thousands of yesses signalled 'over'.

It was a relief to be back on strike as Cummins replaced Lyon from the Kirkstall Lane end. Surveying the field, I pre-meditated the first ball, taking it from round the wicket and chipping it into the leg-side for two. It was important, I felt, to vary the shots I was playing. Becoming predictable would have played into Australia's hands.

A combination of the ground's dimensions – the straight boundaries at Headingley's Rugby Ground end are shorter following reconstruction work – plus the fact that Cummins is another 90 mph bowler persuaded me that a scoop was on. Any bat on such an improvised stroke and it was going for four or six.

Unfortunately, I didn't get any bat on it. However, I still felt confident enough that I could make use of the angle to get another much-needed boundary, and managed just enough elevation on the following delivery to take it from outside off-stump and deposit it over the rope at fine-leg.

A two off the pads and a one behind point off the fourth and fifth balls made it 11 runs for the over and left Jack needing to keep out what was the 10th delivery of his innings. A jab into the leg-side drew a huge cheer from the stands.

My focus was elsewhere. This next one was going to be a big over. Tim Paine had summoned Josh Hazlewood to replace Pattinson. In terms of trying to hit the ball, Hazlewood can be the perfect bowler as he generally lands it on a 10-pence piece, and does not possess the variations that someone like Cummins does. I had to be canny against Cummins, a bowler who can turn to off-cutters, slower-ball bouncers and a genuinely fast bumper. This was a chance to free my arms. Like Lyon, Hazlewood targets one area. An area in which you can swing hard as a batter.

His first delivery was exactly where I wanted it, allowing

me to rock back and power the ball through midwicket. As it scuttled over the rope, I was aware of the reception from the supporters to mark my hundred. I offered a partial wave to the dressing room, touched the peak of my helmet – but there were to be no celebrations.

I cannot tell you how much scoring hundreds for England means to me. Actually, I can – because I did so in the previous chapter – but just as had been the case when my personal tally reached 50, landmarks were immaterial. This innings would only have context for me once the job was done.

Remaining in the bubble was more important than anything, and thankfully I was so immersed in it that instinct completely took over when Hazlewood sent down his next one. When you are in a hitting mode like this, sometimes you see something, react and then ask yourself: *Did I just do that?* This was such a moment.

Firstly, I went deep in my crease. Then, I found myself down on one knee, sweeping a full toss off the stumps over square-leg for six. It just happened. In response to his previous delivery, I thought Hazlewood would either go full or short, and either way being back on my stumps would allow me to swing it away to the on-side.

Still deep in my crease, I managed to get under the next one too, clearing the two fielders posted on the leg-side, in front of the Western Terrace. As they retrieved the ball from the jumping mass, and the ground's scoreboard flashed up the 50-run partnership for England's 10th wicket, I was already plotting my next move.

'Two,' I said to Leachy, as we met in the middle of the pitch.

Three balls: 4, 6, 6. All the fielders were pushed right back and so I wanted to take advantage with a quick change of tempo. I could see in their reactions, in the dropped heads, that the Australians were feeling under pressure. It was an easy couple to third man. The over had begun with 37 required. When Australia allowed me a single to switch ends, the equation was reduced to 18.

Five sixths of the work for the over had been done. *Over to you, Jack.*

He took his time. This did not bother me one bit, as he took his gloves off and polished his glasses. He kept Hazlewood waiting for over a minute. As far as I was concerned, whatever he needed to do to be comfortable was cool. All I said to him from a technical perspective throughout our stand was 'small trigger' – a reminder of the dangers of going back and across too far and being bowled round his legs. Thankfully, the attempted leg-stump yorker that followed lacked direction. Cue more whooping on the terraces.

Australia might have been accused of losing their heads at this point but Tim Paine was thinking clearly from a tactical perspective. He brought back Nathan Lyon, his third bowling change in as many overs. Whereas against the off-spinner it was a case of the runs coming though sixes and singles, the seamers opened up other options: there were choices of twos, singles, boundaries every ball because it was easier to manipulate the pace of the ball. Lyons' return reduced the equation to dot, single, six or out.

People will wonder whether I was thinking of finishing the game in three blows at this point? But a scoring sequence of 6, 6, 6 never entered my mind. As it turned out, I didn't get bat on any of the first three – two attempted reverses, a sweep and a scoop, sandwiching a big turner that flew out of the bowlers' footholes to slip.

What did surprise me, after I played an orthodox drive for none into the off-side, was Paine not bringing the field up for the fifth ball of the over, which allowed me to cut to deep cover for a single. Momentarily, I considered gambling on retaining the strike for the sixth but thought on balance this to be the better option. Head down, I didn't watch Jack Leach's forward defensive stroke. The roar told me it was a sound one.

My next shot was not so sound. Cummins had switched ends and I was lining him up straight down the ground, so when I saw Marcus Harris running in from third man to try to haul in a spiralled chance, I thought: *Oh, God.* He had it in his hands as well. My eyes were on him as it went in and popped out. It was always going to be a difficult catch. *Phew, that was close.*

Forget it. No time to dwell. I had got to within 17 of that 359-run target by playing my way. *Time to crack on.*

Was my heart in my mouth again next ball? No. Why not? Because I had no idea where it had gone. Let alone the fact that a horizontal David Warner could have caught it. I knew I'd made good contact upon impact but lost sight of the ball's trajectory after I swung through the stroke. Not for the first time, the crowd noise told me it was straight through him; a check from the television umpire Kumar Dharmasena confirmed it was four, not six.

My commitment was to hit the ball hard, rather than worry about authentic shots or how it got to the boundary, and the next one was certainly not from the MCC coaching manual – a horizontal-batted crunch powering its way past Cummins' shoelaces and down the ground to beat Hazlewood's desperate dive on the rope. Another piece of instinctive batting had paid dividends.

Not for the first time, though, a misjudgement in running between the wickets left Leach with two Cummins deliveries to keep out. Another huge cheer preceded the bowler pushing off on his run-up. Everyone was seemingly willing the England number 11 on. I stayed in a hunched position 22 yards away until the ball was released from the bowler's hand.

However, I was up in time to see the second of the two deliveries in question strike him on the pad. It drew a huge appeal for lbw from the Australians. Clearly, more in hope than expectation, so obvious was it that the ball had pitched outside leg-stump. There is absolutely no way that Paine would have burned his team's one remaining review had we needed 30 to win. Fact was we needed eight.

To be fair, thinking straight is so much harder in a situation like this when you are out in the middle rather than sat in row H or on the edge of your sofa. You see, it was at this moment, with single figures required, that I didn't know what to do myself.

I had been decisive in my pre-planning of each and every over from the moment that Jack and I were pitched together in the 20th of the afternoon session. Now, though, doubts started to creep in as I questioned myself on how to play going forward. Should I continue in the same manner? I knew we could win it in ones and twos.

Had we needed eight to win at the point when the ninth wicket fell, then I am pretty sure Australia would not have kept the field back. But we hadn't and it was. I decided to stick with the tactics I'd employed throughout. I had got us to a certain point playing a certain way. Why stop?

Don't change what you've done just because we are close to winning, said the voice in my head.

The reason we were in this position was because of a simple enough outlook. *If it is there, hit it, if not, respect it.*

Up until this point, I had been driven by an unflagging belief that we were going to win. Now, though, within sight of victory becoming reality, things took on a slightly different complexion.

Lyon began bowling quicker and into the pitch. I had to wait for my moment. For the third ball of the over. Tossed up. I chose the aerial route straight once again. Down on my knees watching the progress of a towering strike, it was so tight. Australia had put their best fielder Marnus Labuschagne down there, and the ball just cleared his desperate claw in mid-air. A huge intake of breath followed as he hit the turf. Josh Hazlewood, who is several inches taller, had previously been positioned there and might have reached it.

There was real urgency for me now. With two to win, and the field up, I wanted to finish it next ball. I cut hard but could not beat the ring on the off-side.

Nor could I from the next as, employing the same positive attitude, I connected well with a reverse sweep to short third man. I didn't look up, as I had middled it straight to the fielder. All I was focused on was winning the game. So I turned on my heels, swung my bat back round above my head and made my ground.

Unbeknown to me, Leachy was running. I had no idea what made him do it. I only became aware of what had happened when I heard the commotion and looked up. I saw he was halfway down the track. My heart sank. I couldn't believe it. I was watching something unfold in front of my eyes and had no control over it. We had got control of the match and we were about to lose.

I watched the ball on its way from Pat Cummings to Nathan Lyon at the bowler's end. And I could see that Leach was nowhere near making his crease. Then, the real surprise. All he had to do was take off the bails. But Lyon somehow fumbled. I could not believe he dropped the ball. There were so many emotions involved. It was both terrifying and joyous. I couldn't believe what had happened. *How had he fluffed this chance?*

The answer came in one simple word – pressure. Everyone else on that Australian team was screaming at him and it induced a sense of panic. In any other moment of the game, he gathers that throw and Leach is out. How can I describe the relief? It felt awesome.

As we gathered our composure, Jack explained he had charged down the pitch out of habit – because he had been in the rhythm of running from the fifth delivery of an over and he had 'scamper' in his mind.

You might have thought the drama was done for this incredible match. Not so. Next ball, I went to sweep a full delivery and missed. The Australians went up as one. Joel Wilson, the umpire, said not out. Lyon sank to the turf and began rolling around on his back. Others were equally upset, although I didn't follow the thread of Matthew Wade, who led the Australian complaints.

He was barking at Wilson: 'We've got none, they've got one. It's common sense!'

His point, rather oddly, was that because we had one review

left, the umpire should be obliged to give it out. We could then challenge if we so wished. Apart from that's not how the system works.

The ball was angling past leg-stump. The delivery in question did not spin and only changed direction because it struck my front pad. It only struck my back hip because of this deflection. On first impact, the umpire could see two and a half stumps. The ball was on an arc down the leg-side.

Yet the Hawkeye slow motion replays showed it striking my front pad and then somehow changing direction despite there being no suggestion that it had deviated off the pitch.

In my view, there's no way the DRS got this one right. I shudder to think what it would have felt like if Australia had maintained their final review and we'd lost by a single run. Thankfully, Australia were left to rue their decision to challenge that Cummins lbw with eight runs required.

In one final twist to this extraordinary 10-over spell, Jack was now on strike to Cummins once more. I'll be honest, I didn't see a single coming. I thought the way to victory from here was for him to bat out all six balls. So when he got behind his 17th ball and nudged it into the gap, it was the biggest bonus imaginable.

My first thoughts when I got back down to the business end were: *We can't lose, we can still win the Ashes.* Only a defeat would have consigned the final two matches to dead rubbers. The scores were now level; a tie kept things alive.

With this in mind, I half considered running down the wicket to try to hit Cummins for six. I knew he would be bowling a ball to try to get me out so it would be somewhere around off-stump, trying to find the outside edge. I rejected that plan but nevertheless pledged to finish things once and for all that ball.

What a feeling when I rocked back and struck it through a gap in the covers. If you needed to order a ball with one to win this was custom made – short, wide and perfect for the cut shot. I knew I'd hit it for four as soon as the ball made contact on the bat.

The first sign of any emotion throughout my innings came in that moment. I arched my back, threw my arms aloft and let out a scream. It was an outburst that released everything that had been building up throughout that innings. None of the external noise had infiltrated my head throughout my time at the crease, but I had clearly been storing tension somewhere.

I cannot believe I've just done this.

I'm not going to lie; there was that moment of personal indulgence. I love winning games for England and would happily have no influence on a victory rather than put in a great personal performance in a defeat. But to be the one who had performed and stayed there to the bitter end to seal victory filled me with great pride.

For those first few seconds, everything felt so spontaneous. You don't plan for this kind of thing. So the celebrations are at their most natural. For me, moments like these as Jack and I embraced are the best in sport. When everything is on the line and you've achieved something against the odds, it is unbelievably special. Expressions are so natural and emotions so raw. The image of me arched back like that, with the crowd behind crashing up and down like a tidal wave, is one which people will identify with for years to come. See it and I hope they will remember Headingley 2019.

There was no concealing the magnitude of what had been achieved. We had won from nowhere. The game was all but gone when Leach walked out to bat with 73 runs required. It was only the 10th successful chase of a 300-plus target in Test history. Only once had a 10th wicket pair put on more than the 76 runs we had managed between us. The relationship we formed with the crowd that afternoon was awesome. The noise was deafening. I felt gratitude for that and there was a moment when I surveyed the ground and those who had been with us on the journey.

The Australians were gracious in defeat. You expect that in international sport. Whoever wins, whoever loses, you shake hands and respect the opposition's performance. There was a hug and a handshake from Usman Khawaja, who I know from the Indian Premier League, he's a great guy, and Nathan Lyon, because I respected the battle we'd been embroiled in. I made a point of saying 'Great guts' to Marnus Labuschagne. We'd got stuck into him but he played two good knocks and I respected that. Tim Paine was very sportsmanlike as captain. But the sweetest of the handshakes, as you might imagine, was with Warner.

One of the groundstaff handed me a stump as a souvenir. Then, I turned to face the rush of my oncoming teammates, who were all grinning from ear to ear. For once, I was speech-less. All I could manage was some inane giggling.

•

Looking back now, it's strange to realise that we had not started the match well at all. Every time we opened an advantage, we relinquished it.

Due to the atmospheric conditions whichever team won the toss was going to bowl first, and Stuart Broad was as good as he'd been throughout the whole series in the 20-minute period before the first rain break of a seamer-friendly opening day.

It was an incredible performance in which he beat the bat with virtually every single ball he bowled. Arguably, he was doing too much to find the outside edge and it was actually ironic, given how much both he and Jofra Archer were getting the ball to jag off the seam, that the breakthrough from Jofra came from one that didn't do as much. Marcus Harris – picked ahead of Cameron Bancroft – nicked behind as a result of the pressure that had built. Yet aside from the reviewed leg-side strangle of Khawaja, there were no more rewards until the resumption in late afternoon.

In the first hour of that session, we were nowhere as a team. It was inexplicable how bad we were, although these things need to be put into context. Every team has a bad session now and again and this was one of ours. It can be contagious when you start off a session badly. Our bowling wasn't anywhere near as good as it should have been, we lacked energy and the mis-fields and overthrows that littered our fielding said we were nowhere near the standards we like to set for ourselves.

During our worst hour, I bowled an awful five-over spell and to be honest I couldn't put my finger on why things were going so wrong. As a bowler, you do have days in which things just prove to be a struggle and this was one. The ball was not coming out how I wanted it to, and that's really frustrating, because you are obviously not wanting it to go that way. A couple of times Joe Root came down to talk to me and ask me to try to stick in for a bit – to not concede as many runs.

'I'm trying,' I told him. 'It's just not going where I want it to.'

Put simply, I was failing in my execution. Nor was I the only one and we were not happy as a team about how we performed. Safe to say, Joe made his displeasure clear at the drinks break, urging us not to repeat that kind of performance again. Thankfully, we snapped out of it almost immediately.

As soon as we separated the third-wicket pair of Labuschagne and Warner, Jofra got on a roll. When he's in one of his spells, he makes things happen. In contrast to Lord's where he had charged in and reached the speed of light, Jofra used his skills brilliantly for the conditions in Leeds. This was not a ground or a situation in which he had to tear into the crease. The wicket was offering enough in terms of sideways movement for him to reduce his speed somewhat and concentrate on hitting a probing line and length. Outright pace wasn't necessary to dismiss batsmen. Instead, he relied on swing and seam movement, and this time there was no Steve Smith to obstruct his charge. Australia lost their last eight wickets for 43 runs.

If we thought we had got rid of our bad spell in this match, however, we were wrong. Our off-colour performance with the ball was certainly trumped by what we were to produce as a team with the bat. We couldn't give you an explanation as to why we were bowled out for 67. Nor could Australia have told you why they were knocked over for 60 on their previous Ashes tour at Trent Bridge. Sometimes these things just happen. Australia's pace bowlers, led by Josh Hazlewood with five wickets, kept nicking us off.

I would be the first to admit that the shot I played was one of the worst in my career. I'd gone out to bat with the intention of punishing anything loose. If Australia erred, I was going to jump on their mistakes. In my mind, I was looking to pounce on any opportunity to alter the momentum, to switch it from Australia to England. After all, the Australians had only scored 179 themselves and I thought a good hour from me might change things significantly.

One thing about cricket though is that you are judged by the end product of your decisions, not the decisions themselves. If you get dismissed for a sub-standard score, the conclusion inevitably drawn is that it is due to a large proportion of poor shots. I cannot justify my particular downfall. It was a wide ball that I tried to hammer through the off-side. It didn't look good after the event and I was not pleased about it. I didn't have to play at it, and shouldn't have played at it, even though I had that positive mindset of hitting boundaries given half a chance.

We were certainly not bowled out so cheaply because of a lack of ability or a desire to do well. It was just a day we wished had never happened. We had been in a really good position after the first innings and to fall like this totally devalued all the good work we'd done. To walk out and have to bowl again after little more than a session's rest was deflating. There was no choice but to get our heads into the right spaces. We're professional athletes and we don't need reminding of things when we fail.

Australia entered the second half of the game with a 112-run advantage. From our perspective, we knew if we were able to bowl them out for 200 we were still in the game. If they managed as many as 300, we probably weren't.

Stuart Broad took his turn to speak when we huddled on the outfield. He'd spoken plenty of times before, but I don't think I'd experienced him so emotional and fired up like this.

'We need to bowl like we are defending 170,' he said.

Our collective attitude would determine how effective we would be for the second innings and whether we retained a chance of staying in a series which we'd had such high hopes of winning.

Broad followed up his strong words by giving us another strong start, his dismissal of Warner extending a common theme. It was important not to chase wickets, however, because that is when you start leaking runs. At Headingley, you don't have to try so hard, to look to bowl wonder deliveries; you just have to be patient and allow the pitch to provide a helping hand.

After my ropey first-innings display with the ball, I decided to re-evaluate how I went about my bowling. I told Joe Root that in order to get into a decent rhythm I was going to run in and hit the pitch as hard as I could. It's a simple way to drill a decent length and provide the rhythm I had previously lacked. Only after becoming comfortable with bowling in a tight manner would I look to add my skills. In the first innings I tried quite a few variations instead of settling into a spell.

I always enjoy bowling when Broad is at mid-off because he understands me as a bowler and gets a vibe of how things are for me, and of the match situation. His message in a game like this was to try to bowl six balls in exactly the same spot.

Previously, when I've been in one of those spells in which I am making lots of things happen, constantly beating the bat or creating chances, he's jumped in with praise and encouragement.

'Great work, mate. Theatre. Remember the theatre.' He is a great one for sensing the mood and getting his fellow bowlers to sense it too.

Running in to hit the pitch hard uncomplicates bowling. No distractions of trying to hit the seam or get the ball going through the air. It's just a very simple, straightforward process. Even when Root dropped Marnus Labuschagne at first slip, I was undeterred. Yes, I was annoyed that the catch had gone down, but I wasn't going to let it affect how I was bowling because from that perspective I felt very positive. It felt like another opportunity would come around.

Undoubtedly, there was also a bit of me that wanted to take responsibility for the direction in which the match was going. When I am like this, and I was during Alastair Cook's captaincy also, it is difficult to get the ball out of my hand.

This time, my opening spell was eight overs long, economical and accounted for Travis Head. The crowd were with me and that helped. In a summer in which my performances with the bat were the focus of attention, it was pleasing to have an impact during a long spell with the ball. These kinds of scenarios tend to bring the best out of me.

They tend to push me to find an extra 10 per cent. This time, that figure might have been 20–30 per cent because when Jofra Archer got cramp four balls after replacing me, I had no worries about coming back on again. I took my cap off, saying that I was good for another two or three but ended up going all the way to the end of the second day. I had bowled all but four balls in a 16-over spell.

Joe kept checking that I was alright to continue, but as far as I was concerned I couldn't see the point of someone else coming on to bowl three overs. It made sense to keep me on even though a couple of the lads had told me they were surprised I was still standing. To be honest, I love doing the hard stuff. The challenging times are when I want to be judged. I like sending a signal to the opposition, especially in those moments when you are behind in the game, that I am not giving up. These kinds of long spells also send signals to your teammates on how much you will do for them. Of the commitment I have towards the other people in my team.

This England environment, both in Test and limited-overs cricket, is very much all for one and one for all. It is full of people wanting the best for their mates. Take Jason Roy, who had me round the neck and wouldn't let me go after I struck the winning runs on that fourth afternoon. He loves stuff like this. The moments that you will never forget whatever else you do in your career.

Joe Root kept pulling me back, quite aggressively, as I tried to walk off, telling me to take in every last second of the applause. Telling me that what I'd achieved was incredible and that I deserved it all. The crowd's ovation did not dip. It was an incredible response. I was thankful to each and every one of them for the part they'd played in history as I made my way off the field. As my teammates allowed me to leave the field to take the applause, it was quite overwhelming. Such a good moment in my life.

That evening, as the sun dipped, Jack Leach re-enacted the dash for a single that had brought the scores level earlier that day. We drank beer and toasted the against-the-odds success that had kept the series alive.

Later, when we arrived at the hotel bar, I still had my Test cap on back to front and was carrying a sizeable bag of fast food. Asked by security to change my attire, I nipped back to my room with the intention of having a shower and returning quick smart.

When I got there, however, the fatigue hit me. *Sod it,* I thought. I decided to go for a sleep. 'Where the hell have you been?' I was asked when I finally went back to the bar, three quarters of an hour later. To be honest, I felt I deserved it.

I had followed through what I had promised to myself. I remained relaxed, barring a spell when I was next in to bat and, watching the two Joes, Root and Denly in partnership, I was overcome by nerves. To release my anxiety I started biting an old towel. There was no thread in it by the time I'd finished. The other lads had never known me to be so fidgety. When I explained to them that the tension was getting to me, Chris Woakes came back with: 'You should have seen us at the World Cup, then!'

Thankfully, I hadn't. I had been the one at the centre of the action. Just as I like to be. And for the second time in just a few short weeks, I had been there when the team managed to achieve something special. Been there, as I had suggested to my neighbour Chris, when history was made.

England v Australia   Third Test, Headingley, 22–26 August 2019

Result: England won by 1 wicket

AUSTRALIA First Innings	R	B	4s	6s
David Warner c Jonny Bairstow b Jofra Archer	61	94	7	0
Marcus Harris c Jonny Bairstow b Jofra Archer	8	12	2	0
Usman Khawaja c Jonny Bairstow b Stuart Broad	8	17	1	0
Marnus Labuschagne lbw Ben Stokes	74	129	10	0
Travis Head b Stuart Broad	0	6	0	0
Matthew Wade b Jofra Archer	0	3	0	0
Tim Paine (capt) (wk) lbw Chris Woakes	11	26	1	0
James Pattinson c Joe Root b Jofra Archer	2	8	0	0
Pat Cummins c Jonny Bairstow b Jofra Archer	0	13	0	0
Nathan Lyon lbw Jofra Archer	1	4	0	0
Josh Hazlewood not out	1	3	0	0
Extras (nb 2, w 5, b 4, lb 2)	13			
Total (all out, 52.1 overs)	179			

Fall of wickets

1-12 (M Harris, 3.6 ov), 2-25 (U Khawaja, 8.4 ov), 3-136 (D Warner, 31.4 ov), 4-138 (T Head, 32.5 ov), 5-139 (M Wade, 33.6 ov), 6-162 (T Paine, 42.6 ov), 7-173 (J Pattinson, 45.6 ov), 8-174 (P Cummins, 49.6 ov), 9-177 (M Labuschagne, 51.2 ov), 10-179 (N Lyon, 52.1 ov)

Bowling	O	M	R	W
Stuart Broad	14	4	32	2
Jofra Archer	17.1	3	45	6
Chris Woakes	12	4	51	1
Ben Stokes	9	0	45	1

ENGLAND First Innings	R	B	4s	6s
Rory Burns c Tim Paine b Pat Cummins	9	28	1	0
Jason Roy c David Warner b Josh Hazlewood	8	15	2	0
Joe Root (capt) c David Warner b Josh Hazlewood	0	2	0	0
Joe Denly c Tim Paine b James Pattinson	12	49	1	0
Ben Stokes c David Warner b James Pattinson	8	13	1	0
Jonny Bairstow (wk) c David Warner b Josh Hazlewood	4	15	1	0
Jos Buttler c Usman Khawaja b Josh Hazlewood	5	16	1	0
Chris Woakes c Tim Paine b Pat Cummins	5	9	1	0
Jofra Archer c Tim Paine b Pat Cummins	7	8	1	0
Stuart Broad not out	4	5	1	0
Jack Leach b Josh Hazlewood	1	7	0	0
Extras (lb 3)	3			
Total (all out, 27.5 overs)	67			

Fall of wickets

1-10 (J Roy, 3.5 ov), 2-10 (J Root, 5.1 ov), 3-20 (R Burns, 10.4 ov), 4-34 (B Stokes, 14.3 ov), 5-45 (J Denly, 20.1 ov), 6-45 (J Bairstow, 21.1 ov), 7-54 (C Woakes, 24.1 ov), 8-56 (J Buttler, 25.1 ov), 9-66 (J Archer, 26.4 ov), 10-67 (J Leach, 27.5 ov)

Bowling	O	M	R	W
Pat Cummins	9	4	23	3
Josh Hazlewood	12.5	2	30	5
Nathan Lyon	1	0	2	0
James Pattinson	5	2	9	2

AUSTRALIA Second Innings

	R	B	4s	6s
Marcus Harris b Jack Leach	19	39	3	0
David Warner lbw Stuart Broad	0	2	0	0
Usman Khawaja c Jason Roy b Chris Woakes	23	38	4	0
Marnus Labuschagne run out (Joe Denly)	80	187	8	0
Travis Head b Ben Stokes	25	56	3	0
Matthew Wade c Jonny Bairstow b Ben Stokes	33	59	6	0
Tim Paine (capt) (wk) c Joe Denly b Stuart Broad	0	2	0	0
James Pattinson c Joe Root b Jofra Archer	20	48	2	0
Pat Cummins c Rory Burns b Ben Stokes	6	6	1	0
Nathan Lyon b Jofra Archer	9	17	1	0
Josh Hazlewood not out	4	5	1	0
Extras (nb 7, w 2, b 5, lb 13)	27			
Total (all out, 75.2 overs)	246			

Fall of wickets

1-10 (D Warner, 1.2 ov), 2-36 (M Harris, 11.1 ov), 3-52 (U Khawaja, 14.1 ov), 4-97 (T Head, 32.2 ov), 5-163 (M Wade, 52.6 ov), 6-164 (T Paine, 53.3 ov), 7-215 (J Pattinson, 67.6 ov), 8-226 (P Cummins, 70.2 ov), 9-237 (M Labuschagne, 73.3 ov), 10-246 (N Lyon, 75.2 ov)

Bowling

Bowling	O	M	R	W
Jofra Archer	14	2	40	2
Stuart Broad	16	2	52	2
Chris Woakes	10	1	34	1
Jack Leach	11	0	46	1
Ben Stokes	24.2	7	56	3

ENGLAND Second Innings

	R	B	4s	6s
Rory Burns c David Warner b Josh Hazlewood	7	21	0	0
Jason Roy b Pat Cummins	8	18	1	0
Joe Root (capt) c David Warner b Nathan Lyon	77	205	7	0
Joe Denly c Tim Paine b Josh Hazlewood	50	155	8	0
Ben Stokes not out	135	219	11	8
Jonny Bairstow (wk) c Marnus Labuschagne b Josh Hazlewood	36	68	4	0
Jos Buttler run out (Travis Head)	1	9	0	0
Chris Woakes c Matthew Wade b Josh Hazlewood	1	8	0	0
Jofra Archer c Travis Head b Nathan Lyon	15	33	3	0
Stuart Broad lbw James Pattinson	0	2	0	0
Jack Leach not out	1	17	0	0
Extras (nb 1, w 10, b 5, lb 15)	31			
Total (9 wickets, 125.4 overs)	362			

Fall of wickets

1-15 (R Burns, 5.6 ov), 2-15 (J Roy, 6.3 ov), 3-141 (J Denly, 59.3 ov), 4-159 (J Root, 77.3 ov), 5-245 (J Bairstow, 99.1 ov), 6-253 (J Buttler, 102.2 ov), 7-261 (C Woakes, 105.6 ov), 8-286 (J Archer, 114.6 ov), 9-286 (S Broad, 115.2 ov)

Bowling

Bowling	O	M	R	W
Pat Cummins	24.4	5	80	1
Josh Hazlewood	31	11	85	4
Nathan Lyon	39	5	114	2
James Pattinson	25	9	47	1
Marnus Labuschagne	6	0	16	0

11

LEADERSHIP

England v Australia,
Fourth Test, Old Trafford, 4–8 September 2019

It was great to be back in the series after the mayhem and madness of our win at Headingley, but we knew we could not dwell on the past.

In a series like the Ashes, you have to live in the moment, enjoy and appreciate the highs, celebrate and cherish them, but equally the inescapable fact was that there were two games remaining, and without sounding over the top, all those efforts, that extraordinary drama, would be in vain if we failed to back it up as we moved across the Pennines to Manchester.

The message from both Joe Root and Trevor Bayliss as we got together at training at Old Trafford was very clear. We knew there would still be interest, attention and questions about what happened the previous week, but the danger for us was allowing our minds to linger on those crazy days at Headingley instead of moving on. We needed to clear them and focus fully on the fourth Test match, not the third.

Yes, we had kept the Ashes alive into the penultimate

match but we knew that if Australia won one more game then the urn would remain in their hands for another two and a half years. We needed to put a performance together that would give us the best chance of securing another win and gaining control of the series at 2–1.

In the past we'd been very good at drawing a line under poor performances and moving on quickly to start again. 'Bouncebackability' was not required in this situation, though. We just needed to show our most ruthless qualities.

Ideally, that meant us taking the momentum and the positivity from Leeds and going again. Recent history was encouraging as the core of our team had come out on top in must-win games against India, New Zealand and then Australia in the World Cup.

People everywhere were asking me which of the two wins felt better: the World Cup final or Headingley? The honest answer was Lord's because we had a trophy to show for it. We were world champions.

After Headingley we'd only stayed in the contest. It had provided us with a lifeline from a position where the Ashes had almost been lost. It was no more than that. We hadn't got ourselves ahead on the scoreboard. We were just back to where we started, there were no prizes, and we had to go again.

•

I had other things to concentrate my mind upon. There were no rock 'n' roll excesses after my personal display at Headingley.

No, for me, it was straight home to cut the grass. It remained lovely weather throughout that week and it just so happened that the back lawn was in desperate need of attention.

It had been incredibly long, actually, because I had been away with England, and Clare and the kids had also been off elsewhere during the school holidays.

They'd returned home a day or two earlier to find it was a bit of a jungle. The Husqvarna automower that is programmed remotely to patrol our back garden had got stuck in the trees at some point and this wouldn't get the job done.

I'm very particular about my grass looking tidy. So the first thing I did when I got back was to clamber on the ride-on mower and get to work. I find it a meticulous process. You have to cut it to a certain length, then let it settle before going over it again to make it a bit shorter. And so on and so forth.

When Alastair Cook used to go home between Test matches, he would get active on the farm. I am not quite at that level but there is always stuff for me to get on to in the garden. Always some debris or other stuff to clear. I am a bit particular and don't like pine cones, branches or leaves clogging up the place.

•

When we arrived in Manchester it was hard not to notice the effect that our third-Test win over Australia had had on the host city for the penultimate match of the series. The local council's traffic signs on the A56 warned of delays, reading: 'Sir Ben Stokes v Australia, 4–8 Sept, Save minutes off your journey, Take the tram!' I was also aware of a huge advertising poster Ladbrokes had erected outside the Australian team hotel. It was of my celebration moment from the previous week in the style of the 'Carlos Tevez: Welcome to Manchester' posters of 10 years earlier when the Argentina footballer left Manchester United for Manchester City.

I never really know what to think of these kinds of things. I never want to be the centre of attention when it comes to the England team, I just want to be one member of its successes. So while this stuff kind of made me feel good, it made me feel awkward at the same time. I've got as good a sense of humour as the next person, but when you're directly involved there is also a slight sense of embarrassment.

Old Trafford's conditions provided some uncertainty as to what to do over our selection choices. Generally, it is home to the flattest pitch in the country – somewhere the ball doesn't tend to swing as much. It also offers relatively little off the pitch for the seamers.

With this in mind, the selection group opted for a change in our bowling line-up. Chris Woakes had played all four of the Test matches over the previous month and was also a permanent fixture in our World Cup team. Chris is very skilful and had done okay with nine wickets against the Australians at 29 runs apiece, but skilful bowlers tend to get fewer returns here in Tests than at our other international venues. So for a pitch on which taller bowlers tend to extract exaggerated bounce, he was left out in favour of Somerset's Craig Overton, who stands at 6 ft 5 in.

The only other change involved a switch of positions for Joe Denly and Jason Roy within our batting order, reverting to the places I'd argued they should have been in on the eve of the series.

During discussions with Joe Root, I remained adamant that Denly should open and Roy fit in at four. Joe was an advocate of the same thinking. Others with power in the decision-making process clearly thought it best the other way around.

To me, it was a simple case of using Jason Roy's brilliance with the bat most effectively. I know that Jason has come in and dominated the very best bowling attacks at the top of the order in one-day cricket, but in general he has batted at numbers four or five for Surrey in the County Championship.

Jason is far more dangerous down at number four as the ball generally does not tend to move about as much the deeper the innings goes. He'd also strung together a good sequence of first-class scores for Surrey in the previous couple of years. Knowing you have had success in a certain position domestically gives you some confidence.

By the same token, Joe Denly has pretty much spent his entire career in the top three with Middlesex and Kent. It seemed to me that they had been selected for Test cricket and were being asked to do something different to what they had done for their counties in the first place.

It is also an easier switch for someone who's used to batting at number three to move to opener than it is for someone more accustomed to batting at four or five, and Jason Roy is a different proposition to bowl to with a brand new ball in first-class cricket than with one that's 40 overs old.

I honestly believe that Jason can reach the same level that Kevin Pietersen managed because of the way he dominates bowling attacks. He is a fine stroke-player, and as he does while in limited-overs mode, he gives himself a chance to get in before he starts to play a greater number of shots. Once he does get in, he can seriously hurt opponents.

Like Pietersen, he has the potential to be a real game-changer with his flair across all three formats, so from my perspective it was good that the England hierarchy were placing confidence in him by retaining him in the XI.

He would not go on to score the level of runs he would have liked in this particular game, but he appeared a lot more comfortable and assured in what would prove to be his last appearance of the series.

•

Without doubt, it was an important toss to win. The pattern that matches tend to follow at Old Trafford is that you bat first, set your stall out to post a big total, and then take advantage of what generally starts off as a good surface and deteriorates, becoming slower and lower, and a little bit up and down, over time. Towards the back end of the five days, it also spins significantly.

Being asked to bowl on the opening day, and to contend with a wind that would have registered towards the top end of the Beaufort scale, was the hardest challenge I have faced in my career with the ball. All of our bowlers were agreed on how tough the conditions were.

It was a monstrous gale, blowing all over the shop and changing direction intermittently throughout the day. When you are trying to run in, and it's switching like that, it is very disconcerting, knocking you off your length and your line, and exaggerating what the ball does in the air on occasions.

Sometimes, just when you think you have worked out the adjustments required, that you've just about got it, the wind changes direction and you're completely out of rhythm again.

It's constantly taking you back to square one. I would rather bowl in the Arctic than have to contend with that kind of challenge again.

The inhospitable conditions had their effects on all of us England bowlers and it was totally unrealistic of people to expect Jofra Archer to reproduce the level of performance he'd managed at Lord's and Headingley. Most of the people who were suggesting he was ineffective on that opening day seemed to be sat in air-conditioned commentary boxes or cosy front rooms – not running into 40 mph gusts.

Yes, his speeds might have been down to the low eighties rather than the mid-nineties in terms of miles per hour, although there was good reason why he seemed more focused on accuracy than pace and fire. Barbados this was not.

I am not sure how often he would have run into bowl in two-sweater weather, only to be knocked off course. All you can do in this kind of situation is make sure you stay as strong as possible at the crease when delivering the ball, to get it to go as near to the intended target as possible. That's easier said than done, however, because we were either getting pushed in towards the stumps or away from them.

It was perhaps unsurprising that the bowler who coped with it best for us was Stuart Broad, someone playing his 131st Test match. He's played in all conditions, and all weathers. He ran in and bowled as well as he had throughout the series with that new ball to send back David Warner and Marcus Harris early, but unfortunately we couldn't make even worse a position of 28–2 before lunch.

In these kinds of conditions, you want to be the team batting. Coming on and off the field, as the weather dictates, makes it tough for a bowler to develop any rhythm. When, after a three-hour rain delay, we returned to the field for a 4 pm resumption, we did so to the scruffiest of scenes.

Crisp packets, inflatables and cardboard beer carriers flying about the field, added to the fragmented nature of the play, and I had not previously played any kind of senior match in which the bails had been completely dislodged due to the windy conditions, as they were for what amounted to eight deliveries.

Taken aback by the prospect of playing on without them, I made a point of checking with the umpires Marais Erasmus and Kumar Dharmasena what would happen if the ball struck the stumps in different scenarios. Any touch of the ball on them for bowled dismissals and run outs would do, apparently.

Between the gusts, the bails were returned to their grooves in the stumps and then the fourth official Rob Bailey ran on with some heavier replacement ones, manufactured by the groundstaff who attached some screws in a set to weigh them down.

Less than 10 minutes later, Craig Overton knocked them off after nipping one back through Marnus Labuschagne's defence for his first Test wicket on home soil. This was Labuschagne's fourth consecutive 50 in the series, emphasising what an important player he had become for Australia in a very short space of time.

The Australians received a boost to their batting for the match with the return of Steve Smith, who had taken his own sequence of successive half-centuries to eight before rain ended play for the day at 170–3 during a delayed tea break.

Not for the first time, his dismissal was crucial to English prospects. So the advantage swung emphatically back in Australia's favour when Jack Leach produced a beauty that enticed a drive from Smith and found its way into my hands at slip.

As disappointing as it is, and it is because whenever you dismiss Smith it gives you a real boost, no bowler ever means to bowl a no ball. It is just one of those things you have to accept can happen from time to time.

When we saw on the big screen that it was a no ball it provided a deflating feeling, but there is little for you to do as a team other than get back to it to try to find another way of taking a wicket. Obviously, you don't want to be giving a player like Smith an extra opportunity on 118, but you have to play the cards you are dealt on the field and we couldn't change what had happened.

If Leach had stayed behind the line, the game would undoubtedly have taken a different course, with Australia 273–6 shortly after lunch, but you cannot trade on 'what ifs' in cricket.

You know how gutted you would be in that situation as the bowler – to have got their best batter out only to see him take guard again. There's not much anyone can say in that situation. Anything that you could offer would be a bit of a cliché. 'Forget about it, mate,' that kind of stuff. Nor did it help that we put down Tim Paine twice on his way to 50.

I was bowling at the other end but things weren't right. A right-shoulder injury which I had been carrying throughout the series had flared up. It had been sore in the immediate aftermath of the Edgbaston Test but I allowed it to settle, thinking it would be fine after the week's break between the first and second matches, and it had been so. After that it was only an annoyance really, something I would feel now and again rather than a serious concern.

Gradually, though, throwing became more and more painful, and I could feel the issue getting progressively worse throughout each of my bowling spells at Old Trafford. I convinced myself that the problem would loosen up once I'd bowled a few balls every spell, but when I came back for the 11th over with the second new ball it appeared to be worse still. There was only one thing to be done, I thought. I decided to bowl a bouncer, a proper effort ball for the fifth delivery of the over, to see how it would respond.

Immediately, I was like 'nah'. There was no way I could continue. Later, I was to discover that I had experienced a small tear in my rotator cuff. I am someone who would explore all other avenues before opting for a painkilling injection and once we got back the results from the scan, carried out in London a few days later, it revealed an injection would not have helped anyway.

It meant I was no longer a bowling option in the match, although I also knew that if I carried on in the series as a specialist batsman I would have to be available to bowl in some capacity if absolutely necessary. In the short term, it meant rest.

At the time, I thought I had done something horrendous. All I could think as I walked off the field was: *I could be out for weeks and weeks here.* I have a tendency to think the worst at times like these. When I injured my calf against Pakistan, also at Old Trafford, in 2016 I had experienced similar thoughts. Sadly, they were not unfounded. On that previous occasion, trying to muddle through and bowling on resulted in me tearing the muscle. It was actually the worst thing I could have done. This time, I took the sensible route.

•

When an opposing team puts up a score of the magnitude of 497–8 declared, as Australia managed on the back of Smith's double hundred, the objective is to get as close to it as you possibly can. That might sound like stating the obvious but it is important not to get intimidated. Your mindset has to be a belief in your side's ability to match it.

At a ground like Old Trafford, where the pitch starts true but becomes increasingly perilous to bat on by the day, the enforcement of the follow-on is extremely unlikely because, ideally, you want to be the team bowling on day five with a good cushion of runs as an advantage. So for us, the closer we got to Australia's first-innings total, the less pressure we would be under.

Joe Root and Rory Burns ate into the time remaining with some fine application in testing conditions on the third day. It felt like they had broken the back of the batting challenge but one thing that Australia did throughout the series was maintain a brilliant line and length.

Growing up in Australian conditions, on pitches that do not encourage lavish movement, you have to develop great disciplines if you want to bowl fast. And the skills you acquire if you are successful in doing so can be used universally, I reckon.

Wherever you choose to travel in the cricket world, relentless accuracy at the top of off-stump will serve you well. It doesn't matter about the conditions or how unresponsive the pitches are – if you can hit the same area regularly at good pace, you are going to cause batsmen problems. That's the way Pat Cummins and Josh Hazlewood in particular operated throughout the summer.

After the loss of two wickets early in the innings, Burns and Root gave themselves the best chance to lay a platform by batting time. When, as a team, we talk about making big scores and occupying the crease for lengths of time, it is always through the medium of partnerships. We concentrate on getting to 50 together, then 75, 100, and so on.

Our third-wicket pair had gone beyond the third of these little landmarks but unfortunately were separated to spark a spell of three wickets in the final three quarters of an hour. Fair play to Cummins and Hazlewood here, because they backed up spell after spell, never relinquishing the pressure even when they went wicketless for periods of play. Justin Langer, their coach, had spoken of their policy of bowling dry – in other words, they would inflict a run drought – in the hours leading up to the first Test at Edgbaston.

Their bowling attack definitely managed to execute those plans, as it felt like there were fewer four balls on offer than in previous series and you had to work hard for your runs. Here, their patience was rewarded, when the partnership was broken just as it looked like we were on the verge of taking the opposition into the fourth day fatigued rather than with a spring in their steps.

Mitchell Starc, recalled for this match as Australia rotated their pace bowlers, nicked me off next morning with the second new ball: a delivery I felt I had to play that flew to second slip. To their credit, I spent more than 100 minutes at the crease and there were very few scoring opportunities.

Jos Buttler managed to access a few in alliance with the tail and there were huge cheers when a cover drive rifled to the rope off Starc to avoid the follow-on. Australia might have dismissed us with the follow-on in play but had no reviews left when Starc pinned Jack Leach on the pads in his previous over – although the Australians would not have enforced it anyway given the fact they had bowled for more than 100 overs. With plenty of time on their side, despite the equivalent of another session being lost to rain on the third day, they would have been putting extra strain on their four-man attack. They were always going to bat again to give their bowlers a rest.

•

As we made our way back onto the field, trailing by 196 runs, I decided to step forward and lead the team talk. As these happen quite regularly, Joe Root encourages others to come forward and speak. His reasoning is that, although he is captain, he doesn't want to be the lone voice. People get bored when they listen to the same person over and over again. So I will speak every now and again; so will Jos Buttler, Stuart Broad and even Paul Collingwood, one of our support coaches, sometimes.

This, I felt, was my turn. Let's say I was quite aggressive in my delivery. I swore a lot but the message was very clear.

'This is potentially the last time we walk out on the field together with the Ashes still on the line,' I began.

'Knowing this should filter into the rest of this day and however many overs we are out here for as a team.

'That means for bowlers there are no looseners – every ball you bowl is 100 per cent effort – and that all fielders are throwing their bodies on the line to stop everything they can.

'Everyone here has to commit to doing everything possible within their powers and to show the right levels of energy.

'If you don't, then I ask you to look at the bloke nearest to you in the field and realise you've let them down.

'If you don't do this today, if you do not give everything you've got, you're letting your mates down. We have to walk off here later today WITH NOTHING LEFT IN THE TANK.'

My intentions were clear. I wanted to get everybody as revved up as possible. For all 11 of us to feel the passion required for the occasion and to give it one last shot to turn the game around. I very much saw it as a challenging task rather than a lost cause.

On the evidence of the next hour or so, my speech had the desired effect. Or at least the England team displayed each of the traits I had spoken about in our huddle. For example, the way that Stuart Broad and Jofra Archer bowled encapsulated everything that I had said.

They were simply stunning during spells of nine overs apiece in what was a most dramatic start to Australia's second innings. Even though we were so far behind on first innings, our minds started to imagine what might be possible. When you get on a roll on the field like this – as Australia were reduced to 44–4, a lead of 240 – it is natural that thoughts turned to how we might force a position from where we could win the match.

At that stage, with the atmosphere at fever pitch and the stands rocking in echoes of Headingley, we were one more wicket away from potentially getting through Australia and on the way to dismissing them, to set up yet another run chase. We could feel it, so could the crowd. Just one dismissal: one more unplayable delivery from our wholehearted bowlers, one more mistake by a baggy-green batsman.

Once again, this series had produced great theatre. Dismiss Smith early and it would have been a totally different story. During the hour-long period comprising four wickets, deliveries thudded into pads, flew off outside edges and most spectacularly into Travis Head's middle-stump. Four wickets between our new-ball pair – three lbws and a bowled – spoke of their perfect combination of hostility and accuracy.

But the spells of Broad and Archer could not go on for ever. That's saying nothing whatsoever against Craig Overton and Jack Leach, but at whatever point our opening pair were taken off it would provide respite for Australia, while tea 10 minutes later also provided a chance to escape and to nullify the momentum we had built up, and the connection we had made with the crowd. When the atmosphere is like that you just want to keep going rather than have to walk off and return to start again.

Undoubtedly, the 20-minute interval took the sting out of the situation for Smith and Matthew Wade in particular as he had been the subject of a fiery welcome from Jofra.

A Test match involves periods of varying paces and rhythms and Australia could use the leverage they had in building such a big first-innings lead and play exactly how they wanted once they felt that they were in a position from which they were unlikely to lose. Once they had built a lead approaching 300 and thus moving out of realistic range, they chose to attack and go for the positive option of pushing for a win, Smith unsurprisingly leading the way. When he holed out to me at long-off off Leach, he had made 82 at close to a run a ball – his lowest score of the series but an innings which allowed a declaration before the close.

With a target of 383 set, it meant that the only realistic results were going to be in their favour – either a draw that would leave the series at 1–1 heading into the final Test, or an Australian victory that would kill off our challenge.

In contrast to Leeds, there was not much time remaining in the game and so they opted for a short burst at us on a murky Manchester evening. I don't think anyone could envisage what was about to happen when we walked out for the fourth innings of the match.

To lose Rory Burns and Joe Root within the first four balls of this brief period was a devastating blow. There was a sense of disbelief in the dressing room when Rory found the hands of mid-off from a leading edge, having attempted to play a ball off Pat Cummins into the leg-side. Sometimes when cricket is against you, it's really against you. Any batsman will tell you how annoying it is to get out to a leg-stump half-volley.

Rory would eat that delivery for dessert a hundred times out of a hundred in any other match situation and yet it had somehow found its way into the hands of the fielder. No wonder he hung his head as he trudged off; he had good reason to curse his luck.

It's always hard to start an innings against a high-quality, new-ball attack but more so in gloom like this and there was nothing Joe Root could have done about the nut he received first up – one which pitched and left him off the seam to kiss the top of off-stump.

It left Joe Denly and Jason Roy, who negotiated the remainder of the seven overs together, to lead the fifth-day resistance.

When you turn up in a situation like this, with a full day to bat to preserve the series as you know it, there is no need for great speeches or practical plans. Everyone knows what they have to do. It was just a case of going out there with the clear intentions of bat, bat, bat. The longer we spent out in the middle, the harder things were going to get for Australia.

This was obviously not a game situation we wanted to be in but you have to adapt in such circumstances and with 98 overs to combat, and eight wickets left standing, it meant attacking strokes were put away. We were well and truly embroiled in a survival fight.

Of course, as players we get analysed all the time and one of the things that I find mega frustrating is being judged in situations such as this final-day rearguard. Particularly the way in which we are judged.

Survive for a long time, and you have shown a lot of fight. If you don't stick around, you haven't been up for it. The fight image is such a poor one. It's a phrase that I neither like nor see as appropriate. When you are batting in this kind of scenario, you are being tested in the most challenging conditions of the match and it's how you face up to the task technically as much as anything. If your team doesn't repel the opposition for the full day, or whatever proportion of it left, and doesn't succeed with the task in hand, it doesn't mean that they do not care or they weren't fighting – that they lacked in determination.

They just failed to complete the task they set out to achieve. The other team managed their target. That's top-level sport. You cannot fulfil every challenge as you wish.

A typical fifth-day scenario is straightforward to understand when you are looking to secure a draw. First and foremost, you have to survive. That simplifies things in one regard because it reduces the number of shots you are looking to play. Equally, it can feel harder because of the pressure that inevitably comes on you to keep the ball out.

Most of the time as a batsman you set out to score runs, but this was a very different assignment and, frustratingly, it was in not trying to score that I was dismissed.

Lining up a ball from Pat Cummins that was just outside the line of off-stump, I judged it as one to leave but as I went to withdraw the bat the extra bounce resulted in it flicking the toe-end of the bat. As soon as I heard the cheers of the wicket-keeper Tim Paine and the slips behind me, I tucked the bat under my arm and trudged off. There was no point in waiting for the umpire's finger to go up.

Walking in these kinds of situations might be a rare occurrence these days but I felt as though I had smashed it, so what was the point of hanging around? As it happened, the technology only showed it as a feather of an edge, but it showed up clear enough, nevertheless.

I had arrived at the crease 40 minutes before lunch after the partnership between Joe Denly and Jason Roy was ended by Cummins rushing one through the latter's defence. My attitude had to be similar to the one I had employed at Headingley. I had headed into the fourth day there with two runs from 50 balls and I needed to absorb plenty more deliveries here. Sadly, the 17th had done for me.

It meant I was to witness all the things that the lads had talked about in the dressing room in Leeds from four wickets down onwards. All kinds of superstitious behaviour came to the fore as Jonny Bairstow and Joe went back out for the afternoon. People were sat in their nominated seats, others were repeating things that they associated with us doing well such as circling the room or standing up between deliveries or overs, all that kind of stuff.

I was sat in the same seat for a while, next to our team analyst Giles Lindsay, as Jos Buttler and Jonny Bairstow began a partnership together during the second session. Until Starc returned for a new spell and got Jonny out with his first ball. Of course, I then dismissed any superstitious behaviour as a load of old tosh . . . until another stand developed between Buttler, who was showing another side to his batsmanship by digging in for 111 balls, and Craig Overton. I refused to move positions once more.

We had guys in the lower order batting with great powers of concentration, and no little skill, for more than an hour, and in Overton's case almost three, to defy Australia. Jack Leach, his Somerset teammate, showed how organised a batsman he is for a tail-ender – and why he was able to score 92 as a night-watchman against Ireland at Lord's in July. He was getting into line and playing each ball on its merits.

As we attempted to bat out that final day, the atmosphere at Old Trafford was extraordinary: just like it had been at Headingley a fortnight earlier. Each over Overton and Leach saw off was met by huge cheers and pockets of the 26,000 in the crowd burst into the theme tune from *The Great Escape*.

Not that everyone had been enthused by our efforts. On the Saturday evening when Rory Burns had been dismissed, some bloke shouted obscenities at him as he walked up the steps to the home dressing room. Funnily enough, nobody who plays for England ever likes getting out. We are all trying our nuts off for the three lions on our chests.

'What about a bit of support?,' Burns replied, before making the last couple of strides to join the rest of us inside. Already seething at his treatment, further back-chat drove Burns down to challenge his abuser.

Full of heated words between the two, the exchange ended with Rory, who can be a feisty character, suggesting that the disagreement could be settled elsewhere.

'Car park,' he said.

Thankfully, there was no such meeting out on the tarmac and further choruses of *The Great Escape* rang out for the team until that final scheduled hour of the match, when our hopes of another late act of defiance were finally dashed.

It was a sign of how successful Overton and Leach were that Tim Paine felt it necessary to call upon Marnus Labuschagne's occasional leg-spin in a bid to prise them apart, doing so when a big turner from the footholes flashed off the face of Leach's bat to short-leg.

In the end, we took the game into the second over of the final hour of the match. We got so close. Ultimately, though, it was not enough to keep the scoreline at 1–1 as we required.

After having such high hopes that we could follow our World Cup win, and maintain the winnings sequence of home Ashes series, it was tough when Overton's marathon effort came to an end via a DRS-confirmed lbw to Josh Hazlewood. It was not a pleasant sight to see our opponents' celebrations on the Old Trafford outfield, although they deserved our congratulations on how well they had played. Across a five-match series they proved themselves up to the challenge and had defeated us twice.

While acknowledging that Australia had outplayed us, certainly in this particular contest, and were deserving of retaining the urn, we had to get over things quickly. Yes, the Ashes had gone but the series remained alive.

England v Australia Fourth Test, Old Trafford, 4–8 September 2019

Result: Australia won by 185 runs

AUSTRALIA First Innings

	R	B	4s	6s
Marcus Harris lbw Stuart Broad	13	24	1	0
David Warner c Jonny Bairstow b Stuart Broad	0	2	0	0
Marnus Labuschagne b Craig Overton	67	128	10	2
Steve Smith c Joe Denly b Joe Root	211	319	24	2
Travis Head lbw Stuart Broad	19	22	3	0
Matthew Wade c Joe Root b Jack Leach	16	45	2	0
Tim Paine (capt) (wk) c Jonny Bairstow b Craig Overton	58	127	8	0
Pat Cummins c Ben Stokes b Jack Leach	4	9	1	0
Mitchell Starc not out	54	58	7	2
Nathan Lyon not out	26	26	4	0
Extras (nb 4, w 3, b 8, lb 14)	29			
Total (8 wickets, 126 overs)	497			

Fall of wickets:
1-1 (D Warner, 0.4 ov), 2-28 (M Harris, 6.6 ov), 3-144 (M Labuschagne, 39.2 ov), 4-183 (T Head, 48.4 ov), 5-224 (M Wade, 60.5 ov), 6-369 (T Paine, 101.1 ov), 7-387 (P Cummins, 104.6 ov), 8-438 (S Smith, 117.5 ov)

Bowling

	O	M	R	W
Stuart Broad	25	2	97	3
Jofra Archer	27	3	97	0
Ben Stokes	10.5	0	66	0
Jack Leach	26.1	3	83	2
Craig Overton	28	3	85	2
Joe Denly	3	1	8	0
Joe Root	6	0	39	1

ENGLAND First Innings

	R	B	4s	6s
Rory Burns c Steve Smith b Josh Hazlewood	81	185	9	0
Joe Denly c Matthew Wade b Pat Cummins	4	24	0	0
Craig Overton c Steve Smith b Josh Hazlewood	5	15	0	0
Joe Root (capt) lbw Josh Hazlewood	71	168	10	0
Jason Roy b Josh Hazlewood	22	33	3	0
Ben Stokes c Steve Smith b Mitchell Starc	26	62	3	0
Jonny Bairstow (wk) b Mitchell Starc	17	37	2	0
Jos Buttler b Pat Cummins	41	65	7	0
Jofra Archer c Tim Paine b Pat Cummins	1	19	0	0
Stuart Broad b Mitchell Starc	5	29	0	0
Jack Leach not out	4	9	1	0
Extras (nb 4, w 5, b 4, lb 11)	24			
Total (all out, 107 overs)	301			

Fall of wickets:
1-10 (J Denly, 6.5 ov), 2-25 (C Overton, 11.3 ov), 3-166 (R Burns, 64.2 ov), 4-175 (J Root, 66.6 ov), 5-196 (J Roy, 72.4 ov), 6-228 (J Bairstow, 84.5 ov), 7-243 (B Stokes, 88.3 ov), 8-256 (J Archer, 92.6 ov), 9-283 (S Broad, 101.5 ov), 10-301 (J Buttler, 106.6 ov)

Bowling

	O	M	R	W
Mitchell Starc	22	7	80	3
Josh Hazlewood	25	6	57	4
Pat Cummins	24	6	60	3
Nathan Lyon	36	4	89	0

AUSTRALIA Second Innings

	R	B	4s	6s
David Warner lbw Stuart Broad	0	6	0	0
Marcus Harris lbw Stuart Broad	6	16	1	0
Marnus Labuschagne lbw Jofra Archer	11	25	2	0
Steve Smith c Ben Stokes b Jack Leach	82	92	12	0
Travis Head b Jofra Archer	12	19	2	0
Matthew Wade c Jonny Bairstow b Jofra Archer	34	76	2	0
Tim Paine (capt) (wk) not out	23	18	4	0
Mitchell Starc not out	3	6	0	0
Extras (nb 1, w 7, b 5, lb 2)	15			
Total (6 wickets, 42.5 overs)	186			

Fall of wickets
1-0 (D Warner, 0.6 ov), 2-16 (M Harris, 6.1 ov), 3-24 (M Labuschagne, 9.3 ov), 4-44 (T Head, 13.6 ov), 5-149 (S Smith, 38.1 ov), 6-158 (M Wade, 39.2 ov)

Bowling

	O	M	R	W
Stuart Broad	14	4	54	2
Jofra Archer	14	2	45	3
Craig Overton	5.5	1	22	0
Jack Leach	9	0	58	1

ENGLAND Second Innings

	R	B	4s	6s
Rory Burns c Travis Head b Pat Cummins	0	3	0	0
Joe Denly c Marnus Labuschagne b Nathan Lyon	53	123	6	0
Joe Root (capt) b Pat Cummins	0	1	0	0
Jason Roy b Pat Cummins	31	67	4	0
Ben Stokes c Tim Paine b Pat Cummins	1	17	0	0
Jonny Bairstow (wk) lbw Mitchell Starc	25	61	1	0
Jos Buttler b Josh Hazlewood	34	110	4	0
Craig Overton lbw Josh Hazlewood	21	105	2	0
Jofra Archer lbw Nathan Lyon	1	9	0	0
Jack Leach c Matthew Wade b Marnus Labuschagne	12	51	1	0
Stuart Broad not out	0	3	0	0
Extras (nb 2, b 9, lb 8)	19			
Total (all out, 91.3 overs)	197			

Fall of wickets
1-0 (R Burns, 0.3 ov), 2-0 (J Root, 0.4 ov), 3-66 (J Roy, 24.6 ov), 4-74 (B Stokes, 30.2 ov), 5-93 (J Denly, 39.2 ov), 6-138 (J Bairstow, 53.1 ov), 7-172 (J Buttler, 74.2 ov), 8-173 (J Archer, 75.5 ov), 9-196 (J Leach, 89.5 ov), 10-197 (C Overton, 91.3 ov)

Bowling

	O	M	R	W
Pat Cummins	24	9	43	4
Josh Hazlewood	17.3	5	31	2
Nathan Lyon	29	12	51	2
Mitchell Starc	16	2	46	1
Marnus Labuschagne	4	1	9	1
Travis Head	1	1	0	0

12

PRIDE

England v Australia,
Fifth Test, The Oval, 12–16 August 2019

Disappointment was natural after failing to reclaim the Ashes, but with just three days between the fourth and fifth Tests there was no time to lick our wounds. There was still lots for this England team to play for heading into the final game.

Not allowing Australia to leave our shores as winners was a huge motivation. Sure, they had held on to the Ashes but they were partly living off the results they had managed on their own home soil in 2017–18.

They had known from the start that a drawn series would suffice for them. Now the same result was what we were in pursuit of for various reasons. For a start, we felt passionately about the quest to maintain England's unbeaten run against the Australians on home soil, spanning four home wins in 2005, 2009, 2013 and 2015. Not since 2001 had a touring Australian team won in England and we certainly didn't want that happening on our watch.

The podium banner for the post-match presentation reading

'Ashes 2019, Drawn series' was a much more comforting vision than imagining one emblazoned with 'Australia Wins'. This was the biggest driving force for us. This is the most important series that we participate in, and while you are desperate to finish victorious, neither do you want to be defeated.

The Ashes also represented the first series of the World Test Championship and there were points to play for to enhance our position in that. Dead rubbers don't exist when it is England *v* Australia but this provided greater context for another sell-out match at the Oval.

The 24 points available for a victory could potentially decide whether we make the final at Lord's or not in the summer of 2021, and this longer-term view on the match's relevance added another dimension. Although I have to confess the points system baffles me. At the same time as we were playing for 24 win-points per match against Australia, India went to the top of the table with 120 points from a 2–0 win over West Indies. That seems crazy.

It did not alter the bottom line, however: that we want to win as many matches as possible over a 21-month period because whatever the points system – and we will get the chance to play a two-match series carrying 120 points in Sri Lanka in the spring of 2020 – this is Test cricket's equivalent of limited-overs World Cups.

And this group of England players has shown a real hunger to be involved when it comes to global prizes being handed out, having been to the most recent Twenty20 and 50-over World Cup finals. If there is an ICC-sanctioned tournament being contested, we want to win it.

This also presented the chance to finish off an amazing

summer with one last victory. There had been some once-in-a-lifetime moments throughout 2019, I certainly hadn't experienced a period of cricket quite like it before, and the team had made a real connection with the crowds that cheered us on and the wider population who had shown their support from further afield.

Some of those people might have been looking at us and wondering exactly what this series finale meant to us. We knew there would be an examination of our attitude, but they could rest assured we were right up for this game, just as we are for every match in which we represent our country.

It was also Trevor Bayliss' last game in charge of England. We were all very fond of our outgoing Australian coach. We wanted to send him off with something other than the engraved IWC Schaffhausen watch that we clubbed together for and presented him with to mark his four years in charge of the team.

The words we chose for the back of the watch are ones which all those who have played under him since the summer of 2015 will instantly recognise. It became Trevor's catchphrase at training sessions as every time he called a team huddle, he would say in his distinctive Sydney drawl: 'Right, in we come.'

Mark Wood, who is a very good mimic, started taking the rest of us unawares by calling fake Trevor huddles. Then, I started doing it too every now and again. As time went by, when lads sensed we were getting to that time in training, someone or other would provide a phantom shout-out.

We hope that every time he sees on his timepiece the words '"Right, in we come", Trevor Bayliss, 2015–2019' he remembers what we achieved as a group.

Trevor was brilliant for our international team across all three formats but he never wanted to take any plaudits for our success, and so his answer of 'five out of ten' when asked in a pre-match press conference how he would rate his time as England coach was typical of him.

His coaching ethos is very simple. From day one, he stressed: 'You, the players, are the most important people. We, as coaches, are just here to help. Take responsibility for yourselves.'

He believes in allowing cricketers to make their own decisions and for people like him to be there, along the way, with advice and suggestions as necessary. Personally, I have always found that players improve when doing things for themselves rather than relying on being spoon-fed. Coaches are there for opinions, not definitive instructions. He was always an advocate of individuals taking information on board but rejecting it if it didn't feel right. If you take something away from what is said to you, great. At the end of the day, though, we are the ones out there with bat or ball in our hands trying to influence the course of a game.

Obviously, he has left a white-ball legacy with our record of 65 wins and just 26 defeats from 93 completed one-day internationals from 26 May 2015, when he was appointed, to the World Cup final of 14 July 2019. The results during this period were without peer in the history of the England cricket team.

Of course, there are those who sought to turn this excellent long-term form against him. One argument is that he didn't put as much time and effort into the Test team by way of comparison, but that is not informed opinion. It's only based on those results.

The facts were that we were blessed with a very strong one-day team and the quality of players available at this time has quite simply been incredible. In contrast, there was so much chopping and changing within our Test cricket. For example, there were 29 new players given debuts during his stint in charge.

Consistency of selection is going to help any team, and the lack of it at times at Test level has had an effect on the number of wins and losses we have recorded. You are not going to get a consistency of results when you don't keep a consistent XI or consistent squads.

There was no less effort or attention to detail put in by Trevor, it just wasn't as conducive an environment compared to the white-ball series of which he was a part. We have had more world-class performers in the shorter formats than we have in the longer one during his time. Yet for all this, we had still not lost a Test series at home during his tenure.

There really was so much to play for at the Oval. Ultimately, we were representing our country at our chosen sport. We never take international caps for granted. We just couldn't turn up for the game despondent because we hadn't reclaimed the Ashes, go through the motions and allow whatever was going to happen, happen. The message was clear. This game meant plenty.

Ahead of it I faced a fitness test. It wasn't so much whether I could bowl but fulfil my role as an all-rounder. It was soon pretty obvious that my sore right shoulder would not be up to 15 overs a day, although I was confident I could bowl a few later in the match should it be deemed necessary by the captain Joe Root.

It meant I played as a specialist batsman, as high as number four, with Jason Roy the unfortunate player to miss out on selection so that another all-rounder in Sam Curran could be accommodated. Chris Woakes also returned in place of Craig Overton, who had been carrying a mild back niggle in Manchester.

With regard to my batting, I tend to vary the amount of work I do ahead of games, partly due to the schedule dictating it and partly due to the management of my own practice. In the nets, in between international games, you want to work on your game but it's hard. In an instance like this, you have two days of training so you want feelgood nets – ideally lots of decent ball striking to lift confidence for when you get out into the middle.

Focusing on technical stuff tends to be very hard to do in a build-up to a Test match. This kind of stuff is best done at the start of a winter tour or before the English season begins if possible. I believe you should always try to challenge yourself in a net session wherever possible but equally sometimes, to make sure I am performing at my best, I reduce the amount of batting I will do during a series. If it's not contributing to making me a better player, I will pass up the opportunity.

Two days before a match, I will get asked whether I want to bat and if I have any reservations I will respond: 'I will come to you in half an hour.' If I don't feel like I am doing it for a reason then I won't do it. I need to have something to apply myself to. Perhaps it's a case of less is more when you get to a stage in your career where you have lots of experience behind you, and that unless you are working on something specific you might not see value in batting for the sake of it.

On this occasion, with limited bowling work to get through,

I set myself the challenge of not getting out for 40 minutes – something I particularly like to do when the net pitches are hard, or the ball is swinging and nipping around. If you can come out of a net against a couple of your own bowlers unscathed on a tricky surface, then you can feel good about your game.

Good start at the Oval then, when I left the first ball and it duly bowled me, much to Sam Curran's amusement!

'You're batting outside leg-stump,' he chuckled.

'Oh shit, am I?'

Naturally, I thought I was batting on two, my usual guard. With two hundreds to my name over the summer, it was easy to laugh at myself. I felt in decent touch with the bat and felt comfortable at the crease on the opening day after Australia decided to insert us in their pursuit of a first Ashes-winning campaign since 2001. We would have batted first regardless, so both sides began the match the way that they wanted.

One player who had not been feeling so good about his form was Jos Buttler. It was a subject we spoke about at length after he randomly asked me about his cricket. It was during a round of golf in Manchester in which the pair of us were partners – he said he was sick of giving me money, so he wanted to team up for a change.

Don't get me wrong, over the years I have spoken a lot about cricket to Jos, particularly when I have not been feeling great. The other way round, not so much. He has always been the type of person who appears to be uber confident in his approach to the game and this reflects in the style he is known for on the field.

The previous winter, during the tour of the West Indies, I had opened up to the entire England touring group during a team meeting, revealing that I was in a phase with my batting in which I was a bit scared of getting out. I was not walking out there with the same mindset I'd had 18 months previously. I was feeling at odds with my entire approach to batting and it had shown in my contributions in what had been a tough series for a number of us. I'd managed 59 runs across four innings as we went 2–0 behind with one match to play. I explained to everyone that I was still trying to find a way through it and was confident I would but it was proving a struggle. This was the point that Jos picked up on during our round of golf.

'How do you get over it? What do you do?' It was quite clear that he was now in the same place as I had been seven months earlier.

'As soon as I admitted it, faced up to the problems I was having, and put it out there, no longer hiding it away, I felt a weight had lifted off my shoulders,' I told him.

Previously, I had been hiding my fear of being dismissed like an embarrassing secret. Yet as soon as I let my teammates know that was how I was feeling, a sense of relief came over me. It was like I was halfway there to solving the issue.

The other half was taken care of by speaking to Sir Alastair Cook, who was out in the Caribbean working for BBC radio and the *Sunday Times*. Why, of all people, did I turn to him? Pretty simple, really. He was around in the period in which I established myself in international cricket and I'd batted with him lots over the years. He knew what I was like when I played at my best. And how things looked when I was not.

Hearing advice from a coach's perspective was not something I was looking for. I wanted it from someone who knew me well but was no longer around the team. He was the perfect choice.

I'd played 46 Test matches alongside him, 32 of them under his captaincy. There would be a sense of independence to any assessment he gave, too, as he was now outside the England bubble.

His instruction was to go back and watch footage of my hundred against New Zealand at Lord's at the start of the summer of 2015 because, he said, it was me at my absolute best as a batsman. We shared a fifth-wicket partnership of 132 in 26.3 overs and I scored 101 of them. During that innings, and my previous one in that match, of 92, I played every ball on its merits. I had not worried about getting out, even though I walked out to bat at 30–4 on the first morning and the equivalent of 98–4 on the fourth afternoon.

After doing so, I went out and scored 79 and 48 not out against West Indies in the final match of the series, the 232-run win in St Lucia. When I saw how I'd played four years previously, I realised I had to try to replicate it. Partly because it was a clear reflection of the way I play best and partly because I was placing restrictions on my batting by carrying around unnecessary baggage.

When Jos opened up, it was a shock. You just never expect that kind of thing from someone like him. Someone who is such a gifted player. There is not a lot I could help him with, such is his talent, other than pass on the kind of advice that Cookie gave me. I told him to look at the way he batted in one-day cricket.

In that particular format, he goes out and scores runs like he's not even trying. He has such an amazing ability of manipulating the field, of piercing the gaps and of improvising to increase his number of scoring options, such as walking down the wicket to alter a bowler's length.

Turning good length balls into full balls is a particular

strength of his, to the extent that there were no doubts in my mind that he would and will score runs in Test match cricket by implementing similar skills and strategies to that which he uses when in England blue facing a white ball. No bowler likes a batsman that knocks them off their length or makes them think twice about where they're bowling.

He can do this from the moment he takes guard. We have seen it before in Test cricket. Take the maiden hundred he made against India at Trent Bridge in 2018, when we were playing for the draw and yet he still managed to upset the rhythms of the Indian bowling attack. It was typical of his kind of contribution with the bat and I had been lucky enough to witness it from 22 yards away for the equivalent of two full sessions.

This is certainly the way Jos should play in Test cricket going forward.

Like me, just talking about his struggles seemed to relieve a load that he had been carrying. The weight off his shoulders could be seen by the fact there was no longer any tetchiness about his batting. Contributions of 70 and 47 at the Oval each came with strike rates in excess of 70. It's amazing what speaking out can do for your confidence.

Jos had a simple message to the Australia bowlers during the final Test: miss your target, and you're getting hit for four. He's got so much power and he should never forget how devastating that can make him.

He's always busy at the crease too and won't pass up opportunities to score. If you can be like that in the longest form, keep the scoreboard ticking, then the opposition captain is under pressure. Imagine being a bowler and having to bowl to Jos Butler with the score at 300–4.

In the first innings, when he witnessed a deterioration to 226–8 from the position of 176–5 when he arrived at the crease, some of the strokes from his 50-over playbook were being applied to the Test arena. Such as the way he barely moves his feet and strikes the ball perfectly into the gaps on the off-side just by closing his wrists through the stroke. He gets so many runs in ODI cricket by doing this, as he hits the ball so hard in this way that he always seems to miss the fielders. It gave me a real sense of satisfaction to see him make this breakthrough. Three blows into the stands off Josh Hazlewood were breathtaking.

It helped alter the course of things once more, and helped us post 294, after our top three coped admirably with the testing conditions early on. We had lost our way in between. Frustratingly, I managed to get out to Mitchell Marsh in exactly the same manner I did back in 2015 – pulling one straight up in the air, to leave us 130–3 immediately after drinks.

It was a ball that I felt I should hit for four and top-edged it. Any ball back of a length or slightly short, I have exactly the same attitude, and it's not something I am going to shy away from doing again. If it is there to hit, I will go after it, as I have got a hell of a lot more runs playing it in an attacking manner than I have been dismissed trying during my career. Yes, I am going to get out to it from time to time but it's been a major source of runs for me, and I was disappointed this time as I had felt so good in the middle.

•

There had been a lot of scrutiny placed on Jofra Archer during the previous Test match in Manchester and one of the things I brought up with the media in the build-up to this final contest of the series was that all top-level cricketers have bad days. When you see the barely believable level of talent Jofra possesses, the tendency can be to expect exactly the same every day. That's not realistic.

Here, his pace was back up to what it was at the start of the series. Over the course of four matches I think Joe Root got to grips with how to use him effectively in the future. He had bowled an unbelievable long spell at Lord's in the second Test, and at the Oval his first-innings spells of seven, six, seven and four overs were lengthier than the ones that will follow, I feel. As his international career deepens, we will see him move towards being an impact bowler – someone who comes on for a short four- or five-over burst. Yes, there will be the odd long spell from him when it's most needed but it will be quite a natural shift.

There had been a lot of focus on over-bowling him this summer, but people should also remember that this was the start of his England career and it was pretty hard to get the ball out of his hand, so keen was he to make an impression. Once Jimmy Anderson comes back from injury, he will find a more natural home as first change, because I can't see how we would ever break up a duo like Anderson and Stuart Broad. They have such a high skill factor with the new ball, while Jofra is just as good with the old one as he is with the new, if not better.

During Jofra's initial burst of 7–5–7–2 that accounted for David Warner, via a thin nick that we reviewed, and Marcus Harris, Australia managed just two scoring shots off him: an edge for four by Warner and a push through the covers by Steve Smith. He is blessed with such great control as well as pace.

But it is arguably with the older ball that he can do things that nobody else in the England team can. In drier conditions, supporters will see how much reverse swing he can extract later in the innings. So while it is great to see him bowling with a new ball when it's swinging and nipping, later on is the time I feel he will come into his own. Having him follow our most successful opening partnership in history will provide us with a perfect 1–2–3. It's a scarily good combination for us to attack teams over the remainder of the World Test Championship.

There was an additional mode of attack for the bowlers at the Oval too, in the form of traditional swing. The ball had not swung a great deal throughout the series but both myself and Joe Root were rewarded for working hard on getting one side of the ball perfectly smooth and glistening in contrast to the roughed-up side opposite, when Sam Curran in particular got it to move through the air.

I was literally covering the shiny side in saliva and polishing it like mad on my trousers. A couple of the bowlers had mentioned that they felt it was starting to shape more than in previous matches and soon Sam was causing the Australians some problems by moving it back into the right-handers. Even Steve Smith appeared disconcerted, although unusually it was a straight one from Chris Woakes that would account for him for 80, out of Australia's 225.

Others were confounded by the variation Curran was producing, some deliveries ducking in late on their journey, and a number going on with the angle. The danger for batsmen when it starts to swing like this is not only the balls that do plenty but the ones that don't. Playing for swing that wasn't there accounted for Tim Paine.

Because Sam bowls as full as he does, if he gets it around the line of off-stump he creates indecision. Funnily enough, the one bowler on the Australian team that got the ball to swing in this match was Mitchell Marsh, and like Curran he is a bowler that operates in the low to mid-eighties mph rather than the high eighties. Perhaps that had something to do with it? It might also have helped Marsh that conditions on day one were quite a bit different to anything that followed. The pitch was still a little bit damp, and the ball seamed as well as swung.

Unlike at Manchester, where chances had gone begging, we caught well as the series concluded – the catch by a diving Rory Burns very late on day two to end Australia's innings was particularly impressive.

'Good catch that, wasn't it?' I said to Joe Denly, whose spot was next to mine up in the dressing room.

'Yeah, thanks a lot,' he replied, cursing the fact that it meant he and Burns had to go out there and bat for a tricky period of four overs before stumps. Opening batsmen naturally hate having to bat in these kinds of situations when there is little to gain, plenty to lose, the light is dimming and the fast bowlers are tearing in.

Denly experienced an eventful week. I paid a visit to his hotel room the evening before the contest as it had been agreed he would leave the match to be at the birth of his second child; we just didn't know when. A car remained on standby at the ground with the plan being for him to dash down to the Kent coast and return for whatever remained of the match. First, we cleared it with the match umpires as to whether there was any difference if we were batting or bowling when he left the ground. We were told it didn't matter, as this kind of situation was considered an extreme circumstance.

It meant he left at the close of play on day one to be with his wife Stacy and, despite getting little sleep, returned to London around lunchtime the next day after welcoming his daughter into the world.

And he was agonisingly close to making it a stunning double celebration, getting to within six of a maiden Test hundred. A few of us were saying how much we'd love to see the baby-rock celebration to complete the week for him as he headed out with Rory Burns on the third morning.

He fell short but it was nevertheless an important innings within the greater scheme of things in relation to his career. At the age of 33, Denly might have been viewed as the most vulnerable of the batting group when it came to selection for the 2019–20 winter tours, with Dominic Sibley and Zak Crawley pushing for places and Ollie Pope back fit, so to hit a score of this magnitude, following half-centuries in the previous two Tests, solidified his place.

In partnership with him I just wanted to get the team to a place where we were safe. We were ahead of the game but, after opening up a 69-run lead on first innings, I told Joe Root at the tea break that I would be looking to press on a little more after it, to try to take the game forward.

Immediately, he attempted to temper my intentions, perhaps anticipating that I was about to start running down the wicket to try to thrash everything for four or six. Far from it: I knew we were nowhere near the stage in the game for doing that. It was just a case of having a bit more positive intent than I had shown up until this point. His message was not to get stumped and not be satisfied with a 300-run lead, either. As it turned out we opened up one close to 400.

It was a good contest between myself and Nathan Lyon. I managed to middle a few, he induced a few false shots, and had some chances missed before he bowled me what was a pretty unplayable delivery to a left-hander by an off-spinner: drifting in and then spinning away sharply to beat the defensive push.

The real long handle would come some time after my contribution of 67. There is nothing more exciting than a tail-ender pumping the world's number one bowler for two sixes in an over as Stuart Broad did to Pat Cummins. That provided a good feeling and turned the tables on Australia a little, if I am honest. James Pattinson had done this to our weary attack at Edgbaston, as had Mitchell Starc in the previous week's defeat at Old Trafford.

Sealing victory was important for all the reasons I mentioned earlier, but also because there had been a few murmurs about Joe Root's captaincy between the penultimate and final matches. As far as I was concerned, however, any doubting he was the best man for the job was nonsensical. It's always the captain that takes the flak.

I know Joe well. I have known him since we were 15-year-olds and I have witnessed several times over how he rises to challenges. He will have learned a heck of a lot from this summer and will look back on it as a period that helped shape him, I have no doubt.

He will be the first to admit he doesn't get everything right, but along with trying to improve his batting conversion rate (he got to 50 in the first innings at the Oval once more without going on) he will be determined to drive this England team – *his* England team – forward. He's incredibly strong-willed and the experience of what we went through across five matches will undoubtedly shape his future leadership. You don't learn a huge amount when things are going swimmingly, you learn in moments of adversity and when you are challenged.

Joe is determined to be the man to go to Australia in 2021–22 as England captain and get those Ashes back. As a team, we were just as determined to make sure that the scoreline for this series would be 2–2 as we defended a 399-run target.

Some things didn't change throughout the five matches: Stuart Broad made mincemeat of the opening batsmen, David Warner and Marcus Harris, once again. Crucially though, one thing did. On the 24th day of the scheduled 25 days of Ashes cricket in 2019, Steve Smith finally hit a ball to leg-slip. There had been numerous close calls along the way and in every other game the ball had flown to the left or right of this rather old-school fielding position. On 23, however, he did not lob it into a gap. I caught it, diving to my left, to provide Broad with the third of his four wickets.

Test cricket is attritional with the bat at times. For us this was being about attritional with the ball, staying patient and waiting for mistakes. Yet our generally disciplined approach did also comprise a fast-bowling duel for the ages between Jofra Archer and his Hobart Hurricanes captain Matthew Wade. It was proper viewing to witness a bowler capable of such extreme speed giving everything at the death of a five-match series, as fiery and threatening as he had been at its start. Credit to Wade too as he took on some shots, swayed out the way of others and wore one on the arm to boot. Here were two guys neither of whom were going to stand down.

Wade proved a very feisty character throughout the series, and you might be surprised to hear, given that he was portrayed as Australia's chief irritant (mainly through his words being picked up by the stump microphones), that the consensus from our changing room was that he was a guy you would like to have on your team. The recurring word used by us to describe him throughout the summer was niggly.

A heated atmosphere was developing between certain players and it was undoubtedly due to the fact that the end of the series was in sight. I actually enjoyed the spikiness. You might not have thought so when some choice words of mine towards David Warner were picked up by the Sky Sports effects microphones as we left the field on Saturday tea-time. I'd had enough of him about two matches earlier. Both teams were getting stuck into each other, more than in any other game of the series. The umpires stepped in on a few occasions when there was a bit of verbals, but nobody got a stern telling off. The stuff the players were dishing out wasn't exactly of the highest intellectual calibre. I mean, we are cricketers not A* students.

Sometimes no words are necessary when you are getting stuck into an opponent, something that Jofra demonstrated when he extended his follow-through by walking towards the centurion Wade with his arms behind his back, with a dramatic, emphasised closing of his mouth.

What can an umpire object to in that? It's just good old-fashioned intimidatory fast bowling. At 24 years old Jofra has developed these menacing mannerisms out in the middle without needing to cross into the realms of put-downs or smart comments. Rarely do you see him say anything after he's bowled a ball.

In contrast, Wade has verbal diarrhoea. And so it was amusing during his 166-ball 117 that he appealed to the umpires about the level of chat we were directing towards him.

'Come on, they're going at me here,' he said to Marais Erasmus.

Marais simply replied: 'Turn around and bat, mate.'

In other words, you've been dishing plenty out, you will have to take some in return. I'd never seen an umpire spray a player like that before. You can imagine that we didn't just let it lie, either, taking the chance to say stupid stuff like 'Help, Marais, help!'

A little over 24 hours earlier, he had been asked to calm down by the on-field officials while I was batting with Joe Root on what was to be the penultimate morning. Erasmus and Kumar Dharmasena are probably the two best umpires to have in this kind of situation. They understand it is international sport, let a lot go, but have to be seen to be taking action if it threatens to go too far or becomes too prolonged. What Wade found was that it wasn't one rule for one, another for someone else.

It was inevitable that Joe Root was going to be the bowler to dismiss him. He got quite a few boundaries away at first, but it was a bit of a waiting game because of the way he had decided to play with the tail for company. Using his feet was a positive option, but with the ball turning quite prodigiously off the surface it was only a matter of time until he ran down to one that pitched a bit shorter, was fired in a bit quicker, and spun like it did. It was the kind of dismissal that you feel you have already seen when it happens.

Meanwhile our main spinner, Jack Leach had become a crowd favourite during the summer due to his surprise contributions with the bat: the nightwatchman's 92 against Ireland at Lord's, and even more so with Test cricket's most talked-about one not out at Headingley. What he had been able to do for us in terms of his primary role in the team, though, was be a spinner who on balance contained more than he attacked. It certainly helped his bowling this summer that we played on pitches that assisted spin and he has shown that he is capable of doing an excellent job in both disciplines.

In fact, he ended up taking some really important wickets and headed for New Zealand in November on a hat-trick after wrapping up victory and sealing the series stalemate with two wickets in as many balls.

Leach is a character who has made a good habit of overcoming adversities in his life. Some big, some small. Others make more of a deal than he does of the fact that he has to bat in glasses rather than contact lenses because of his astigmatism. But as we saw with his regular polishing during his batting effort in Leeds, it is not straightforward doing so when your sight can be affected by your glasses steaming up.

No fuss, the cloth comes out, and within a beat he's ready to go. He just gets on with things. To his credit, he never moans about the Crohn's disease which he suffers from, even though what he eats can severely affect him.

Let's be honest, he seized his opportunity this summer, and the thing I like most about him is that he is always looking to put extra work in with our spin-bowling coach Saqlain Mushtaq. He is never content with where his game is, always wanting to push it on further, learning techniques to improve his bowling.

One of the things I discovered is that he bowls seamers first thing in the morning for 10–15 minutes before play.

'Why you doing that?' I asked him, genuinely bemused by what I was seeing when he came into the fold at Lord's. He explained that getting used to his arm coming over fast was beneficial when he came to bowl his customary spin in matches, as arm speed allows a bowler to impart more revolutions on the ball.

•

Knowing we were going to win as we cut through Australia's lower order felt good, although there was a bittersweetness about it too. As Stuart Broad said, there is still something incomplete, something unsatisfactory about a win when it doesn't come with the Ashes at the end.

Neither had we lost though, so when Joe Root took two tumbling catches, in different positions, off Leach to wrap things up as the evening sunshine dipped behind the Oval's stands, our victory by 135 runs meant we finished the summer in exactly the manner as we had started it – on a high.

Afterwards, the Australians joined us in our dressing room. There is a great picture of us all that was posted on the England team's Instagram feed which reveals what it is like to be an English or Australian cricketer at moments like these. Every series is the same. No matter the levels of antagonism between the players on the field – and in truth there wasn't too much in this particular series – you are always going to see a picture like that at the end. No matter what, there will be respect for your opponents at the close of a series.

The conclusion of a summer like this also provides time for reflection and as I toasted it with one or two cold beers I knew that both myself and the England team had fully committed to achieving our aspirations in this most wondrous of cricket years. I had been at the forefront of making things happen for England and that's where I want to be. We had given it our best shots and we had been just good enough to achieve one of our goals, but not quite good enough to achieve the other.

The margins had been of the narrowest variety at times; the smiles some of the widest; the laughs some of the longest. The dates of 14 July and 25 August will be etched in my memory for ever. I am so proud to have been part of a year like this. People said the drama of 2005 would never be replicated. I think this England vintage of 2019 managed to do so.

I promise to do all I can to make the years ahead just like it too.

England v Australia Fifth Test, The Oval, 12–16 September 2019

Result: England won by 135 runs

ENGLAND First Innings	R	B	4s	6s
Rory Burns c Mitchell Marsh b Josh Hazlewood	47	87	7	0
Joe Denly c Steve Smith b Pat Cummins	14	26	2	0
Joe Root (capt) b Pat Cummins	57	141	3	0
Ben Stokes c Nathan Lyon b Mitchell Marsh	20	36	2	0
Jonny Bairstow (wk) lbw Mitchell Marsh	22	55	3	0
Jos Buttler b Pat Cummins	70	98	7	3
Sam Curran c Steve Smith b Mitchell Marsh	15	13	1	1
Chris Woakes lbw Mitchell Marsh	2	5	0	0
Jofra Archer c Tim Paine b Josh Hazlewood	9	16	2	0
Jack Leach b Mitchell Marsh	21	43	3	0
Stuart Broad not out	0	5	0	0
Extras (nb 2, w 5, b 3, lb 7)	17			
Total (all out, 87.1 overs)	294			

Fall of wickets

1-27 (J Denly, 8.3 ov), 2-103 (R Burns, 30.5 ov), 3-130 (B Stokes, 39.5 ov), 4-170 (J Root, 56.1 ov), 5-176 (J Bairstow, 59.4 ov), 6-199 (S Curran, 63.6 ov), 7-205 (C Woakes, 65.5 ov), 8-226 (J Archer, 70.4 ov), 9-294 (J Buttler, 86.1 ov), 10-294 (J Leach, 87.1 ov)

Bowling	O	M	R	W
Pat Cummins	25.5	6	84	3
Josh Hazlewood	21	7	76	2
Peter Siddle	17	1	61	0
Mitchell Marsh	18.2	4	46	5
Nathan Lyon	4	0	12	0
Marnus Labuschagne	1	0	5	0

AUSTRALIA First Innings	R	B	4s	6s
David Warner c Jonny Bairstow b Jofra Archer	5	8	1	0
Marcus Harris c Ben Stokes b Jofra Archer	3	15	0	0
Marnus Labuschagne lbw Jofra Archer	48	84	10	0
Steve Smith lbw Chris Woakes	80	145	9	1
Matthew Wade lbw Sam Curran	19	31	2	0
Mitchell Marsh c Jack Leach b Jofra Archer	17	44	2	0
Tim Paine (capt) (wk) c Jonny Bairstow b Sam Curran	15	15	0	0
Pat Cummins lbw Sam Curran	0	1	0	0
Peter Siddle c Rory Burns b Jofra Archer	18	39	2	0
Nathan Lyon b Jofra Archer	25	30	4	1
Josh Hazlewood not out	1	1	0	0
Extras (w 5, b 1, lb 2)	8			
Total (all out, 68.5 overs)	225			

Fall of wickets

1-5 (D Warner, 1.5 ov), 2-14 (M Harris, 5.5 ov), 3-83 (M Labuschagne, 29.2 ov), 4-118 (M Wade, 36.4 ov), 5-160 (M Marsh, 48.4 ov), 6-166 (T Paine, 53.4 ov), 7-166 (P Cummins, 53.5 ov), 8-187 (S Smith, 61.1 ov), 9-224 (N Lyon, 68.1 ov), 10-225 (P Siddle, 68.5 ov)

Bowling	O	M	R	W
Stuart Broad	12	3	45	0
Jofra Archer	23.5	9	62	6
Sam Curran	17	6	46	3
Chris Woakes	10	2	51	1
Jack Leach	6	1	18	0

ENGLAND Second Innings

	R	B	4s	6s
Rory Burns c Tim Paine b Nathan Lyon	20	48	4	0
Joe Denly c Steve Smith b Peter Siddle	94	206	14	1
Joe Root (capt) c Steve Smith b Nathan Lyon	21	26	2	0
Ben Stokes b Nathan Lyon	67	115	5	2
Jonny Bairstow (wk) c Steve Smith b Mitchell Marsh	14	24	3	0
Jos Buttler c Marnus Labuschagne b Peter Siddle	47	63	6	0
Sam Curran c Tim Paine b Pat Cummins	17	26	2	0
Chris Woakes c Steve Smith b Mitchell Marsh	6	16	1	0
Jofra Archer c Tim Paine b Pat Cummins	3	9	0	0
Jack Leach c Josh Hazlewood b Nathan Lyon	9	32	1	0
Stuart Broad not out	12	9	0	2
Extras (nb 1, b 7, lb 11)	19			
Total (all out, 95.3 overs)	329			

Fall of wickets

1-54 (R Burns, 16.3 ov), 2-87 (J Root, 27.2 ov), 3-214 (B Stokes, 63.6 ov), 4-222 (J Denly), 5-249 (J Bairstow, 72.3 ov), 6-279 (S Curran, 80.4 ov), 7-305 (C Woakes, 86.6 ov), 8-305 (J Buttler, 87.1 ov), 9-317 (J Archer, 92.3 ov), 10-329 (J Leach, 95.3 ov)

Bowling	O	M	R	W
Pat Cummins	21	5	67	2
Josh Hazlewood	19	5	57	0
Nathan Lyon	24.3	5	69	4
Peter Siddle	13	4	52	2
Mitchell Marsh	11	1	40	2
Marnus Labuschagne	7	1	26	0

AUSTRALIA Second Innings

	R	B	4s	6s
Marcus Harris b Stuart Broad	9	15	2	0
David Warner c Rory Burns b Stuart Broad	11	22	2	0
Marnus Labuschagne st Jonny Bairstow b Jack Leach	14	39	1	0
Steve Smith c Ben Stokes b Stuart Broad	23	53	4	0
Matthew Wade st Jonny Bairstow b Joe Root	117	166	17	1
Mitchell Marsh c Jos Buttler b Joe Root	24	67	4	0
Tim Paine (capt) lbw Jack Leach	21	34	4	0
Pat Cummins c Jonny Bairstow b Stuart Broad	9	41	1	0
Peter Siddle not out	13	18	2	0
Nathan Lyon c Joe Root b Jack Leach	1	8	0	0
Josh Hazlewood c Joe Root b Jack Leach	0	1	0	0
Extras (nb 2, b 2, lb 12, pen 5)	21			
Total (all out, 77 overs)	263			

Fall of wickets

1-18 (M Harris, 4.6 ov), 2-29 (D Warner, 6.4 ov), 3-56 (M Labuschagne, 16.3 ov), 4-85 (S Smith, 26.3 ov), 5-148 (M Marsh, 43.3 ov), 6-200 (T Paine, 55.6 ov), 7-244 (P Cummins, 70.6 ov), 8-260 (M Wade, 75.1 ov), 9-263 (N Lyon, 76.5 ov), 10-263 (J Hazlewood, 76.6 ov)

Bowling	O	M	R	W
Stuart Broad	15	1	62	4
Jofra Archer	16	2	66	0
Sam Curran	8	3	22	0
Jack Leach	22	8	49	4
Chris Woakes	7	1	19	0
Joe Root	9	1	26	2

ACKNOWLEDGEMENTS

This unbelievable year in my life would not have been possible without the dedication and commitment of others. To these people I offer my heartfelt thanks.

To my England teammates and the support staff who all contributed towards 2019 being so exciting and so rewarding – the hours of hard work paid off. Without the efforts of all of you guys it would not have been such a summer to remember.

To Neil Fairbrother and all at Phoenix Management: we are like a family, and the combination of time and effort you put into looking after the interests of each player in this family is nothing short of remarkable.

To Jonathan Taylor and Tom Whiting and all at Headline Publishing Group, for giving me the opportunity to be able to relive these events in my own words.

To Richard Gibson, for helping me put it all together. It was a pleasure working with you again.

To Clare, Layton, Libby, Mam, Dad and my mother-in-law Jane – you've been through all the highs and lows with me. I love you all.

PICTURE CREDITS

The World Cup

Page 1: Nigel French/PA Wire/PA Images (top and bottom); Stu Forster-ICC/Getty Images (middle)

Page 2: Philip Brown/Popperfoto/Getty Images (top); Robbie Stephenson/JMP/Shutterstock (middle); James Marsh/BPI/Shutterstock (bottom)

Page 3: Adam Davy/PA Wire/PA Images (top); Gareth Copley-ICC/Getty Images (bottom)

Page 4: Jon Super/AP/Shutterstock (top); Matt West/BPI/Shutterstock (middle); Adrian Dennis/AFP/Getty Images (bottom)

Page 5: Clive Mason/Getty Images (top left and bottom); Michael Steele/Getty Images (top right)

Page 6: Stu Forster-ICC/Getty Images (top); Glyn Kirk/AFP/Getty Images (middle); Nick Potts/PA Wire/PA Images (bottom)

Page 7: Paul Ellis/AFP/Getty Images (top left); Clive Mason/Getty Images (top right); Tom Jenkins/Getty Images (middle); Matt Dunham/AP/Shutterstock (bottom)

Page 8: Philip Brown/Popperfoto/Getty Images (top left); Aijaz Rahi/AP/Shutterstock (top right); Gareth Copley-ICC/Getty Images (middle right); James Veysey/Shutterstock (bottom and inset)

The Ashes

Page 1: Mike Egerton/PA Wire/PA Images (top left); ESPA Photo Agency/CSM/Shutterstock (top right); Matthew Impey/Shutterstock (bottom left and right)

Page 2: Javier Garcia/BPI/Shutterstock (top); Philip Brown/Popperfoto/Getty Images (middle); Graham Hunt/ProSports/Shutterstock (bottom left); Glyn Kirk/AFP/Getty Images (bottom right)

Page 3: Mike Egerton/PA Wire/PA Images (top and bottom right)); Matt West/BPI/Shutterstock (bottom left)

Page 4: Allan McKenzie/SWpix.com/Shutterstock (top); Alex Davidson/Getty Images (middle left and bottom); Stu Forster/Getty Images (middle right)

Page 5: Mike Egerton/PA Wire/PA Images (top); Allan McKenzie/SWpix.com/Shutterstock (bottom left); Alex Davidson/Getty Images (bottom right)

Page 6: Philip Brown/Popperfoto/Getty Images (top); Allan McKenzie/SWpix.com/Shutterstock (bottom left); Stu Forster/Getty Images (bottom right)

Page 7: Mike Egerton/PA Wire/PA Images (top); Martin Rickett/PA Wire/PA Images (middle); Visionhaus/Getty Images (bottom)

Page 8: Graham Hunt/ProSports/Shutterstock (top left); Adrian Dennis/AFP/Getty Images (top right); Graham Hunt/ProSports/Shutterstock (middle); Philip Brown/Popperfoto/Getty Images (bottom)